Research: An Introduction

About the Author

Robert Ross has a BA in English from the University of Oregon and an MA in English from Texas Christian University, where he has also completed some doctoral work. He has taught English composition and literature at Texas Christian University, Pan American University at Edinburg, Texas, and Clatsop Community College in Oregon.

Research:
An Introduction

ROBERT ROSS

BARNES & NOBLE BOOKS

A DIVISION OF HARPER & ROW, PUBLISHERS

New York, Hagerstown, San Francisco, London

First BARNES & NOBLE BOOKS edition published 1974.

LIBRARY OF CONGRESS CATALOG CARD NUMBER: 73–13439

ISBN: 0-06-460141-2

81 82 83 84 85 86   10 9 8 7 6 5

Preface

The emphasis on independent research is becoming increasingly widespread, and rightly so. After all, what we discover and analyze ourselves usually stays with us much longer than that which is handed to us. It is on this premise that this book is based. Aimed directly at the individual engaged in a research project, it is intended as a practical guide to research, not as a treatise on the philosophy of research. The plan has been to explain and to illustrate the essential parts of the research task in their logical order. Special emphasis has been placed on organization, analysis, and synthesis of evidence, an area that too often remains a mystery in research manuals. Thus, considerable attention has been given to forming a hypothesis, making an outline, determining an organizational approach, and using specific developmental materials.

In addition, both written and original sources are considered, as well as visual materials. The technical matters pertaining to documentary and bibliographical forms are presented separately in the appendixes, as are bibliographies of selected general and specific reference works. Chapter 6 is devoted entirely to writing the rough draft, revising it, and preparing the final paper. Chapter 9 includes sections on tone, style, and mechanics of form. Care has been exercised to define all terms as they appear in the text so that the user of the book will know exactly what is intended in any given passage.

Although the book is directed in particular toward the beginning researcher, it is likely that the upper-level or graduate student can make use of certain sections, especially those dealing with organization, reference materials, and documentation. Because this manual is not limited strictly to the academic in its approach, it should also prove helpful to the individual conducting research outside the college or school environment.

It is difficult to acknowledge the many persons who directly or indirectly assisted in the writing of this book. In order to cover part of my indebtedness, however, I must mention the following people: the many students whose problems and triumphs in research work served as a basis for what went into the book; the helpful and patient librarians who answered scores of questions and located materials; the various friends, who, at times unwittingly, served as editorial advisers; Mrs. Roberta Anderson, head librarian, Clatsop Community College, Astoria, Oregon, who assisted in compiling the bibliographies and gave editorial criticism on the chapter concerned with library use; and Mr. Jerry Solomon of the U.S. Department of Agriculture, who provided materials and assistance for the chapter on writing reports.

And to my wife, Anita, who always knew that the work would be completed, I dedicate the book.

Contents

1
Planning the Research

Chapter 1

Understanding Research

*It is our perpetual yearning to overcome difficulties
and dangers, to see the hidden things, to penetrate into
the regions outside our beaten track—it is the call of the
unknown—the longing for the Land of Beyond, the divine
force deeply rooted in the soul of man which drove the
first hunters out into new regions—the mainspring
perhaps of our greatest actions—of winged human
thought knowing no bounds to its freedom.*
Fridtjof Nansen, Adventure and Other Papers

It is a basic desire of man to want to add to his own knowledge
and ultimately to the world's knowledge. Man is by nature a
question asker and an answer seeker. Sometimes his search for
answers through acquiring knowledge is motivated by the sheer
necessity of solving an immediate problem; at other times it is
motivated by the higher need of understanding his being and
his world.

The elementary methods of acquiring knowledge are chance,
trial and error, and generalizing from experiences. A more complex approach is the use of logic, which leads to certain conclusions based upon previous generalizations. In addition to
chance, trial and error, generalizing from experiences, and logic,
modern man adds to his knowledge through a systematic method
called *research*, which incorporates aspects of all these methods
and adds a dimension of its own. Here is a definition of this
many-sided function:

Research is essentially an *investigation*, a *recording*, and an
analysis of *evidence* for the *purpose* of gaining knowledge.

INVESTIGATION

Research involves, specifically, an investigation into a particular matter or problem. (The word is derived from the French *rechercher*, meaning "to search back.")

Qualities of the Investigation

Certain qualities distinguish this investigation.

Thoroughness. The necessity for thoroughness is particularly obvious in scientific research, but it must not be overlooked in written research. When the scientist approaches a problem—for example, the eradication of cattle disease—he must examine all aspects of the problem and investigate many possible solutions in order to arrive at an effective one. Similarly, the person carrying on written research must make an exhaustive investigation. Relying on a single source is a practice that is often confused with research, but using information from one book or periodical or general reference work is not sufficient.

Exactness. In research work there is no room for carelessness of any kind: guesswork, inaccuracy, unfounded assumptions, or hasty conclusions. The investigation must be characterized by careful attention to details and mental alertness in analysis. Only then will accuracy be assured, assumptions firmly based, and conclusions valid.

Honesty. Sometimes intentionally and sometimes inadvertently, dishonesty creeps into the investigation in the form of falsification or plagiarism. Using spurious evidence or documenting false sources destroys the validity of the investigation. And plagiarism, the undocumented and uncredited borrowing from other works, is in direct opposition to one of the main purposes of research: originality.

Approaches to the Investigation

Traditionally, there are two approaches to research: the *deductive method* and the *inductive method*. The modern approach, called the *scientific method*, utilizes both traditional methods but also has distinctive properties of its own.

Deductive Method. Developed to a high art by the ancient

Greeks, the deductive method covers reasoning from the general to the specific. That is, the process is a matter of reasoning from certain reliable preliminary statements, or *premises*, to conclusions that may be drawn from such premises. The basis of this method is the *syllogism*, which is illustrated by the following classic example:

1. All men are mortal.
2. Socrates is a man. } **Premises**
3. Hence, Socrates is mortal. } **Conclusion**

Aristotle, the leading proponent of this method, stressed that the premises must be sound and must be based on the direct observation of nature. If the premises are untrue, any conclusion drawn from them is also untrue. In this fact lies the inherent danger of total reliance on the deductive method.

Inductive Method. The inductive method uses facts as evidence to prove a conclusion. In other words, the inductive process begins with the gathering of specific facts that are then assembled in order to arrive at general conclusions or generalizations. Leonardo da Vinci (1452–1519) and Francis Bacon (1561–1626) were early proponents of this method.

Scientific Method. Modern researchers have discovered that it is impossible to rely exclusively on either the deductive or the inductive method. Based on the work of Aristotle, Bacon, Charles Darwin (1809–1882), and countless others, the scientific method is the approach that is most often employed by researchers today.

The American educator and philosopher John Dewey (1859–1952) provided the following analysis which may be used as a guide to understanding the scientific method:

STEPS IN REFLECTIVE THINKING

1. The occurrence of a felt difficulty
   a) In the lack of adaptation of means to end.
   b) In identifying the character of an object.
   c) In explaining an unexpected event.
2. Definition of the difficulty in terms of a problem statement.
3. Occurrence of a suggested explanation or possible solution

—a guess, hypothesis, inference, or theory.

4. The rational elaboration of an idea through the development of its implications, by means of the collection of evidence.

5. Corroboration of the idea and formation of a concluding belief through experimental verification of the hypothesis.[1]

The five steps Dewey presented roughly parallel the steps the research writer takes in preparing a written work:

1. Choosing a subject
2. Forming a statement of the problem
3. Forming a hypothesis or theory
4. Collecting and organizing the evidence
5. Drawing conclusions and writing the paper

RECORDING AND ANALYSIS

The recording of the evidence falls into two parts: (1) It is recorded during the investigation. (2) It is put into an acceptable form once the investigation has been completed and the evidence has been analyzed.

During the Investigation

It is a waste of time to read extensively without making any record of your reading. In addition, the bibliographical information concerning the sources should be recorded completely and accurately. Similarly, it would be foolish for the person engaged in scientific research to conduct experiments without recording the results.

After the Investigation

Having formed a hypothesis or theory early in his work, the researcher must *analyze* the evidence carefully when the investigation has been completed to be sure that it supports his original hypothesis or theory. If it does, the hypothesis or theory becomes a thesis statement that governs the direction of the written work. If it does not, the writer should not cling

1. John Dewey, *How We Think* (Boston: D. C. Heath, 1933), p. 12.

stubbornly to his original hypothesis or theory. Rather, he should revise and restate it as necessary.

The next step is to *synthesize* the evidence, that is, to assemble the parts and elements of the evidence into a readable form that substantiates and develops the thesis statement and its logical parts. The results of the investigation and analysis will be synthesized in one of four basic kinds of written works.

Research Paper. This written work is variously called the *term paper,* the *library paper,* the *long paper,* or the *documented paper.* In this book it will be called the *research paper.*

Usually running from 3,000 to 5,000 words, the research paper contains one general statement (frequently called the *thesis statement*) and its logical parts; these parts are developed and substantiated by evidence drawn from the sources. The research paper is the most elementary form of research writing, but this fact does not make it a lowly or inferior work. Anyone who has mastered the undergraduate research paper can easily apply these skills to the more demanding graduate-level research tasks.

Report. Many books on research use the descriptive terms *research paper* and *report* interchangeably, but this book will make a distinction between the two. Although they have much in common, they differ in two ways. (1) The research paper depends mainly on evidence drawn from written sources; whereas the report relies primarily on empirical or field-study evidence. (2) The research paper is philosophical in nature; whereas the report tends toward the derivation of principles or the solving of problems. There are two kinds of reports.

1. REPORT BASED ON EMPIRICAL EVIDENCE. Usually associated with science and psychology, empirical evidence is gathered through experimentation or direct observation. Properly guided by a hypothesis, a researcher will arrive at conclusions, derive principles, or solve problems by observing certain phenomena and occurrences in nature or human behavior. On the other hand, the laboratory is, in a sense, a reproduction of nature; in it the researcher may observe phenomena and behavior in a controlled atmosphere. His observations, conclusions, or principles serve as the basis for the report. Most likely the researcher will rely partially on printed material, but his main source will be the empirical evidence that he has gathered.

2. REPORT BASED ON FIELD-STUDY EVIDENCE.   The main methods
for gathering field-study evidence are through interviews, questionnaires, tests, experimental and control groups, and observations. Used most often in the social sciences, these data lead
to the formation of conclusions or principles or to the solving
of problems. The written report, based primarily on field-study
evidence and partially on printed sources, presents the conclusions, principles, or solutions, as well as the evidence from which
they have been derived. Graphs, statistical tables, and other
illustrations are often used in addition to the written presentation.

Master's Thesis.   The word *thesis* means a proposition advanced and defended by argumentation. (It is derived from the
Greek word meaning "to lay down.") The *traditional thesis*
still fulfills this definition to a certain extent. However, graduate
education today has expanded in so many directions that the
traditional thesis is not always appropriate for all areas of study.
Therefore, several variations on the traditional thesis have been
introduced: the creative thesis, the scientific thesis, and the field-
study thesis.

The *creative thesis* may take the form of a recital; an exhibit
of sculpture, paintings, or other art works; a dramatic production; or an architectural design. And for an advanced degree in
creative writing, the student may submit poetry, a novel, or a
play in place of the traditional thesis.

The *scientific thesis* may be based on a single experiment or
on a series of experiments and observations; it includes the
descriptions, conclusions, and principles drawn from the collected data. It is likely that the scientific researcher will refer
to printed materials and make use of them in his thesis.

The writer of a *field-study thesis,* usually in the social sciences
or education, gathers information from interviews, questionnaires, tests, control groups, and observation. Like the scientific
researcher, the writer will probably draw evidence from written
sources, too.

Essentially, the master's thesis, which has no standard length,
is an expanded and more sophisticated research paper or report.

Doctoral Dissertation.   There is no exact definition of the
dissertation; it takes as many forms as the thesis, if not more.

It is usually substantially longer than the master's thesis and treats its subject in greater depth. Mainly, though, greater emphasis is placed on the dissertation's original contribution to knowledge, which is, after all, its ultimate purpose.

The form, organization, approach, and evidence are all dictated by the academic area for which the dissertation is being written. But even in this advanced research work, the principles underlying the research paper still apply.

EVIDENCE

The varieties of evidence that the researcher will gather for his written work have all been mentioned in the preceding paragraphs. However, it may be helpful at this point to list the kinds of evidence in an organized manner.

Library Materials

Most undergraduate researchers will rely mainly on library materials, which consist of printed and audiovisual sources.

Printed Sources. The basic printed source is the reference work that provides a general outline of a subject and/or a list of materials pertaining to the subject. Included in this list are books, pamphlets, periodicals, and government documents.

Audiovisual Sources. A new kind of source has come into its own in recent years in the form of microfilms, microfiches, tapes, slides, filmstrips, video tapes, and other devices. Materials not otherwise available have become easily accessible through audiovisual materials, and new research projects have evolved as a result of these materials. (Chapter 8 is concerned with audiovisual materials and special projects based on these sources.)

Field Study and Experimentation

Direct observation (field study) and experimentation provide for the gathering of new information concerning man and nature.

Studies of Man. Modern researchers have heeded Alexander Pope's admonition that "the proper study of mankind is man" by devising numerous ways to study man and his society through

tests, control groups, questionnaires, observations, and interviews.

Studies of Nature.   No longer content to accept the mytho-
logical, religious, or traditional explanations of natural phenomena, pioneering scientists like Galileo (1564–1642) observed
nature and arrived at certain conclusions and explanations. Although their efforts did not win immediate acceptance, these
early scientists paved the way for the modern scientific researcher who views nature as an arena for research and who
has gone even further and isolated aspects of nature in the
laboratory.

PURPOSE

The highest purpose of research is to gain knowledge, and
that knowledge is either used for the solving of problems
(*applied research*) or prized for its own sake (*pure research*).
C. P. Snow distinguishes between the two approaches in this
manner: "The scientific process has two motives: one is to
understand the natural world, the other is to control it."[2] The
traditional distinction between pure research and applied research is an oversimplification because the two cannot be separated. It is true that some research is conducted for the exclu-
sive purpose of solving a problem—perhaps social, industrial,
or educational in nature. But once the problem is solved, the
knowledge remains, either for solving new problems or for its
own sake.

Through research, be it applied or pure, new information is
obtained, new relationships established, new concepts created,
and existing concepts verified.

New Information

The researcher continually uncovers, discovers, and reevaluates information. The work of the archaeologist is an example
of uncovering information, often literally. From his diggings
and his careful examination of his findings, he can reconstruct

2. C. P. Snow, *The Two Cultures and a Second Look* (New York: New
American Library, 1964), p. 64.

ancient civilizations or fill in historical gaps. The social scientist conducting a survey on how urban renewal affects displaced families discovers new information on a new problem. The biographer reevaluates information, along with searching for the new, in his attempt to present an unvarnished picture of his subject.

New Relationships

The researcher establishes new relationships by analyzing and synthesizing established evidence or by discovering new evidence. In the process, he adds to the overall understanding of a subject. Historians look into the past and shed light on the present. Scientists set out to establish new relationships by searching for links, such as the supposed connection between smoking and disease. Educational researchers seek special kinds of relationships that they call correlations, such as the one between the drab surroundings of underprivileged children and their defective object perception that leads to poor reading.

New Concepts

There are times when an existing concept needs to be replaced by a new concept or when a new concept should be created. The theologian, the philosopher, the literary scholar, and the historian are involved in creating new concepts. Some educational, social, and scientific research falls into this category; the researchers often seek new concepts, hoping that they might be translated into practical use.

Verification of Existing Concepts

A concept is a generalized idea, often one that has been reached through the process of deduction. Therefore, it is sometimes necessary to reexamine the premises in order to verify the concept. This reexamination may engage the theologian, whose research and writing often represent attempts at rational verification of religious concepts. The philosopher is also involved in this activity when he probes the depths of a subject.

One purpose of the literary scholar's works is to verify concepts, such as the standing of a particular author in the overall development of literature.

DESIRE FOR KNOWLEDGE

The goals are different and the techniques vary, but the ultimate purpose of research remains the same: man's desire to know. He may want to discover new information or re-evaluate existing information. He may want to create new concepts or verify existing ones. He may want to establish new relationships or solve problems. But essentially, he wants to know. And that is what research is all about.

Chapter 2

Beginning the Investigation

*Error may flourish for a time, but truth will prevail
in the end. The only effect of error ultimately is to promote
truth. Theories, speculations, hypotheses, are started;
perhaps they are to die, still not before they have
suggested ideas better than themselves.*

John Henry Newman,
"Christianity and Scientific Investigation"

Beginnings are usually difficult, and beginning the investigation that will lead to a research paper or report is no exception. Because the beginning is the most subjective step in the investigation, it is also the most elusive to define and describe in order to give specific directions. Unlike other steps in the investigating and writing process, such as taking notes or organizing the material, there are no specifics, only guiding principles.

Obviously, you must first choose a subject. Once you have chosen the subject, consider it carefully to be sure that you can handle it. If the subject passes this test, the next steps are to form a statement of the problem and to survey the evidence. All this work will lead to the final step: the forming of the hypothesis.

The guiding principles, then, for beginning the investigation are as follows:

1. Choose and consider the subject.
2. Isolate and state the problem.

3. Survey the evidence.
4. Form the hypothesis.

CHOOSING AND CONSIDERING THE SUBJECT

The necessity for choosing a subject is so apparent that it sometimes does not receive the careful attention it demands. Many unfinished papers or uninspired ones are simply the result of haphazard choices.

How the Subject Is Assigned

Student research is most often undertaken to fulfill an assignment in a course or to complete a requirement in a degree program. Consequently, many limits on the subject have already been set.

Undergraduate Level. On the undergraduate level you usually receive considerable guidance in the selection of subjects. Frequently, the instructor will make the choice for you. If this happens and you do not understand or like the subject that has been assigned, you should confer with your instructor. Never allow yourself to be pushed into a research project for which you are not suited. On the other hand, you should not expect the instructor to select and plan your research project for you or to act as an editor.

Sometimes you will choose from a list of suggested subjects. It is imperative in this case that you understand the exact nature of the subject before you commit yourself.

Perhaps the ideal situation exists when you are given the freedom to explore any area you wish within the bounds of the course for which you are writing the paper or report. But, as always, with freedom comes responsibility, and you must exercise special care when going out on your own.

Graduate Level. It would seem that by the time you reach this level, you would no longer find it difficult to choose a subject, but the problem still exists.

There may be times when you are virtually forced into a project by a professor who wants someone to perform research tasks for him. If this situation cannot be avoided, you will likely feel stifled by the lack of freedom. However, too much freedom can also cause problems. Extensive background in an academic discipline makes it more difficult to determine a specific area for research, and you might find yourself inundated by the diverse possibilities that a particular subject offers.

If you are in a seminar, you will probably be assigned a specific aspect of the seminar subject for your research project. This procedure is usually satisfactory because you probably would not be taking the seminar if you were not interested in the subject.

How to Choose the Subject

If you have been given the freedom to choose a subject and are at a loss, you can employ one of the following methods to help you make a choice.

Reading a Magazine Article. A current newsmagazine, a scholarly periodical, or another publication can direct you to a subject. You may read something with which you violently disagree. This would be a good start because you could then set out to disprove the ideas in the article through research. On the other hand, you may discover an article that opens up an aspect of a subject that interests you, thus leading into a research project.

Drawing upon Past Experiences. Personal experiences, such as travel and direct observations, might lead you to a subject. Upon recalling an automobile trip across the United States, you may decide to investigate the development of the interstate highway system. Or a street-corner conversation with a person involved in a particular religious movement may start you on an investigation of the history or influence of that sect. The memory of a spectacular electrical storm in the Midwest or the recollection of poverty in an urban area might suggest a project employing scientific research or field-study methods.

Relying on Previous Knowledge. Books, academic courses, and previous research projects can sometimes provide a subject. If you have recently read a book on ecology, for example, some of the ideas in it may direct you toward a subject. Possibly a course you took introduced ideas that you could consider for a paper. Or an earlier research project may have suggested ideas that you were unable to pursue at the time; thus, a review, *not* a reworking, of an earlier paper or report might result in a new research work.

Communicating with Others. Conversations, discussions, and even arguments can be the geneses of research papers. A casual conversation with a friend about a book he has just read might cause you to read the book and develop an interest in the subject. By discussing ideas in a group, you may hear a new approach to an old problem that could evolve into a subject. An argument on the political situation with a person of opposite persuasion may encourage you to check into the soundness of your own views; such an investigation could form the basis for a paper.

Using Reference Works and Guides. Reading about a particular subject or about several subjects in a general reference work such as an encyclopedia can give you ideas and lend you some background for the investigation. Referring to the Dewey decimal or Library of Congress system of library classification, especially in their more detailed forms (see pp. 28–29), can direct you toward a subject and to sources concerning it. Some books on research include lists of suggestions for research projects. Even though such lists may appear somewhat sterile and uninviting, they might help you find a subject or at least stimulate your thinking.

How to Consider the Subject

Once you have chosen a general subject, you should apply the following commonsense rules to be sure that the subject is an actual possibility.

Interest. You must be interested in the subject because you will be deeply involved with the investigation and writing for a considerable period. If you are bored, your paper will probably reveal this unhappy fact.

Background. You must have sufficient background to handle the subject. Certainly you should not avoid a challenge or stay away from new subjects, but it is unwise to select a subject requiring extensive preparation before the actual research and writing. You should not attempt to treat a highly technical subject, for instance, without adequate preparation; nor should you plan to write a paper on "The Major Influences in Nineteenth-century Russian Literature" unless you have already read fairly extensively in this body of literature.

Availability of Sources. You must be able to locate the necessary sources with a minimum of difficulty. Relying on the holdings of campus or city libraries is usually preferable for short-term projects because obtaining materials from out-of-town libraries is often time consuming. Similarly, if you are going to depend primarily on empirical or field-study evidence, you should be sure that the equipment and other resources are available.

Involvement. You must be involved in your subject, but not to the extent that your paper becomes subjective and argumentative. Obviously, you should avoid a highly denominational and evangelistic treatment of a religious subject or a biased and opinionated discussion of a political topic. It is not necessary to shy away from all controversial subjects, but try to approach such matters objectively. Always keep in mind that a research paper is impersonal in nature.

Appropriateness. The subject must be appropriate. Even though you may be extremely interested in a particular topic, a research paper on it might not fulfill the specific assignment. This factor does not really limit your freedom; rather, it serves as a disciplinary and broadening factor. For example, your real interest may lie closer to chemistry than to English literature. Certainly a paper on chemistry would not fulfill the assignment for a literature class, but you could capitalize on your interest by investigating a somewhat related subject such as "Alchemy in English Drama."

The exercise of good taste also plays an important role in choosing a subject. Of course, the bounds of so-called good taste differ from person to person. A detailed study of Roman orgies might delight one history professor and horrify another. In such instances, you must use your judgment and common sense to discriminate.

ISOLATING AND STATING THE PROBLEM

Generally speaking, "all scholarly studies are undertaken to solve specific problems."[1] The word "problem" is used here

1. Tyrus Hillway, *Introduction to Research* (Boston: Houghton Mifflin, 1964), p. 76.

in its broadest sense, meaning "a perplexing question." Therefore, after you have chosen and considered the subject, you must isolate the problem or a question about the subject that you find perplexing. Next, you form a statement of that problem which will guide you in developing the hypothesis, analyzing the subject, and surveying the evidence.

How to Isolate the Problem

The best method of isolating the problem is asking questions. Although it helps to be familiar with the subject, it is not absolutely essential at this point because the first questions will be general. Gradually, the inquiries become more specific, growing so logically from the general ones. Here is an example of a series of questions leading to the isolation of the problem:

GENERAL SUBJECT

An Investigation of the Interstate Highway System

GENERAL QUESTIONS

What is its purpose?
How is it financed?
What is the master plan?
When will it be completed?
What will the effects on the United States be?

SPECIFIC QUESTIONS

1. What is its purpose?
   1.1 For defense?
   1.2 For better transportation? —Commercial and/or private?
   1.3 For industrial development?
2. How is it financed?
   2.1 How much by the federal government?
   2.2 How much by the state governments?
   2.3 Has the financing been adequate to finish it?
3. What is the master plan?
   3.1 Is the plan effective?
   3.2 Has local and political influence affected the planning?
   3.3 Will it become obsolete soon?

3.4 Is it well constructed?
4. When will it be completed?
    4.1 Is it on schedule?
    4.2 Why is it spotty in its completion?
    4.3 Why have some states finished while others have not?
5. What will the effects on the United States be?
    5.1 Will it destroy the countryside?
    5.2 Will it isolate small towns?
    5.3 Will it result in more accidents?
    5.4 Will it lead to more pollution?

How to State the Problem

Numerous questions have been raised in the preceding example, certainly too many for one research project. The next move, then, is to select the one question that will receive your full attention. This choice is sometimes an arbitrary one because all the questions or many of them might be logical possibilities. Your background and preference enter into this choice. If you are interested in economics, you will likely choose the question concerned with finances; a concern with the environment will probably lead you to investigate the effects of the system on the United States. When you have made your choice, isolate the problem in a statement. Here are two examples:

STATEMENT OF THE PROBLEM: FINANCES

The interstate highway system in the United States, financed partially by the federal government and partially by the state governments, has not progressed as planned.

STATEMENT OF THE PROBLEM: EFFECTS

The interstate highway system will affect the environment.

These statements are so general that at first they may not appear to be very significant discoveries. But closer study shows that a giant step has been taken in limiting the subject and directing it toward the formation of a hypothesis. Certainly the financial aspects or the environmental effects of the interstate highway system are more specific than the broad subject of the system itself.

Although this example concerns a subject that would be

developed primarily through the use of library materials, the same process of discovering and stating the problem is applicable to reports based on empirical or field-study evidence.

In some instances you may be confronted with a topic about which you know so little that you are unable to ask questions meaningful enough to result in the formation of a statement of the problem. You should then check a reference work for an overview of the subject.

SURVEYING THE SOURCES

The statement of the problem will direct you in surveying the sources from which you will gather the evidence. Unless your survey is focused on a single aspect or question, you will waste time looking over sources that are related to the broad subject but not directly concerned with your specific problem. Similarly, you need to consider some preliminary materials when you plan to gather evidence from scientific research or a field study.

Library Materials

Begin the survey of library materials by checking the card catalog for books on your subject. Next, go to the reference room and use the *Readers' Guide to Periodical Literature* to get an idea of which periodicals contain articles pertaining to your subject. Besides using this basic guide, look into some other bibliographies of periodicals and books. (See chapter 3 for discussion on use of library materials.)

Because you now have a good idea of what you are looking for, you will be able to eliminate many titles immediately. Make bibliographical notes on some of the titles that sound interesting and relevant. These notes will be helpful in forming the preliminary bibliography.

Next, you should glance through some of the available sources and possibly take a few notes to use later when you form the hypothesis.

Remember that you are making a survey or a preliminary investigation of the sources. You will be forming a more extensive bibliography and recording more detailed notes after you have formed the hypothesis; hence, you should not spend excessive time on this survey.

Empirical and Field-Study Evidence

Before gathering empirical or field-study evidence, you will most likely refer to printed materials for background information. In addition, you will probably study records of other investigations similar to the one you are planning in order to get an idea what has already been discovered regarding the particular problem.

If you plan to conduct scientific experiments, be sure of the accessibility of equipment and materials. If you want to gather evidence from a field study, decide what method or methods you are going to employ and be sure that subjects or opportunities for observation are available.

ARRIVING AT THE HYPOTHESIS

You will find that once a hypothesis emerges, the research will take on direction and purpose. The hypothesis is a map, a chart and compass, a set of blueprints, a voice in the wilderness—or whatever your favorite metaphor happens to be.

Distinction of Terms

Although the terms *hypothesis* and *theory* are often used synonymously, there is a slight distinction in their meanings. Essentially, the hypothesis is a "less certain conclusion" than the theory. However, it should be noted that a theory is never totally certain either; even one that has been accepted for centuries can be disproved by new information.

Dewey, in his "Steps in Reflective Thinking" (see pp. 5–6), lists two other terms: *inference*, meaning a conclusion drawn from premises or evidence, and *guess*, meaning an opinion based on probability.

In order to simplify matters, the term *hypothesis* will be used in this book to embrace the varying concepts of the theory, inference, and guess, as necessary.

The hypothesis, then, advances a temporary and provisional idea, based on a limited amount of evidence. Once the evidence has been gathered and the hypothesis has been tested, it becomes the thesis statement that the research work sets out to defend, proposes to develop, and attempts to prove. However, in spite of all the defense, development, and proof, the thesis statement still is not totally certain. It is more so than the hypothesis, but it is not absolute because new evidence could destroy its validity.

It is possible to write a research work without a hypothesis, and subsequently without a thesis statement, but the result would be nothing more than a compilation of facts. A worthwhile study consists of fact-finding (guided by a hypothesis) and fact interpreting (guided by a thesis statement).

Formation of Hypotheses

While stating the problem and surveying the sources, you should have raised several questions and discovered some evidence to direct you toward the formation of a number of hypotheses. If not, retrace your steps by once again analyzing the problem and surveying the sources.

The following example illustrates the process you should follow in forming the hypothesis:

STATEMENT OF THE PROBLEM: FINANCES

The interstate highway system in the United States, financed partially by the federal government and partially by the state governments, has not progressed as planned.

GENERALIZATIONS FROM THE PRELIMINARY INVESTIGATION (SURVEY OF SOURCES)

1. Some states have not borne their share of the financing.
2. The federal government has not allocated sums to the states fairly.
3. There have been cases of suspected corruption on the part of contractors.
4. Partisan politics has entered into some of the decisions regarding allocation of money to various states.

The generalizations concerning the finances of the interstate highway system were formed after the survey of sources and were based on the limited amount of evidence examined. More extensive research may prove or disprove them. Hence, the careful writer does not reach a hasty conclusion and write a scathing paper on "Corruption in the Building of the Interstate Highway System." Instead, he will consider all four generalizations carefully and maybe even form hypotheses for each of them before he selects the one he will develop.

Proposed hypotheses

1. *Based on Generalization 1:* When all the states are willing to provide their share of financing for the construction of the interstate highway system, it will be completed.
2. *Based on Generalization 3:* If the corruption on the part of contractors is eliminated, the construction of the interstate highway system will continue at a more rapid rate.
3. *Based on Combined Generalizations 2 and 4:* When partisan politics is eliminated from the allocation of funds to states for the building of the interstate highway system, its completion will become a reality.

Each of the foregoing hypotheses provides a solution to the incompletion of this elaborate highway network. The hypothesis, then, gains another dimension; that is, in addition to stating the problem, it suggests a solution to the problem. Note the construction of the foregoing hypotheses: All three sentences are complex. The dependent clause states the problem and the solution; and the independent clause states the outcome.

Problem and solution stated in the dependent clause

If the corruption on the part of contractors is eliminated, . . .

Outcome stated in the independent clause

. . . the construction of the interstate highway system will continue at a more rapid rate.

Although there is no hard-and-fast rule that all hypotheses must be expressed in complex sentences, it is generally preferable and advantageous to do so. Not only does a hypothesis so worded set forth the problem, solution, and outcome, but it also lends a natural organization to the paper.

Selection of the Hypothesis

Choosing the most defensible hypothesis is the next step. This choice is based on your preference and on further investigation of the evidence. Once the selection has been made, you are ready to begin the full-scale collection of evidence.

This same process applies to the forming of a hypothesis for a report based on field-study or empirical evidence.

Construction of a Rough Outline

It is helpful to make a rough outline that will lend direction to the research and organization of the evidence as it is collected. If it does not seem possible at this point to make a rough outline—and sometimes, because of lack of evidence, it is not—you can form the outline when you have learned more about the subject and its logical parts.

Here is an example of a rough outline for the first hypothesis:

1. Discussion of the history of the interstate highway system
2. Discussion of the financial policies of the federal and state governments regarding the system
3. Examples of uncooperative states
4. Results of lack of cooperation on the progress of the construction
5. Possible solutions

During and after the research, you could add the subdivisions under the main points.

CONTINUING THE INVESTIGATION

Some students find the beginning—choosing a subject and limiting its scope—to be the most difficult step in the investigative process, but it need not be if it is approached in an orderly manner and if the mental tools of questioning, analyzing, and hypothesizing are put to good use. Once the idea is fixed, it will direct the remaining steps and gradually lead to the truth.

2

Gathering the Evidence

Chapter 3

Investigating Documented Sources

The true function of scholarship as of society is
not to stake out claims on which others must not trespass,
but provide a community of knowledge in which others
may share.

F. O. Matthiessen, *American Renaissance*

At this point the investigative process begins in earnest, as you look into the "community of knowledge" available to you. The subject analysis and the hypothesis formation, which have already been accomplished, give direction to locating and selecting library materials. However, these steps are only preliminary ones; you must also evaluate and take notes on the evidence after you collect it. Hence, the four parts of this procedure are as follows:

1. Locating the materials
2. Selecting the materials
3. Evaluating the materials
4. Recording the evidence

It would be incorrect to suggest that each of these is an independent activity; they are usually carried out simultaneously. However, for purposes of analysis, the four parts will be considered one at a time.

LOCATING THE MATERIALS

The key to knowledge is not so much what you know but how skillful you are at finding answers. Therefore, in order to become a good researcher, you need to develop the ability to locate the materials required to answer your questions and develop and substantiate your ideas.

Library Use

Although research is not limited to the library, it usually begins there. Understanding the library's organization and using its services and reference materials will help you to form a list of promising sources, that is, a *preliminary bibliography*.

Classification Systems. Classification systems have been developed in order to facilitate the arrangement of library materials in an accessible manner. Under these systems, each work is cataloged and labeled with a call number. The *Dewey decimal system* is the most commonly used, although it is sometimes modified in small libraries. The more detailed *Library of Congress system* is used by a number of college and university libraries. Although you should be thoroughly acquainted with the systems of classification, it is not necessary to memorize or to be able to interpret all the subtleties of either the Dewey decimal or the Library of Congress system.

Here are profiles of the two systems, with sample call numbers from each:

DEWEY DECIMAL

000 General works	500 Natural science
100 Philosophy	600 Useful arts
200 Religion	700 Fine arts
300 Sociology	800 Literature
400 Philology	900 History

SAMPLE CALL NUMBER FROM DEWEY DECIMAL SYSTEM

Book: Bradbook, M. C. *The Growth and Structure of Elizabethan Drama.*

Call number: 822.09
              B81
              g

Explanation: The "8" denotes literature, and the other numbers indicate that it is a critical-historical work on English drama. "B" stands for the first letter of the author's last name; "81" is a code number for the author's full name; "g" stands for the first letter of the first word of the title, excluding "the."

LIBRARY OF CONGRESS

A	General works	M	Music
B	Philosophy, religion	N	Fine arts
C	History	P	Language and literature
D	Foreign history	Q	Science
E, F	American history	R	Medicine
G	Geography	S	Agriculture
H	Social sciences	T	Technology
J	Political science	U	Military service
K	Law	V	Naval science
L	Education	Z	Library science, bibliography

SAMPLE CALL NUMBER FROM LIBRARY OF CONGRESS SYSTEM

Book: James, William. *Talks to Teachers on Psychology and to Students on Some of Life's Ideals.*

Call Number: LB
              1051
              J34
              1958

Explanation: "L" stands for education, thus, the book would be found in the education section. "B" is added to denote philosophy. (The double letters are a common practice in this system.) The subject of the book, then, is educational philosophy. The numbers on the second line denote a subdivision under education. On the third line, "J34" is a symbol for the author's last name; the numbers are a special code. On the fourth line, "1958" is the year of publication; this date is omitted if the book is a reprint.

The method for identifying authors used by both the Dewey decimal and the Library of Congress systems was developed by Charles A. Cutter (1837–1903), a Boston librarian. It is flexible and adaptable to the specific needs of any library. Small libraries often omit the author symbols entirely. However, in large libraries, a number of books may have the same subject designation; therefore, a further identification is necessary.

Card Catalog.   There are two ways to obtain call numbers. One is to refer to the floor plan of the library, go to the stacks, locate the books on your particular subject, and then browse. The second is to use the card catalog. In some libraries the first alternative is immediately eliminated because the stacks are closed except to library personnel and other authorized individuals. In order to obtain a book under these circumstances, you must fill out a *call slip* based on the information in the card catalog and turn it over to an attendant, who will secure the book for you. Even when the stacks are open, it is advisable to begin with the card catalog unless you are reasonably certain of the books you need.

A good card catalog provides a cross-index to the *author*, *title*, and *subject* of all books and bound pamphlets in the library. Therefore, each work will have at least three cards; works with two or more authors, titles, or subjects will have additional cards. In many libraries the subject cards are in a separate catalog, and the author and title cards are filed together. In others all three cards are in the same catalog or are divided into three catalogs.

The *author card* is filed alphabetically by the first letter of the author's last name. The cards of major writers are arranged as follows: (1) collections, (2) selections from collections, (3) individual works in alphabetical order by title, (4) single works with one or more coauthors, (5) edited or translated works, and (6) works *about* the author, in alphabetical order according to *their* authors' names.

Here is a typical author card:

	AUTHOR CARD
Library Call Number, based on Dewey Decimal or L. of C.	]]]]]]]]]]
Author	Jones, Ernest, 1879–1958
Title Other details on contents Publisher & date	The life and work of Sigmund Freud. Edited and abridged by Lionel Trilling and Steven Marcus. With an introduction by Lionel Trilling. New York, Basic Books [1961]
Number of pages; illustrated; size	541 p. illus. 25 cm
Other heading in catalog	1 Freud, Sigmund, 1856–1939.

Author's full name	Full name: Alfred Ernest Jones
L. of C. & D. D. classification numbers	BF 173.F85J612* 926.1

* Both Freud (the subject) and Jones (the author) are identified in the author code.

The *title card* is placed in the catalog according to the first word in the title, excluding "a," "an," "the." The placement of the *subject card* is determined by the first letter of the subject. Subdivisions of a topic can provide an instant bibliography on the subject; under the heading "Science," for instance, you may find cards listing books that cover such topics as "Abbreviations," "Concepts," and "Dictionaries." Sometimes at the ends of subject listings there are "see also" cards that supply convenient cross-references.

Ideally, the card catalog should follow the foregoing description without variation and guide you to the exact book you need without fail. Unfortunately, this is not always the case; card catalogs are sometimes faulty. You should understand the intricacies and makeup of the filing system thoroughly enough to step around its omissions and errors and still locate the material you need. And you should not be surprised to find a particular book cataloged differently in various libraries because the complex classification system is subject to varying interpretations.

List of Periodicals.   Most libraries provide a list of periodicals to which they subscribe currently and to which they have subscribed in the past. Usually, this list indicates to what date the file extends and whether the copies are loose, bound, or on microfilm. In addition, there are various guides to periodical literature. Libraries usually mark these to show which periodicals are available in that particular library.

Guide to Audiovisual Materials.   If the collection of audiovisual materials is not extensive, it will probably be cataloged in drawers placed at the end of the regular card catalog. In the case of a large collection, such materials will be cataloged separately in the audiovisual department. In other instances, the audiovisual materials will be cataloged, usually by title and subject, within the regular card catalog.

Union Catalog. In addition to their regular catalogs, some libraries have a *union catalog*, which holds duplicates of the cards in the Library of Congress catalog and some other American libraries. If a library does not have a union catalog, it may have copies of the Library of Congress catalog on microfilm.

The main branch of some city and county libraries that have several branches or are cooperating with other libraries in the immediate area will have a union catalog covering the holdings of all the branch or cooperating libraries.

Assistance in the Library. Both beginning and experienced researchers will occasionally find themselves bewildered by the complexities of library organization. It is then time to turn to a librarian for assistance in locating materials. Most librarians are extremely cooperative, but you should not expect them to form your bibliography or carry out your basic research.

Many libraries publish a guide to their organization and resources. These brochures are helpful in orienting you to a library you have not previously used.

Interlibrary Loans. Most libraries offer access to the resources of the state library and cooperating college libraries through interlibrary loans. However, these loans often take several weeks and should not be relied upon for short-term projects.

Reserving Books. In case the book you want is not on the shelf, ask at the circulation desk if it has been checked out. If it has not, the library staff will instigate a search for the book. If it has been checked out, you may place a hold on the book to reserve it when it is returned.

Reference Materials

The classification systems and the card catalog will guide you to many of the materials you need. But they should be supplemented by reference works, especially for periodic literature that is not indexed in the card catalog.

Reference materials fall into two classifications: (1) *general reference works* (such as a general encyclopedia) that provide bibliographical and/or factual information on a variety of subjects; (2) *specific reference works* (such as a handbook of literature) that give bibliographical and/or factual information on a single subject.

In a small library both general and specific reference works are kept in one reference room. But in a large library the general reference works are usually in the main reference room, and the specific reference works are in special reference sections in the various divisions of the library. For example, all the reference works pertaining to the social sciences would be found in the social science section.

A reference work will help you to form a preliminary bibliography and will often provide you with an overview of your subject as well.

The following discussion is concerned with both general and specific reference works. Selected bibliographies of these reference works are provided in appendix A (p. 253) and appendix B (p. 260).

Books about Books. Because several thousand books are published each year in the United States alone, there is a necessity for systematic guides called *bibliographies* to lead the right person to the right book at the right time. *Basic bibliographies* list the author, title, publisher, and city and date of publication. *Annotated bibliographies* give this information and also provide some comments about each book's contents and organization. *Annotated-critical bibliographies* add critical or analytical comments to the basic information. The proliferation of bibliographies has led to the compiling of *bibliographies of bibliographies*.

Lists of sources, including both books and periodicals, are not found only in bibliographical works. They also appear at the ends of many encyclopedia articles, textbooks, and scholarly works. In addition, trade publications provide bibliographical information. The major American trade publication is *Books in Print*, which lists its entries by author, title, and subject. Publishers' lists are cumulated once a year in *Publishers' Trade List Annual*. Other sources include book reviews, cumulative indexes to these reviews, government publications, library publications, and specialized lists.

Books about Periodical Literature. *Periodicals*, or *periodical literature* (usually called *serials* by librarians), include all regular publications, such as general-interest magazines, newspapers, newsmagazines, scholarly journals, and house organs.

There are numerous guides to articles in periodicals, the most basic index being the *Readers' Guide to Periodical Literature.* Some publications, such as the *New York Times*, print their own indexes covering the contents of each issue. There are also specialized indexes to periodicals in specific fields, such as the *Index to Legal Periodicals* and the *Education Index*.

Monthly publications devoted entirely to *abstracts* are another guide to periodicals. Abstracts index current articles and give summaries of their contents, thus serving somewhat the same purpose for periodical literature that annotated-critical bibliographies serve for books.

When the library you are using does not have a periodical that you need, you should refer to one of the serial-holding lists to find out what libraries have this particular periodical. The two main works that show the periodical holdings of major libraries are the *Union List of Serials* and the *New Serials Titles*. Once you learn where the periodical is available, you may be able to arrange to borrow it through an interlibrary loan. Often, upon your request for a certain periodical, the librarian will do the checking in the serial-holding lists for you.

Books about Audiovisual Materials. Guides to the increasing kinds of audiovisual sources—films, microfilms, recordings, and graphic materials—are similar to those concerning books and periodicals. Examples of such guides are specialized film catalogs such as the *Educator's Guide to Free Films* and the *American Film Catalog* and Schwann's monthly *Record and Tape Guide*, a basic listing of audio materials. Catalogs from companies producing and renting audiovisual materials are also helpful.

Books of Collected Information. *Encyclopedias* are the standard collections of information. General encyclopedias, ranging from one volume to twenty or more, cover every conceivable topic in varying degrees of depth. Most encyclopedia publishers issue supplements periodically in an effort to keep the sets up to date. The specialized encyclopedias, sometimes called *dictionaries*, provide general and specific information about a certain field. The *Dance Encyclopedia*, the *Concise Encyclopedia* of *Western Philosophy,* and *Grove's Dictionary of Music and Musicians* are typical of such specialized works. Most of these are in one volume; some, such as *Grove's Dictionary,* comprise several volumes.

Handbooks, a catchall designation, cover nearly every facet of knowledge. There are handbooks to assist readers, writers, and speakers; examples are the *Oxford Companions* to literature and *Bartlett's Familiar Quotations. Yearbooks,* another species of handbooks, are annual compilations of general or specialized information; they include titles as diverse as *Commodity Year Book* and *Social Work Year Book.* In addition, there are yearly guides to almost everything, including colleges, research in progress, television and film productions, debate topics, and literary markets. Special series on authors, how-to books on projects and hobbies, college catalogs, play catalogs, and government publications represent other kinds of handbooks.

Books about Words. Ranging from the pocket-size dictionary to the monumental *Oxford English Dictionary* in thirteen volumes plus supplements, books about words contain information on all aspects of the history, meaning, connotation, use, origin, and pronunciation of words. A dictionary such as *American Pronunciation* deals solely with pronunciation, and one such as the *Chemical Dictionary* defines only terms related to a specific field. Some dictionaries specialize in slang, synonyms and antonyms, derivations, and regionalisms. In addition to English-language dictionaries, there are dictionaries of foreign languages in most reference rooms.

Books about words include *concordances,* which are alphabetical indexes of the principal words found in a book, with reference to the passage and context in which they appear. Concordances prove helpful in using the Bible or studying the work of a major writer such as Shakespeare.

Books about People. Extensive reference material exists on important persons—worldwide, past and present. Besides the general *Who's Who in America* and its companion *Who Was Who in America,* numerous *Who's Who* books contain information on people from a particular state, region, or foreign country. Biographical information on persons in fields ranging from the arts to labor may be found in specialized biographical works, often called *dictionaries of biography*. These surveys frequently include bibliographies of books and articles concerning their subjects.

Even a city telephone directory may be helpful in locating information, and most major cities' directories are in reference rooms.

In addition to the reference works on people, all libraries have biographical sections, and encyclopedias contain biographical materials and sometimes related bibliographies.

Books about Places. A variety of books provide geographic information. They are usually concerned with one or more of the following aspects of geography: physical, economic, human, ecological, governmental, and historical. For information on a limited scope, *almanacs* are useful. They contain data on countries, states, and other regions, as well as statistical information on mountains, rivers, lakes, and other specific places. *Gazetteers*, or geographic dictionaries, are comprehensive books consisting of descriptive entries under geographic place names; the names are arranged alphabetically and the descriptions include basic geographical data. Collections of maps, called *atlases*, fall into two categories: *historical* and *current*. General historical atlases contain maps showing the world or parts of it at different periods in history; specialized historical atlases include works such as *The Official Atlas of the Civil War* and the *Atlas of the Bible*. Current atlases depict the modern world by showing the changes in national boundaries. (Needless to say, such atlases can become outdated quickly.)

In addition to these standard works, information on places may be obtained from guidebooks for tourists, geographic handbooks, and government publications, especially the pamphlets from the Department of the Interior and the chambers of commerce of major cities. General encyclopedias also provide extensive geographic information.

Other Works

Written sources other than reference materials fall into five categories: literary works, nonfiction books, pamphlets, government publications, and unpublished works.

Literary Works. *Literary works* appear either in single volumes or in *anthologies*, which are collections of literary works.

Obviously, such works are indispensable to someone writing about literature. Although students have been known to prepare literary papers without referring to the basic sources (plays, poems, novels, and short stories), this practice is not recommended.

Nonfiction Books. The following kinds of books may be classified under the general heading of *nonfiction:*

1. IN-DEPTH TREATMENT OF A LIMITED SUBJECT. Examples include biographies, such as Nancy Milford's *Zelda* (New York: Harper & Row, 1970), which is an account of the life and times of F. Scott Fitzgerald's wife, and studies of specific problems, such as Charles E. Silverman's *Crisis in the Classroom* (New York: Random House, 1970), which is an investigation of contemporary public education.

2. SURVEY OF A GENERAL SUBJECT. An example is a one-volume history of the United States from 1607 to 1972.

3. COLLECTIONS OF ESSAYS OR ARTICLES. These are frequently unified by a single theme. Examples are *Mark Twain: A Collection of Critical Essays* (Ed. Henry Nash Smith; Englewood Cliffs, N.J.: Prentice-Hall, 1963) and *The Vanishing Landscape: A Collection of Critical Essays on Pollution and Environmental Control* (Eds. Donald G. Douglas and John R. Stewart; Skokie, Ill.: National Textbook Co., 1970).

4. PHILOSOPHICAL WORKS. Examples are Martin Buber's *I and Thou* (New York: Scribner's, 1958), a book of religious thought, and Ernest Becker's *Beyond Alienation: A Philosophy of Education for the Crisis of Democracy* (New York: George Braziller, 1967).

Pamphlets. Essentially short books, usually under 100 pages in length, *pamphlets* fall into the same categories as books. Some libraries bind pamphlets of special value and shelve them with regular books. They may also be kept in vertical files, arranged under subject headings. Bound pamphlets are cataloged, but pamphlets in vertical files are not. Pamphlets cover a variety of subjects; they may be compilations of facts, religious or political discussions, reprints of articles from other sources, or the texts of speeches or symposia.

Government Publications. The governments of the United States and other countries publish a wide variety of books and pamphlets. These materials—sometimes free, otherwise generally inexpensive—are accurate, up to date, and objective. (The last is significant because most of the publications are written not by officials on a political level but by experts employed in specific departments.)

Many U.S. government publications are the result of requests by the public for information on specific matters. When the same information has been requested often enough, the agency may prepare a booklet on the subject. Other titles include statistical reports (based on the census or other studies) and the reports of special presidential commissions.

State and local governments in the United States also publish materials on their particular regions.

Many foreign governments distribute English-language pamphlets containing information on travel, industry, geography, and other aspects of their respective countries.

Nearly every library has some government publications; those designated as depository libraries receive all U.S. government issues except those restricted for security reasons. Guides to government documents are listed in appendix A, Selected Bibliography of Basic Reference Works (p. 254).

Unpublished Works. The libraries of colleges and universities that have graduate schools usually hold copies of the theses and dissertations completed by students seeking advanced degrees there. These works are not often cataloged in any manner and are usually shelved according to either subject matter or the writer's last name. Of course, they vary in quality, but in many cases they are useful for research work.

The *Dissertation Abstracts International* (formerly called *Dissertation Abstracts*) is a descriptive and current listing of 95 percent of the doctoral dissertations produced each year at over 250 colleges and universities. It now includes dissertations from major European universities (under the old title, it consisted of work only from U.S. schools). Also, approximately 350 abstracts of selected master's theses are published each year in *Masters Abstracts*. A service called DATRIX provides direct access to reference information from doctoral dissertations. This computerized service, which will produce a list of dissertations related to a particular topic, is available through University Microfilms, Ann Arbor, Michigan.

Some libraries have collections of mimeographed or typed

articles on matters of local interest, including geography, biography, and history. In addition, letters, diaries, and journals
often contain valuable historical or personal information; these
materials are available in many libraries, museums, historical
societies, and private collections.

Periodical Literature

Ranging from general interest to the esoteric, *periodical literature* is a basic source for research work. Much of the material
is more current than that found in books, and much of it never
appears in books.

"Periodical" describes something that recurs at intervals of
time; thus periodical literature is published at recurring intervals—daily, weekly, monthly, bimonthly, and so forth. The
publication time is usually regular, but not in all cases. Some
periodicals recur at undetermined intervals, and some never
recur at all.

It is impossible to describe all periodical literature, but the
following paragraphs examine those sources that are most valuable for research purposes.

Newspapers. Regional daily or weekly *newspapers* may
sometimes contain helpful material; however, newspapers with
a broader scope (such as the *New York Times*, the *Christian
Science Monitor*, and the *National Observer*) usually provide
a more comprehensive coverage and analysis of current events
and problems.

Newsmagazines. The major newsmagazines—*Time*, *U.S.
News & World Report*, and *Newsweek*—offer a roundup of the
week's events and usually a detailed treatment of at least one
subject.

General-Interest Magazines. Although the general-interest
magazines are vanishing, some that remain still contain good
articles. *Harper's*, *Atlantic Monthly*, and the *New Yorker* all treat
varied topics on a fairly intellectual level.

Scholarly Journals. Especially useful in research, scholarly
journals contain articles on limited aspects of the particular subject to which each journal is devoted.

Special-Interest Magazines. Nearly every subject under the
sun is covered in the so-called special-interest magazines: travel,

religion, politics, human relations, gardening, cooking, meta-physics, bottle collecting, to name a few. Not all these maga-zines are reliable for research purposes; some are superficial or biased in their treatment of subjects. However, publications such as *Psychology Today* and *Arizona Highways* exemplify special-interest magazines that could be considered worthwhile research tools.

Reproductions and Audiovisual Materials

In some ways the advent of twentieth-century communication technology is as significant to research and scholarship as the invention of the printing press was several hundred years earlier. Through reproductions of printed matter and the audiovisual materials (recordings and graphics), a wealth of knowledge has been preserved and made easily accessible.

Reproductions of Printed Matter. A leader in the field of reproducing printed matter is University Microfilms, founded in 1938 to provide researchers and librarians with scholarly materials that are difficult to obtain or to keep in their original forms. Today there are several other companies providing sim-ilar or slightly different services.

Microfilms, small reels of films which are placed in machines that enlarge the photographic reproduction of the page to a readable size, are the most common of the new information storage devices. Also becoming popular are film cards, called *microfiches*, which are inserted into a machine that projects a readable image on a screen. Some of the reading machines are equipped with reproducing devices that will print the material for use at a later time. In addition, *facsimiles*—actual, full-size reproductions of books or periodicals—are available. Of special interest are the facsimiles of older works because they preserve the typography and makeup of the original.

Microfilmed sources include general periodicals, books, and special collections. The University Microfilms catalog of recent and back-file periodicals currently consists of more than 5,000 titles, with publication dates beginning as far back as 1669. Many government documents are also available, as well as news-papers ranging from the *New York Times* to the *Japan Times*. All the periodicals on microfilm are indexed.

One or more copies of over 37,000 out-of-print books may be ordered from University Microfilms through the On-Demand Publishing program. The books are reproduced either on microfilm or as facsimiles. Reproductions of early books from Great Britain and America are immediately available.

The service offers special collections of microfilmed materials on specific topics such as *Source Materials in the Field of Theatre*, a compilation of books, periodicals, manuscripts, journals, and diaries concerned with world theater, and *The March of America*, a survey of American history from 1493 to 1893.

The ERIC materials consist of selected articles from current educational publications. This information is indexed and reproduced on microfiches.

The availability of reproductions of printed matter varies, but more and more libraries are taking advantage of these materials. The problems of providing storage space for back-file periodicals, obtaining out-of-print and rare copies, and preventing deterioration of such materials are solved by reliance on microfilm and reproductions.

The total impact of the reproduction of printed matter on microfilms and microfiches (called *micrographics* in the industry) will not be realized for some time. However, a *Saturday Review* article on the subject offered some predictions.

No one is quite sure where micrographics is going, or how it will solve some of its tougher problems, but there is no question that it is coming to play a larger part in American life every year. Already microfilm is in hospitals, law offices, department stores, churches, banks, automobile service centers, factories, offices, police stations, schools, and government offices. By the end of the century, it is estimated, only 50 per cent of our records will be on paper. . . . Before that time, micrographics may well become a prime factor in education and an entirely new means of bringing information and entertainment into everybody's home.[1]

Recordings. *Records* and *tapes* often contain information not obtainable in printed form; for example, Tyrone Guthrie's lecture "Directing a Play," which is in the Folkways Records series, is not available elsewhere. Similarly, Caedmon Records

1. John Tebbel, "Micrographics: A Growing Industry," *Saturday Review*, 10 July 1971, p. 50.

and other companies have produced recordings of authors reading and discussing their own works. Record albums and the
booklets included in many of them are excellent sources of information on the music and the artists.

Recordings of speeches, musical performances, and theatrical
productions are available. Still another growing field is the recording of standard printed works, such as the Bible, and of
periodic literature. Much of this material has been recorded on
cassettes, small tapes that are inserted directly into specially designed devices.

Many libraries have extensive record and tape collections
from which you may borrow. If the record or tape cannot be
taken from the library, the audiovisual department provides
listening facilities.

Graphics.   Other valuable sources are *graphics*, or visual materials, including films, filmstrips, slides, video tapes, and photographic collections.

The uses for graphic materials in research are varied. A student of American painting, for instance, would benefit from
viewing the National Art Gallery's collections of slides of representative American masterpieces. These slides may be ordered
directly from the National Gallery, or they might be available
through a library or museum nearby. Some libraries have collections or can obtain selected films for a student researching some
aspect of the art of film making. Usually a rental fee is charged.
Video tapes of original, commercial, or educational television
productions sometimes contain specialized information. These
tapes are often available through a college television department
or an educational television station. Filmstrips contain excellent
surveys and give information on matters ranging from use of
the library to highway safety. Most libraries hold collections of
filmstrips, or you may obtain them from other sources such as
businesses and some government agencies.

Libraries and museums often have collections of old and
rare photographs and documents that can be especially helpful
to the historian. (Certainly the Brady photographs have played a
unique part in the historical record of the American Civil War.)
The process for copying such photographs and documents has
become simple and inexpensive. Copies are often on sale in the
shops connected with museums, or it might be possible to order

copies through the museum facilities. Naturally, museums or libraries seldom lend rare photographs or documents to individuals for copying purposes.

Recordings and graphic materials add another dimension to research. And as a result of these developments, new kinds of research projects have evolved that are presented primarily through audio and/or visual materials rather than the written word. (The preparation of such projects will be discussed in chapter 8.)

Sources for Audiovisual Materials. Although libraries are increasing their holdings of audiovisual materials, many of the ones you need may not be available in your particular library. These materials are frequently expensive and difficult to store. In an attempt to overcome these problems, several systems have been set up. Sometimes the various departments in a college or university will have their own audiovisual libraries. The materials may be available only to faculty for classroom or research uses, but if you are engaged in a project under the supervision of a faculty member, he can usually help you obtain the materials you need. Many public schools have formed city- or countywide audiovisual centers, and it may be possible to borrow or rent from their holdings. States, too, often have centers where audiovisual materials are available for lending and renting. The contents of such centers are usually cataloged in widely distributed and up-to-date publications.

Other sources for audiovisual materials are businesses and government agencies that either distribute materials free or sell them at a minimal cost for promotional or educational purposes. Renting from commercial services or buying materials outright are other possibilities. (Catalogs and guides for obtaining audiovisual materials from various sources are listed in appendix A under "Books about Audiovisual Materials," p. 255.)

SELECTING THE MATERIALS

Too often a beginning researcher locates a number of sources pertaining to his topic and thinks that he must read them all in order to decide which ones will be applicable. There are several tools, however, that help determine the amount, value, and kind of information a book or pamphlet contains. And there is a way to get to the main idea of an article by surveying it. Similarly, it is possible to determine the usefulness of audiovisual materials without listening to them or viewing them in their entirety.

Books and Pamphlets

Most books, many pamphlets, and some unpublished works have part of or all the following tools as an aid in surveying them.

Preface. In the *preface*, which is seldom more than three or four pages long, the author usually states his purpose, his methods, and his debts. For example, Silverman, in the preface to *Crisis in the Classroom*, sets forth his purpose on the first page by advancing the idea that the public school classroom is a reflection of, and a contributor to, the larger crisis in American society and that in order to solve this specific crisis, everyone must be alerted to what is wrong and what needs to be done. He then tells how he visited schools, observed teachers, and gathered information; he concludes by thanking numerous people for assistance. Through reading Silverman's preface, you get a good idea of what the book will cover and how the information was collected.

Foreword. The *foreword* is a brief comment on the work by someone other than the author. Because the writer of the foreword (whose name appears at its close) is often an authority in the field, his remarks can give important clues about the reliability of the work.

Introduction. The *introduction*, which is usually written by the author or editor, may be defined as a preview of the material that follows. In the introduction to *The Vanishing Landscape*, the editors point out that the current issue on the environment is no longer how to exploit the resources but how to protect ourselves from their exploitation. This central idea is developed more fully in the articles that constitute the main part of the book. Some introductions, especially to literary works, are extensive, offering specific information and critical comments not given elsewhere in the book.

Table of Contents. Useful as a synopsis or overview of the book's scope, the *table of contents* is a listing (with beginning page numbers) of the titles of parts (if the book is divided in this manner), chapter headings, and sometimes divisions within chapters. For example, in the table of contents to *Beyond Alienation*, the following entry appears:

Textual Aids.   Especially common in survey books, *textual aids* are helpful in locating specific information. The main kinds are division headings, paragraph headings, glosses (now more commonly called *marginal notes*), and chapter summaries (at either the beginning or the end of a chapter).

Epilogue or Afterword.   The *epilogue*, or *afterword*, is a concluding comment on the work. Written by the author or editor, it is often a challenge, sometimes a final question, and in other instances a summation of a problem. The epilogue in Silverman's *Crisis in the Classroom* is a combination of all three.

Appendix or Appendixes (*Appendices*).   The *appendixes*, placed at the end of a book, contain supplementary material, usually of an explanatory, documentary, statistical, or bibliographical nature. Appendixes are not particularly common except in educational and scholarly works. One example of their use in a work of general nonfiction is Joe McGinnis's *The Selling of the President* (New York: Trident Press, 1969), which includes as appendixes communications, data sheets, and other documents from the planning of President Nixon's 1968 campaign strategy—material that illuminates some of the events described in the text.

Index or Indexes (*Indices*).   The *index* is an alphabetical listing of names, places, and topics, along with the numbers of the pages on which they are mentioned or discussed. For example, the following entry in the index to *Zelda* gives immediate help to someone studying Fitzgerald's *Tender Is the Night* (New York: Scribner's, 1951):

Tender Is the Night (F. Scott Fitzgerald, early titles, *Doctor Diver's Holiday; The Drunkard's Holiday*), 139–40, 152, 153, 172,

190, 217, 224, 234, 260, 261, 266, 267, 268, 281, 284, 286–87, 292, 298.

In some instances different categories (names, places, topics, authors and titles) are indexed separately, but in shorter works the index is usually collective. In a well-indexed book, there may also be subheadings under the main headings, directing the reader to specific aspects of the topic, as well as cross-references directing him to related entries.

Periodic Literature

Because guides to periodicals list the name and page number of an article, you can locate the material with a minimum of effort. Once you have located it, you must determine whether you need to read the entire article. Usually you can find a statement of the main idea in the first paragraph or so. Scanning subsequent paragraphs and making use of division headings, if there are any, will help you to determine the content and appropriateness of the article. For example, if you were studying Ibsen's dramatic technique, an article entitled "Ibsen as a Stage Craftsman" would likely prove significant. At the end of the first paragraph in this article, the author states: "The following examination of his [Ibsen's] experience as a stage craftsman endeavors to assess the influence of the practical theater on his work as a dramatist."[2] On the other hand, you could eliminate for your purpose an article entitled "Ibsen's Conception of Truth." In the third paragraph of this study, after an introductory discussion of truth in German drama, the writer states:

His [Ibsen's] aim is to establish "a new truth" which, in spite of the relativity of its content, imposes a much greater responsibility upon the individual than either the "ideal demand" or submission to the generally accepted codes and norms.[3]

Obviously, this study is more concerned with Ibsen's philosophy than with his dramatic technique.

2. P. F. D. Tennant, "Ibsen as a Stage Craftsman," *Modern Language Review*, 34 (Oct. 1939), 557.
3. F. W. Kaufmann, "Ibsen's Conception of Truth," *Germanic Review*, 32 (Apr. 1957), 84.

Reproductions and Audiovisual Materials

Because reproduced material consists of books and periodicals, you could apply the same methods mentioned in connection with the originals for determining usefulness. Annotated bibliographies and catalogs provide some information on what audiovisual materials contain. The brochures that accompany such materials are also useful; however, keep in mind that these brochures are often written for promotional purposes.

EVALUATING THE MATERIALS

Selecting a variety of materials is a worthy goal, but you must consider their quality, too. The techniques for evaluating printed and audiovisual materials are approximately the same.

Recency

The criterion of *recency* does not apply in all cases because in some fields the date of the source is not important. In fact, in historical research, the older the document is, the more valuable it may be.

However, in fields such as science and technology, recency is of great importance in many instances. Even in disciplines such as literature and philosophy there may be new ideas and fresh insights that are significant. For example, some of the early biographies of Mark Twain tended to convey a "nice old man" image; whereas more recent studies have examined all sides of his complex personality.

Checking the back of the title page for the date of original publication (not the reprint date) is easy with most books. Some standard works are revised periodically, and for these you should note the date of the most recent revision. The publication date is not always given in older books, but you can often determine an approximate date through internal evidence. In some instances, pamphlets of a questionable nature, such as one devoted to propaganda, may not show publication dates; however, this information is practically always provided in dependable works.

Reliability

Although probably a more difficult factor than recency to determine, *reliability* is at the same time the more important. Even though it may appear presumptuous, you should examine the credentials of the writer. The fact that he had something published does not automatically make him an authority. The experienced researcher in a specific field becomes acquainted with the names of scholars whose works are usually reliable. Any student of American literature, for instance, soon learns that Robert E. Spiller's studies are responsible, and American history students know that they can bank on the soundness of Charles and Mary Beard's work. On the other hand, if you pick up a book on political and economic conditions in Africa's emerging nations and you are not familiar with the author's qualifications and background, you should consult a dictionary of biography to learn something about him. Another example along this line is a recent book on regional theater in the United States. Because its author was a New Yorker whose experience had not gone beyond the New York theater, people in other parts of the country might justifiably question his qualifications to write about theater in areas largely foreign to him. Also, a recent trend has encouraged persons with unrelated backgrounds to become instant authorities on public education. Although experience does not necessarily make for reliability or eliminate bias, the observations, conclusions, and solutions of the inexperienced are often questionable.

Comparing views held by various authorities on a particular subject is another important aspect of determining reliability. In addition, when you are using a work that required research, you should determine the extent and methods of the research that went into it. You can usually obtain this information by studying the preface, other introductory material, and the bibliography.

In some cases you might want to check the publisher's standing and the appropriateness of the book's being issued by a particular company; library guides to publishers contain this information.

Reference guides can also help you check the reliability of a work; annotated-critical bibliographies, abstracts, and book review digests contain opinions of qualified persons regarding the scholarship in various works.

Finally, instructors and librarians, through their broader experience, can help you locate reliable sources.

Checklist for Evaluating Materials

Although other methods might present themselves in special instances, the following checklist is a standard guide to the evaluation of sources:

1. Know the subject under investigation.
2. Use the tools provided in the materials.
3. Sample the materials.
4. Check the publication dates.
5. Investigate the authors' and publishers' qualifications.
6. Compare sources on the same subject.
7. Determine the extent and methods of research that went into the work.
8. Use reference guides.
9. Rely on instructors' and librarians' experience for guidance.

RECORDING THE EVIDENCE

Once the materials have been located, selected, and evaluated, you then need to record the bibliographical information of the sources and make notes on the evidence.

Working Bibliography

Form a *working bibliography* by recording each entry accurately and completely on three-by-five-inch index cards. The following illustrations show typical bibliography cards for a book and a periodical article. (Forms for listing other materials are given in appendix E, "Forms for Bibliographical Entries," p. 288.)

BIBLIOGRAPHY CARD FOR A BOOK

> Bobker, Lee R. Elements of Film.
> New York: Harcourt, Brace &
> World, Inc., 1969.

BIBLIOGRAPHY CARD FOR AN ARTICLE

> Alpert, Hollis. "The Diversification
> of Shirley MacLaine." Saturday
> Review, 27 Feb. 1971, pp. 43-45.

The importance of making a complete bibliography card immediately after selecting a source cannot be stressed too much because the cards will serve to relocate sources, document references, and compile a final bibliography.

Note-Taking

Notes record facts taken from the sources. When you begin writing, you will use these facts to support and develop the ideas in your paper. At that point the facts will evolve into developmental materials, including details, examples, direct quotations, statistics, definitions, and analogies. (A complete discussion of developmental materials begins on p. 106, chapter 6.)

• *Materials for Notes.* Three-by-five-inch index cards, which are usually sufficient for bibliographical information, are generally too small for note cards and might be confused with the bibliography cards. Beyond this word of warning, nothing more need be said about the materials for note-taking except that they should be acceptable to you. In view of the fact that the quality of the notes takes precedence, they may be recorded on any size of index card, half sheets of paper, or full sheets of paper. Sometimes, however, an instructor may request that you submit your note cards for examination and may require that you use a specific size of card.

• *Rules for Making Note Cards.* The cardinal rule for note-taking is never to record more than one note on a single card. The necessity for following this rule is difficult for the beginner to grasp, but strict adherence to this principle will assure ease in sorting and organizing the notes as the paper is being written.

Another important rule is to write legibly because you will not use the note cards immediately and will need to be able to read them later. Generally, it is a waste of time to scribble the notes and then type them.

The third rule covers the bibliographical information for the note's source. It is not necessary to include all of the bibliographical data because the source can be easily identified by the author's name or a code number leading to the bibliography card that contains the complete information. The note cards on p. 54 illustrate these procedures.

Fourth, record the number or numbers of the page or pages from which the note was taken. If the note was derived from two or more pages, place a slash mark within the note to indicate at what point the page number changes.

Fifth, indicate the subject of the note at the top of the card in order to facilitate sorting and organizing the cards at a later time. It is best, whenever possible, for each note card to bear a designation of the outline subdivision to which it pertains. If the outline is not complete enough to follow or is nonexistent, then you should place a descriptive word or phrase at the top of the card.

If you are lost in a maze of technique, you may almost lose sight of the real purpose for making note cards: to record spe-

cific facts from the evidence in an accurate and complete manner.
In summary, the rules for making note cards are as follows:

1. Place one note only on each card.
2. Record the information legibly.
3. Identify the source.
4. Record the page number or numbers.
5. Identify the subject of the note.
6. Record the information accurately and completely.

Parts of a Note Card. The following illustration shows the
three essential parts of a note card:

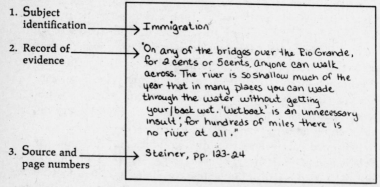

1. Subject
   identification ——————→ Immigration

2. Record of ——————————→ "On any of the bridges over the Rio Grande,
   evidence   for 2 cents or 5 cents, anyone can walk
                           across. The river is so shallow much of the
                           year that in many places you can wade
                           through the water without getting
                           your | back wet. 'Wetback' is an unnecessary
                           insult; for hundreds of miles there is
                           no river at all."

3. Source and —————————→ Steiner, pp. 123-24
   page numbers

Here is an explanation of the parts of this note card:

1. SUBJECT IDENTIFICATION. If you formed a rough outline before the note-taking, you can identify the subject with the
Roman numeral and subordinate symbols from the outline.
Then, by referring to the outline, you will be able to determine
the subject of the note card. Otherwise, you will have to use a
descriptive title, such as the one on the first line of the card
above, and add the symbols after you form the outline. The first
method is preferable because it saves time, but if you have
difficulty making a rough outline prior to the research, you will
have to rely on the second method.

2. RECORD OF EVIDENCE. The record of evidence in this example is a direct quotation, so it is set off by quotation marks.
Note the single quotation marks ('. . .') around *wetback* on the
note card. This word was originally set off by double quotation
marks (". . ."), but they were changed because of the use of

double quotes around the entire passage. The slash mark indicates the point at which the page numbers change.

3. SOURCE AND PAGE NUMBER.   The third part consists of bibliographical information leading to the note's source. It is not
necessary to record on the note card all the data that you would
include on the bibliography card. The author's last name will
lead to that complete information. Here is the bibliography card
for the quotation from Steiner:

Steiner, Stan. *La Raza: The Mexican
Americans.* New York: Harper
& Row, 1969.

If you are using more than one book by the same author or
books by writers with the same last names, then include both
the title and the author's name. Another method of identifying
the source is by using a code; you simply number each bibliography card and then place that number at the bottom of the
note card, thereby forming a cross-reference system. It is usually wise, however, to circle the source number so that you do
not confuse it with the page number. The bibliography card
shown previously has a code number that is used instead of the
author's name on the paraphrase note card (p. 54).

Kinds of Notes.   Notes fall into three categories: (1) direct
quotation, (2) paraphrase, (3) summary or synopsis.

DIRECT QUOTATION.   Quoting directly may appear to be the
easiest and safest method. It should not be relied on too extensively, however, because once your notes are cold, you may
wonder exactly what the quotation means and why you thought
it was significant. Thus, when quoting directly, be sure that the
passage is significant and self-contained. Always place quotation
marks around the passage.

Here, again, is the example of a direct quotation recorded on a note card:

Immigration

"On any of the bridges over the Rio Grande, for 2 cents or 5 cents, anyone can walk across. The river is so shallow much of the year that in many places you can wade through the water without getting your/back wet. 'Wetback' is an unnecessary insult; for hundreds of miles there is no river at all."

Steiner, pp. 123-24

PARAPHRASE. The second kind of note, the paraphrase, involves restating or rewording a particular passage. Do not rely too heavily on the original phrasing. In a paraphrased note you do not have to use complete sentences, but it is usually advisable. Sometimes part of the note may be paraphrased and the rest quoted. Here is a paraphrased version of the material quoted directly on the preceding note card:

II. A. 1.

The term "wetback" is "an unnecessary insult" because for a few cents anyone can walk across the Rio Grande bridges, there is little water in most parts of the river, and for several hundred miles there isn't any river border.

This note card makes use of outline symbols for subject identification and the circled number for source identification.

SUMMARY OR SYNOPSIS. The *summary* or *synopsis* note, which is a brief statement or outline that recapitulates the main ideas in a long passage or complete work, is not used extensively in research work. Most note cards carry specific evidence rather than general restatements or outlines, but sometimes it might be necessary to summarize or outline a complete chapter or work for inclusion in the text of the research paper.

The use of the summary or synopsis note is most common in literary papers. For example, if you were writing a paper on *The Inferno* from Dante's *Divine Comedy*, you might want to summarize the characteristics of each of the circles in the inferno.

Second Circle

When Dante and Virgil visit the second circle, they see the unlawful lovers, the carnal sinners guilty of lust, blown about by the wind, which is symbolic of their surrender of reason to lawless passion. Virgil points out famous lovers. Dante hears the story of Francesca da Rimini and Paolo Malatesta and is so filled with pity that he faints.

Dante, Canto V, pp. 73-91

Machine Copies

Making copies from noncirculating library materials such as reference works and periodicals may be helpful in some instances. Of course, this practice should not be substituted for note-taking. Furthermore, the cost and trouble involved should be enough to prevent indiscriminate use of the copying machine. Even if you took time to copy page after page of sources, at five or ten cents per sheet, you would still have to make notes on the material because it would be impossible to incorporate it into the paper in its entirety or even to manipulate it for organizational purposes. But there are instances when the text of an article or selected pages from an article or a book might be a valuable aid in writing the paper, especially if the source is a key one. The 1976 copyright law permits photocopying for this purpose. Another use is copying charts, statistical tables, and other illustrative matter.

SHARING THE COMMUNITY OF KNOWLEDGE

In some ways the actual research is the most challenging and exciting step in the preparation of a research paper. It is in this part of the work that you discover, compare, evaluate, and gather knowledge. Although just a portion of the knowledge that you have gained will eventually be used in writing the paper, the rest is not lost. It has now become a part of your own experience.

Chapter 4

Obtaining Original Evidence

> *The scientific method is concerned with how things
> do happen, not how they ought to happen. Knowledge
> of the way things do happen, with no ifs, ands, or buts,
> allows us to deal more effectively with our environment.*
> Stuart Chase, *The Tyranny of Words*

The search for evidence to support and ultimately to prove a
hypothesis need not be limited to documented sources. The
evidence may be original, drawn from questioning, observing,
or experimenting. These field-study methods seek validation in
present experience rather than in past authority. And they show
"how things *do* happen, not how they *ought* to happen."

An analysis of these approaches to obtaining original evidence
sets forth several distinct methods:

Questioning
    Interviews
    Oral History
    Questionnaires
    Measurement questionnaires
    Tests
    Personal documents
Observing
    Noncontrolled observation
      Nonparticipant and participant
    Controlled observation
Experimenting

Often a single study, usually called a *survey*, will rely on several of these techniques. For example, a survey of educational needs in a community may derive its facts, figures, and opinions from questionnaires (both personal and measurement), interviews, tests, and observation.

The scientific method, as generally understood, is nonhistorical in that it looks to current experience, not to past authority, for support and proof. Usually, though, the scientific researcher will examine secondary sources (either accounts of similar studies or related works) in order to gain some background or to determine the need for a study.

QUESTIONING

If you want to know something, find someone who can tell you about it. Here is a tested research method, one that a child uses when he first learns to talk, and one on which both the novice researcher and the seasoned scholar rely. The principal devices for questioning include interviews, oral history, questionnaires, measurement questionnaires, tests, and personal documents.

Interviews   *authoritative*
             historical
             field

The basis of the interview is the reliance on another person's verbal response for information about himself, his opinions, his experiences, or his knowledge. In other words, you are asking someone to respond to specific questions, and you are recording his responses for possible inclusion in the research work. As an interviewer, you should always bear in mind that this verbal report may or may not be taken at face value; after all, the respondent usually relates experiences and describes events that you have not directly observed. Sometimes, however, the skillful interviewer may learn as much about his subject from what is left unsaid as he does from what is stated directly.

The form of the interview is largely determined by its purpose and the person interviewed. If the subject of the interview is a well-known figure—prominent in politics, for instance—you may ask him about his personal background and his opinions on subjects related to his experience. Or if the interviewee is a recognized authority on a particular subject—say, industrial relations—you might limit yourself to questions dealing with his specific field. Sometimes the individual interviewed may be a representative of a larger group; for example, if you were conducting a study on the causes of alcoholism, you might talk to several alcoholics and former alcoholics, eliciting their responses and opinions on alcoholism and its causes.

Kinds of Interviews. Because the interview is totally unpredictable, dependent as it is on human personality, it is difficult to name definite kinds of interviews and to list all their pitfalls and advantages; however, interviews generally fall into three broad categories: authoritative, historical, and field.

AUTHORITATIVE INTERVIEW. Interviewing an authority in a particular field is one of the most common kinds of interviews. Although the basic purpose of such an interview is to gather information, it may be expanded to include the person's observations and opinions on the subject. For example, you might interview a banking authority regarding the exact procedures for extending loans to businesses. In addition to gathering the facts on this subject, you could draw out unexpected statements on the condition of the economy or on the inner workings of bank financing.

This kind of interview is probably the easiest to conduct. In the first place, you are talking to someone about something in which he is interested, and a person usually speaks of his interests with ease. Second, since you are not probing into personal matters, it is unlikely that the subject will be hostile. Furthermore, you will not have to be concerned with factual accuracy, for the most part, because a recognized authority in a particular field usually will not disseminate incorrect information. Unlike other kinds of interviews, the authoritative interview lends itself to validation because you can check on the facts at a later time through other sources.

However, before conducting the authoritative interview, you need to prepare yourself carefully and thoroughly. Mainly, you must brief yourself on the subject at hand so that you can ask questions which will give you the information you want. Well-phrased inquiries, thought out in advance, will help you to gather not only the basic information but additional material, sometimes in the form of valuable observations and opinions.

During the interview, you should also be careful to record the information exactly in order to assure your understanding of the material later and to prevent attributing supposititious matter to the person you have interviewed.

HISTORICAL INTERVIEW. The essential purpose of the historical interview is to gather information about a specific event from an individual who was present at the time or about a particular person from someone who knew him. Most likely, the interviewer was not a witness to the event or did not know the person. Thus, he is usually at a disadvantage because he is subject to the whims of memory, honesty, emotional involvement, and personality on the part of the interviewees. Numerous literary works (e.g., Robert Browning's *The Ring and the Book*) have taken as their theme the fact that several persons can witness and be involved in a single event and yet recall it differently when asked to tell or to write about it. Unfortunately, the matter of differing accounts is not just a literary device. Anyone who has carried on historical interviewing would agree that generally there are as many versions of what took place as there are witnesses.

But this problem does not lessen the value of the historical interview. Quite the opposite; it is its basis, so long as you are aware of the possible discrepancies. Alertness to this fact will prevent you from misconducting and misinterpreting the historical interview.

The following suggestions, adaptable to varying circumstances, will aid you in conducting historical interviews that are both effective and profitable. First, never dispute what someone is telling you, even if you suspect that his account is confused, prejudiced, or inaccurate. Tactfully point out that another witness had reported something different and that you would appreciate it if he would explain his version more fully, perhaps suggesting subtly that the other person is the one who is confused. Such an approach, if handled skillfully, might shed even more light on the event. Second, at every important point in the interview, establish where the interviewee was during the event being recalled, in order to ascertain how much of his information is direct and how much is based on the reports of others.

Taking the negative approach is another device that will produce differing opinions. For example, if you are asking someone about a pioneer schoolteacher, do not phrase your question: "I have always heard that Miss Lion was kind, sympathetic, and intelligent. Do you agree with this estimate of her character?" Most people will not want to shatter someone's opinion of another person even if they violently disagree. In this case, you will probably get a noncommital answer to your question. On the other hand, you will pave the way for a fuller answer by asking a more negative question: "In spite of Miss Lion's reputation for kindness, sympathy, and intelligence, I understand that she could be quite overbearing and stubborn at times." If the person admired Miss Lion, he will immediately defend her, probably relating a story to prove why such a statement is wrong. If not, he will agree with the negative statement and augment his agreement with material illustrating Miss Lion's unpleasant side.

FIELD INTERVIEW. The field interview is conducted to learn how people feel about themselves and others, about their environment, and about specific issues and problems. Such an interview is often the most difficult to conduct because a person may be reluctant to talk about himself, his environment, or his personal opinions and beliefs. Sometimes he may not be able to discuss such matters, even if he wants to do so.

The most valuable and most common kind of field interview is the in-depth investigation, possibly including several sessions, with a respondent who is very much involved in the specific environment or problem. A research project on prison conditions, for instance, might include a series of interviews with former and present prisoners, who would be better prepared to discuss specific penal problems than the man on the street. However, the man on the street should not be excluded; asking specific questions of a cross section of people is another phase of the field interview that can provide useful data.

The salient factor in determining the success of the field interview is the attitude and conduct of the interviewer. You must assure the respondent that you are taking him and his responses seriously, without saying as much directly. Remember that if you are taking the situation seriously, your attitude will be evident. In all cases, you must make the respondent feel that his information is vitally important to the overall success of the project and even to the advancement of knowledge itself.

As the person responds, do not react if you are shocked, dismayed, or offended. On the other hand, you must not be so blasé that you give the respondent the impression that you are totally detached and uninterested. Again, taking the person seriously and showing honest interest in him and his responses will help you to tread the line between overreaction and aloofness.

How structured your questions are depends on the situation. Although you should have a general outline to follow, you must not be afraid to veer from it if the respondent is providing useful information. When preparing questions, keep in mind that some questions are *open* and others are *closed*. An open question allows the respondent a choice. For instance, you could ask a former prisoner: "What conditions in the prison did you find most difficult?" He could answer the query in a number of ways and could expand into several areas, depending on his attitude and verbal ease. Conversely, a closed question does not give the opportunity for a variety of answers. For example, you might inquire: "What aspect of prison life did you find to be most degrading to you as a man?" The response to such a question would be limited because the question itself limits and specifies. When interviewing a person who has difficulty expressing himself, you could use the closed question to advantage.

A variation on this technique would be allowing the respondent to choose from a number of closely related questions. He could then select the question that seemed to suit him best or that appeared to be least threatening.

Another approach is *funnel questioning*, which begins with open questions and gradually leads into closed ones. In other words, you begin with the generalities, build a framework, then get to specifics, and fill in the empty spaces. This procedure may also help to put a reluctant interviewee at ease or to bring vague responses into sharper focus.

Techniques of Interviews. Whatever the purpose of the interview and whoever the subject, a few guidelines will help you to conduct meaningful and worthwhile interviews.

TIME. Whenever possible you should arrange for the interview in advance. Once you have done this, be sure that you are on time, and preferably a few minutes early. Be friendly at the outset, but get to the point of the interview as quickly as possible. Usually one hour is the maximum time for an interview. In some instances, however, you may want to spend less time, as in the case of an elderly person who finds it difficult to concentrate for a long period. Or if you are simply gathering opinions from a cross section of people, you may spend only a few minutes per interview.

TECHNICAL DEVICES. Electronic equipment has advanced the art of the interview, and you can make good use of these devices. Recording the interview has obvious advantages because you will have an exact record of the questions and answers. More than this, however, you can listen for pauses, inflections of the voice, and other subtleties that cannot be noted on paper.

Of course it is sometimes physically impossible to use electronic equipment, but the most important consideration determining its use is the person being interviewed. The mere presence of a recorder could destroy all rapport between you and the respondent. Obviously, you should obtain permission in advance when you plan to record the interview.

When recording is impossible or inadvisable, you will have to rely on note-taking. One method is to write each question on the left sheet of a spiral notebook, leaving the blank right sheet for the answer. Take down the information as quickly and as inconspicuously as possible, but do not be afraid to ask the person to repeat something, especially a date, or to spell a name. Because the person you are interviewing might request to see what you have written in your notebook, be sure to keep personal opinions in your mind only.

STAYING ON THE SUBJECT. Digressions can be interesting and valuable, but if the digression has neither of these qualities, tactfully get the person back on the track. Do not interrupt him, but at the first opportunity say something like: "Let's go back to what I asked you a moment ago." Then repeat the question.

PRESENCE OF OTHER PEOPLE. Ideally, no one should be present except the interviewer and interviewee. When someone else is present and attempts to correct or add to the remarks, you must be kind but firm, explaining that you want the original interviewee to tell the story himself. This problem often arises during the historical interview. You may find yourself talking to a pioneer logger who is weaving fascinating stories about his early days in the lumber camps but whose wife is correcting him or refreshing his memory.

OFF-THE-RECORD REMARKS.　One of the main problems in interviewing is the request that certain remarks should be considered off the record. The fact is that if the major portion of the material you have gathered from the interview cannot be used, then you have not added much to your research. When someone asks not to be quoted and proceeds to make off-the-record remarks, your job is to get him back on the record as tactfully and as quickly as possible. Otherwise you will have filled your tape or notebook with unusable material.

QUESTIONS.　The nature of the questions has been discussed previously in relation to the specific kinds of interviews, but some general rules do apply for all interview questions. Ask questions that are clear, concise, and pertinent, and ask them one at a time. Remember, too, that the purpose of the questions is to guide the responses, not to convey your ideas and prejudices. Phrase the questions so they will elicit more than a "yes" or "no" reply. Never ask: "Did you understand the lecturer's remarks?" Try something like this: "What did you think the lecturer was trying to say?"

CONTROVERSIAL MATTERS.　In some interviews, you will be confronted with opinions and values differing from your own. When this happens, never argue with your respondent or condemn his opinions. Keep in mind that the interview is a learning situation for you, not an instructional session for the person you are interviewing.

TALKING.　As an interviewer, remember that you are drawing information from another person, not informing him of your experiences and ideas. Needless to say, the major portion of the talking should be the responsibility of the interviewee, *not* the interviewer.

Oral History

The distinction between the standard interview and oral history is not always clear, but the main difference lies in the purpose of each. Interview material has an immediate and specific use, either to form a hypothesis or substantiate an established thesis. Data gathered in oral history is intended for future and general use by a number of historians. Defined by its purpose, then, oral history is broader in scope than the interview.

Background. Although oral history is hardly new, its modern use and development got under way at Columbia University around 1950 when a group of historians decided to record the history of the 1930s in the United States. They felt that an oral record of this decade would supplement the written documents, preserving a richer record of a unique historical period. Since that original project, the oral-history files at Columbia have grown steadily, covering subjects ranging from autobiography to the oil industry. Through oral records, numerous universities, individual scholars, historical societies, and other groups interested in history are today preserving the history of organizations, movements, individuals, industries, political events, to name a few.

Often the tapes and/or transcriptions are not generally available to the beginning researcher, but this situation does not always prevail. You should not overlook the possibilities of oral-history files in your area. Also, you might consider conducting your own oral-history project. Extensive material on the techniques of oral history is available; one of the best publications for the beginner is Willa K. Baum's *Oral History for the Local Historical Society* (available through the Conference of California Historical Societies, University of the Pacific, Stockton, California).

Techniques. The basic technique of the oral-history approach is similar to that of the interview: The questioner directs the respondent in recording data. Because the oral-history interviewer is not the only person to make use of the material, he often evaluates the interviewee regarding his cooperation, apparent veracity, and general attitude. These comments and observations are attached to the material so that the future users will have some idea of the interview conditions.

It is necessary to ask more penetrating questions in oral history recording than in the traditional interview. In order to assure that the material will not be a partial or surface treatment of the subject, the interviewer must attempt to examine all sides of the subject and see that it is amplified as fully as possible. Otherwise the future user will be left with gaps he will probably not be able to fill. Some oral historians speak of the necessity for cross-examining, much the way a lawyer questions a witness.

Another function of the interviewer is selectivity. Although full details are the object, they must not be so abundant that they obscure and confuse the subject at hand. The interviewer necessarily guides the respondent into this selectivity when he wanders into irrelevant gossip, family genealogies, health problems, and the like.

The destiny of the material from an oral-history interview varies. It may become readily available, either on tape or in typescripts; or it may be sealed and stored, to be opened at a future date, usually determined by the person interviewed.

Uses.   Not all the material from oral history has been filed away for limited use; a generous amount has found its way into printed form.

One such example is Oscar Lewis's anthropological study *The Children of Sanchez: An Autobiography of a Mexican Family*. This work records the story of each member of the family in a word-by-word transcription. According to the author, such an approach "gives us a cumulative, multifaceted, panoramic view of each individual, of the family as a whole, and of many aspects of lower-class Mexican life."[1] The tremendous appeal of this book and subsequent works by Lewis that use the same method is that the subjects speak for themselves, permitting the reader to draw his own conclusions.

In his biography *Huey Long*, T. Harry Williams also relied heavily on oral history. Williams pointed out in the preface to the work that he conducted part of the research through conventional written sources but that much of the information, including what was most valuable, came from the men and women who knew Long. The reminiscences of 295 of these people served as the basis for his book and will continue to serve scholars of Long, his dynasty, and Louisiana history. Williams placed the typescripts in the Louisiana State University Library, Baton Rouge, under a time seal; that is, the material will not be available to other scholars until a predetermined date. This condition is frequently imposed on oral-history records in order to protect living persons from embarrassment or recriminations.

1. Oscar Lewis, Introduction, *The Children of Sanchez* (New York: Random House, 1961), p. xi.

Regarding the value of oral history, Williams wrote:

As I continued with the research, I became increasingly convinced of the validity of oral history. Not only was it a necessary tool in compiling the history of the recent past, but it also provided an unusually intimate look into that past. I found that the politicians were astonishingly frank in detailing their dealings, and often completely realistic in viewing themselves. But they had not trusted a record of these dealings to paper, and it would not have occurred to them to transcribe their experiences at a later time. Anybody who heard them would have to conclude that the full and inside story of politics is not in *any* age committed to the documents.[2]

A White House Diary by Lady Bird Johnson (New York: Holt, Rinehart & Winston, 1970) is another example of oral history turned into printed form. Based on a series of tapes made by Mrs. Johnson during her five years as First Lady, this book offers an unparalleled look into a presidential administration. Undoubtedly, Mrs. Johnson recorded incidents, comments, and responses that she would not have had time or the inclination to put into writing. This work illustrates another form of oral history: the totally undirected response. Even though the tapes were edited before being published in book form, they were originally made without any specific direction. Mrs. Johnson recorded whatever she thought was important and relevant.

Recording a free reminiscence, without asking questions or directing the course of responses, may not always be effective. The material could be extraneous or irrelevant. On the other hand, the nondirected recording may lead the respondent into giving a richer, fuller, and more honest account.

Oral history, obtained primarily through the directed interview and occasionally through the undirected reminiscence, is a research tool that will continue to prove its worth as a supplement to written documents and as a method of acquiring personal accounts of history.

Questionnaires

The questionnaire consists of specific written inquiries. It is submitted to individuals so that their responses can be analyzed for usable information. Although more limited than the interview

2. T. Harry Williams, Preface, *Huey Long* (New York: Knopf, 1970), p. ix.

in some respects, the questionnaire is still a valuable tool for research. In spite of its limitations—less knowledge of the respondent, lack of personal contact, and possible misunderstanding of the questions—the questionnaire has strong points of its own. It can be distributed widely without considerable expense, thereby reaching a larger number of respondents than would be possible through the interview. The fact that the inquiry is in a set form makes it more consistent than oral questioning, which usually possesses an element of variation.

Construction. The preliminary planning that has gone into the research project will logically determine what information you want to gather through the questionnaire. Suppose that the purpose of the study is to determine the attitudes of college students toward required lower-division courses. A study of this nature could examine students' attitudes toward the courses with regard to their value and interest; and it might develop into seeking suggestions for improvement. Directed by these general topics, you would have a good idea what information you are seeking.

Another factor to consider is how much personal information you will need concerning the respondents. In the college study, for example, you may want to learn about majors, reading habits, interests, and high school backgrounds. These facts could add another dimension to the study: the relationship between the attitudes and suggestions regarding the courses and the respondents' educational and personal background.

Once you know what information you are seeking, the next step is to decide how to gather it. The form of the questions depends on the educational and social background of the respondents and the intended analysis and interpretation of the material. Regardless of the background of potential respondents or the planned uses of the information, however, clarity and simplicity should always govern question preparation. Basically two kinds of questions exist: (1) direct ones that ask explicitly for single answers (e.g., "What is your major?") and (2) indirect ones that call for evaluations and/or opinions (e.g., "How did you benefit from the world history course required of all freshmen?"). In some instances additional information may be inferred from the answer to the indirect question.

Every question is valuable, intended specifically to draw a

response that can be analyzed for useful information. Therefore, you must examine each inquiry carefully before including it in the questionnaire. Here is a guide for evaluation:

Is the question useful in gathering the desired information?

Will it be clear to the respondent?

Will the respondent have the necessary background and information to answer the question?

Is the question too general? Is it too specific?

Is the wording of the question unfair or objectionable (tricky, too personal, prejudiced, biased, and the like)?

Should the question be direct or indirect?

Equal in importance to the question is the method for answering it because the person who completes the questionnaire must be able to do so quickly, effectively, and accurately. The methods for response should be determined by the respondent's ability, the amount of time he has to complete the questionnaire, and the information sought.

The simplest form for response is the check answer, which takes one of the following forms:

1. Yes. No.
   Did you feel that your freshman literature course helped you to gain a fuller appreciation of literature?
   ———Yes ———No

2. Agree. Disagree.
   The freshman literature course gives the student a fuller appreciation of literature.
   ———Agree ———Disagree

3. Rating.
   Lower-division required courses are
   ———not worthwhile at all.
   ———not very worthwhile.
   ———somewhat worthwhile.
   ———very worthwhile
   ———extremely worthwhile
   (Place "1" on the line in front of the phrase that most closely reflects your opinion of the courses, "2" before the next, and so on.)

4. Multiple choice.
   ———The lower-division required course most beneficial to me was (1) composition, (2) biology, (3) history, (4) physical education.

Poor checklists are a common fault in the construction of questionnaires. They should not be ambiguous (i.e., full of such terms as "quite," "sometimes," "fair," "average," "usually"), nor should they be so incomplete that they lack sufficient alternatives to give the respondent an opportunity to record his opinions accurately. And the responses in the checklist should never be tricky, loaded, extreme, or irrelevant.

Another method is the short answer, which consists of a single word or phrase. The question "How valuable were the lower-division required courses to you?" could be answered by responses such as "extremely valuable" or "totally worthless." Such an inquiry suggests two possible follow-up questions: "What course was least valuable?" "What course was most valuable?"

The most inclusive response is the long answer, which may range from one sentence to several paragraphs. The advantages of the long answer are obvious: It might include fuller details, qualifications, personal reactions, and opinions. On the other hand, the long answer sometimes results in vagueness, extraneous matter, and difficulties in analysis and interpretation. When you intend to employ the long-answer response, consider the respondent's writing ability, the amount of time he can spend on the questionnaire, and the kind of information you are seeking.

A questionnaire may rely on a single method of response, or it may combine the three methods, depending entirely on its purpose and scope.

Whenever possible, you should try out the questionnaire on a group of subjects in order to determine the usefulness and clarity of the questions and to eliminate unclear or objectionable phrasing. After the trial run, experiment with the information to determine if what you have learned can be analyzed and interpreted in relation to your study.

Sampling. Rarely are you gathering information from a group so limited that you can administer a questionnaire to each of them. Therefore, you will most often use a sampling; that is, you will depend on the responses of a representative number of the larger group and through this sampling of responses attempt to determine the opinions, attitudes, and so forth of the entire group. The validity of your results will be determined in large measure by how carefully based your sampling techniques are.

The approach to sampling is naturally governed by the nature of the problem, resources, time, and availability of respondents. But even in conducting the simplest research project, you should strive to sample as extensively as possible.

Suppose that you are studying the role of small-town mayors in national politics. After you have determined an approach and have formed the questionnaire, your next step is to set up a guide to sampling. Realizing that it would be impossible to send a questionnaire to every mayor in the United States, you must decide how to avail yourself of information from a representative group. The logical approach is to develop criteria such as the following:

1. Mayors of towns with populations of 1,000 to 5,000
2. Mayors of towns in each state (or possibly a region or even a county)
3. Mayors of towns near metropolitan areas
4. Mayors of towns in rural areas

Directed by these four points, you could plan a strategy something like this one:

1. Questionnaires to three mayors in each state (or region or county) whose towns are near metropolitan areas and are 1,000 to 5,000 in population
2. Questionnaires to three mayors in each state (or region or county) whose towns are in rural areas and are 1,000 to 5,000 in population

Administration. The method of administering questionnaires depends on the purpose of the study, the immediate availability of respondents, the method of sampling, and the resources of the researcher.

The questionnaire may be administered to one person at a time, in some instances as a supplement to the interview. The more common method, however, is to administer the questionnaires to a group. The advantage of this method is obvious, in that you can gather all the information at one time. Another system is to mail questionnaires to a selected group of possible respondents. If you follow this plan, always include a stamped, preaddressed envelope for the respondent. Never count on a high percentage of response, however, when you are relying on the questionnaires to be returned by mail.

Measurement Questionnaires. Thus far the discussion of questionnaires has centered on personal responses based on experience and opinion. Another kind of questionnaire, directed toward measurement, is used for gathering statistical data. The construction of the measurement questionnaire follows the principles mentioned earlier because, once again, the questions must be absolutely clear before they can act as agents in gathering the data. The fact that the responses are in numbers makes them definite, thus eliminating the problem of deciding what method of response to use. Here is a sample from a questionnaire that might be employed in a management study:

1. How many people report to you? _____
2. What is your annual salary? _____
3. How long have you worked for the company? _____
4. How long have you been in your present position? _____
5. How long has each of the people who report to you worked for the company? _____ _____ _____ _____

Once the information sought in this kind of questionnaire has been gathered, it can be presented in its totality to give a complete picture, and/or it can be analyzed according to statistical formulas (based on the theory of probability) that show correlation, central tendency, and variability.

It should be added at this point that opinions may also be measured. For example, the study on lower-division required courses (given as an earlier example) may include a section showing what percentage of the students interviewed indicated satisfaction, need for change, and so forth.

Statistical information may often aid in developing and specifying a research work, and you should utilize it to bring generalizations into sharp focus. However, the purely statistical study, complete with formulas and computer programming, is far afield from written research. You should avoid including too much statistical information, especially in the form of tables, in a written research work. Instead, either work the statistical data into the flow of the text, or translate it into graphic presentations. (Chapter 8 includes a discussion of graphic materials.)

Tests

Another method of gathering original data is through the administration of standard tests intended to measure such areas as general intelligence, reading levels, occupational interests, and emotional development. Testing is an exacting field, and in order for a test to be a valid tool in gathering information, it must be administered by qualified persons under the right conditions (a fact that at least one state legislature has recently noted by forbidding indiscriminate intelligence and psychological testing in the public schools). The results from testing are handled in the same manner as the data assembled through questionnaires.

Personal Documents

In essence the personal document is a nondirected questionnaire. As its name implies, at its best it is a private revelation of an individual's thoughts, feelings, and/or experiences.

The use of the personal history or reminiscence (one form of the personal document) in historical research has long been widespread. Either written voluntarily and preserved or composed on request, the personal written reminiscences can be of infinite value to the historian. However, when the historian relies on a personal document, he must have some clue to the work's reliability. The following criteria are those most often used:

1. Was the ultimate source of the detail (the primary witness) able to tell the truth?
2. Was the primary witness willing to tell the truth?
3. Is the primary witness's account regarding the details under examination reported accurately?
4. Is there any external corroboration of the detail under examination?[3]

Personal documents that aid in historical research are usually autobiographical or biographical or are records of specific events. For example, someone studying California's Imperial Valley

3. Louis Gottschalk, Clyde Kluckhohn, and Robert Angell, *The Use of Personal Documents in History, Anthropology and Sociology*, Bulletin No. 53 (New York: Social Science Research Council, 1945), p. 38.

could make extensive use of personal documents. The history of this agricultural area, developed in the midst of the desert in the early 1900s, has been richly preserved in personal histories and documents. In addition, numerous people who settled in the area during its early days are still living and could be called upon for personal histories or reminiscences. If you were conducting research of this kind, you could direct the content of the current documents by asking the writers to concentrate on specific persons, events, or conditions. In some cases, the use of oral-history techniques might seem more advisable than the written documents. Ideally, however, one approach could enrich the other.

Social scientists and psychologists also use personal documents extensively. Differing in purpose from historians, sociological and psychological investigators are more concerned with the expression of intrinsic personal values and how they reveal the individual, his relationship with his peers, and the overall structure of the group. For example, in a study attempting to discover why teen-agers run away from home, you could request personal histories, reminiscences of experiences, or records of opinions from the subjects, hoping that these documents would shed some light on their problems, which in turn could lead to determining the causes.

OBSERVING

Everyone, in varying degrees, observes his environment. But scientific observation includes more than casual viewing and haphazard absorption of the sights, sounds, and smells that assault the senses. In order for observation to be scientific, it is necessarily methodic and analytic. The observer approaches the field of his observation with definite objectives in mind. In order to fulfill these objectives, he views the phenomena from a mental standpoint as well as from a physical one, and he records the data in a precise manner.

This kind of perceptive observation may be carried on in an uncontrolled situation in which the observer is either a non-participant or a participant. For example, someone studying life on skid row—an ever-popular sociological exercise—could observe this urban tradition in action as an outsider, watching but not participating. Or he could pose as a member of skid-row society and conduct his observation from the inside as a participant.

Controlled observation, on the other hand, places the subjects in a specific situation; and rather than viewing the entire group at random, the observer studies the sample group in depth. Educational research, in particular, has taken full advantage of controlled observation. In a study of retarded children, for instance, the researcher (possibly hidden behind a screen or one-way glass) may observe a group of youngsters in a specific situation and record their activities, reactions, and interactions.

Principles of Observation

In order to assure that he sees with both his eyes and his mind, the observer should follow certain basic principles of observation.

Definite Objectives. Just going out to watch people, whether they be habitués of skid row or first-nighters at the civic opera, is not true scientific observation. Before initiating any observation, the observer first needs to form definite objectives to guide his research. Here are some questions that will help to get the observation on the right track:

1. Exactly what is being looked for?
2. Why is it being observed?
3. How will the results of the observation tie into the overall research project?

Answering these questions in detail (i.e., determining the exact purpose of the observation) will help to eliminate haphazard and uncoordinated procedures and will lead to establishing definite objectives.

Lack of Bias. Scientific observation demands a lack of bias—that is, true objectivity—on the part of the observer. If he begins his observation already convinced that he will discover only degradation on skid row or only sham at the civic opera, then he might as well stay at home. Generally speaking, when someone has his mind firmly set on a particular idea, no amount of evidence to the contrary will change his preconceived opinion. The scientific observer, however, must enter any observational task as free of bias as is humanly possible.

Awareness of the Larger Setting. The scientific observer seeks specific evidence, and in so doing, he usually limits his observation to a definite area and to a particular group. For example, in a study of a mining town disrupted by the closing of the major mining activity, the observer may examine the effect of this situation on a single family. But even though this family may be representative of a hundred other families in the town, the observer should not become so involved in the single unit that he loses sight of the larger setting. He must grasp the whole picture first, then enlarge on a particular aspect of it, at the same time keeping the larger setting in mind.

Kinds of Observation. There are three basic kinds of observation: noncontrolled-nonparticipant, noncontrolled-participant and controlled.

● NONCONTROLLED-NONPARTICIPANT OBSERVATION. The simplest and least scientific kind of observation is the noncontrolled-nonparticipating approach. The politician who visits a foreign country for a few days and returns as an authority, the social reformer who walks through a ghetto and reports it in detail, the eastern newspaperman who observes a Midwest farm area briefly and writes about it "in depth," the psychologist who tiptoes through a homosexual community and prepares a paper—these are a few examples of nonparticipating observers in noncontrolled situations.

One of the major pitfalls in this kind of surface observation is the tendency for the observer to appear to be more of an authority than he actually is, thus becoming dishonest from a scientific standpoint. Another problem is subjectivity. When a person is not totally absorbed in the observed phenomena, he tends to bring his own emotions into play in the interpretation. This problem is understandable, especially when what is observed is so vivid and real and even startling that it is difficult to exclude emotional reactions.

Another difficulty that arises through the lack of understanding inherent in casual observation is the misreading of the minds of those observed, thus characterizing their response to the environment in terms of the observer's values rather than the values of the persons actually involved. For example, what may appall the observer of a guerrilla band in South America might go unnoticed or be accepted by the participants.

However, noncontrolled observation, in spite of its short- *pros*
comings, can play a significant role in data gathering. First,
because such observation does give a partially accurate picture
of a segment of life, it could pave the way for a more systematic
approach to observation by suggesting specific areas for closer
analyses.

Long-term noncontrolled observation can be effective in some
instances. The observer remains in the environment for several
days or even weeks (preferably the latter) and watches the
group over a span of time. This procedure enables the observer
to grasp the environment more fully and to see the observed
under varying circumstances.

Second, it has been suggested that much can be learned about
a community by observing in a noncontrolled manner several
aspects of community life, including school activities, church
services, organizational meetings, police work, and weddings.

Thus, noncontrolled-nonparticipating observation is not totally without value. But if misused, it can be a highly unfair
and inaccurate approach.

● NONCONTROLLED-PARTICIPANT OBSERVATION. In this kind of observation, the observer becomes a participant in the noncontrolled situation and shares, in varying degrees, the experiences
of the group he is observing. In some instances, the observer's
identity is known to the group; in other cases, he passes as a
participant. Even though the second technique is preferable,
either approach will provide the observer with opportunities for
close studies of the persons involved.

A classic example of this kind of observation is John Griffin's
Black Like Me (Boston: Houghton Mifflin, 1962). The author,
through medical treatment, changed his pigmentation and joined
the black community in the Deep South, traveling by bus,
working at various jobs, and experiencing in depth the rigors
of black life.

● CONTROLLED OBSERVATION. The major benefits derived from
noncontrolled observation (both nonparticipant and participant)
is that the results lay the groundwork for further study utilizing
the greater preciseness of controlled observation. Even though
the control of human behavior is neither possible nor desirable,
the environment can to some extent be controlled. This point
is the essence of controlled observation: The social scientist

places an individual or group in a specific situation and observes the reactions. For example, a sociological researcher, striving to prove that young men who have been sentenced to prison on first offenses should be treated from a rehabilitative standpoint rather than from a punitive one, could form two matched control groups, one to be treated traditionally and the other to be treated innovatively. Through observation, relying on some of the instruments of observation, the researcher could reach some definite conclusions on the relative values of the two approaches.

Instruments of Observation

Especially in controlled observational situations, but in noncontrolled instances as well, the observer will utilize one or more of the instruments for observation described in the following paragraphs.

Recorders, Notes, Diaries. Taping the conversations of a group or the comments of an individual, preferably without the speaker's knowledge, is one technique that supplies intimate data. For example, in a study of social mores in a city neighborhood bar, the observer could tape some of the conversations of regular patrons. From such records, he would likely discover threads of the relationships, views, and backgrounds of the people who regularly patronize the bar.

If using a recorder is not feasible, then note-taking would have to suffice, but the latter is obviously not so complete or reliable. In the case of long-term observation, the observer often maintains a diary in which he records the day-to-day events and his comments on these events.

Films and Photographs. The power of the picture should never be denied, nor does a good picture lie. Facial expressions, environmental conditions, and physical appearances sometimes cannot be depicted effectively by words alone. The photographic essay and/or the film can often aid in showing what is beyond the capacity of the written word. A good example of the photographic approach is Michael Sexton's doctoral dissertation on education, which was featured in a *Saturday Review* article entitled "Who Is the School?" (27 May 1972, pp. 32–37). Completed in 1971 at the University of Iowa, this pictorial "exposé of 'educational' bureaucracy and the ivory tower," as Sexton describes it, contains over 3,000 prints of teachers, students, and administrators in a Denver inner-city school. (See chapter 8 for further discussion of the use of films and photographs in research projects.)

Schedules. Formalized charts, called *schedules*, for recording minute bits of information help to standardize the record of observation and to isolate specific elements. For example, in studying a worker over a given period of time, an efficiency expert will record on a schedule each movement that the worker makes. Or someone observing teen-age boys in a reformatory in order to tabulate relationships, adjustments, and activities could choose one boy and record on the set schedule his behavior over a particular span of time.

One-way Screens. Observing a specific group in a controlled situation by watching through a one-way screen is a popular technique. The advantages are obvious because the group (or individual) is not aware of the observer, who can then watch them in a natural situation free from distractions. This technique has been used extensively in educational research for classroom observation, but it can also prove useful in other cases, especially in social situations.

The stimuli may be either natural or artificial. Classroom observation, for instance, may be carried on with the students working in an ordinary situation, or it can be conducted to determine the students' reactions to some unusual situation that has been created by the observers.

Use of Observational Techniques

Although a valid approach to data gathering, observation is rarely the only source of information for a study. As mentioned previously, the results of observation, both noncontrolled and controlled, are most often the basis for further investigations that include interviews, questionnaires, and testing.

EXPERIMENTING

In some ways, experimentation is an extension of the observational approach. The controlled observation of the social scientists approximates the laboratory experiment of the physical scientists. However, in the physical sciences, the conditions can be controlled to a greater extent, or they can even be simulated. Of course, the physical scientist relies to some degree on non-controlled observation, but the core of his work takes place in the artificial setting of the laboratory.

Setting up, designing, conducting, and evaluating a laboratory experiment often entail elaborate preparation, the construction of special equipment, extensive observation, and exact recording of data, sometimes in the form of photographs or scientific illustrations. The purpose of the experiment is the same one that motivates the gathering of data through questioning and observing: to produce original data for forming, testing, or substantiating a hypothesis.

The actual procedure for carrying out an experiment varies, depending upon its complexity, purpose, and field. You should refer to texts in your own field for procedural instructions.

DEALING WITH THE ENVIRONMENT

Finding out "how things *do* happen, not how they *ought* to happen" is the goal of the scientific researcher, either in the physical or in the social sciences. By gathering original data through questioning, observing, and experimenting, the scientific investigator no longer needs to rely on historical or logical approaches in order to reach conclusions. He can discover "how things *do* happen" in his environment by dealing with it directly and learning from it.

3

Presenting the Evidence

Chapter 5

Organizing the Research Paper

> *The great men of culture are those who have had*
> *a passion for diffusing, for making prevail, for carrying*
> *from one end of society to the other, the best knowledge,*
> *the best ideas of their time; who have laboured to*
> *divest knowledge of all that was harsh, uncouth,*
> *difficult, abstract, professional, exclusive, to humanise it,*
> *to make it efficient outside the clique of the cultivated and*
> *learned, yet still remaining the best knowledge and thought*
> *of the time, and a true source, therefore, of sweetness*
> *and light.*
>
> Matthew Arnold, "Sweetness and Light"

Everything will finally fall into place: the hypothesis, the un-developed ideas, the rough outline, the information on the note cards. Assembling these disconnected pieces into a coherent written work—one that humanizes the knowledge and makes it efficient—is not always easy. But the task does offer the possibilities of genuine satisfaction and worthwhile accomplishment. And it will be easier if you approach it from an organized standpoint.

First, by surveying the evidence, you can test the validity of the hypothesis, keeping in mind that a valid hypothesis leads to a thesis statement. Next, you need to decide how to approach the subject. Then, guided by the organizational pattern that the approach suggests, list all parts of the thesis statement in the conventional form of the outline. Determining the approach and making the outline lead directly into writing the rough draft. The parts of this step are as follows:

1. Testing the hypothesis
2. Forming the thesis statement
3. Determining the approach
4. Making the outline

TESTING THE HYPOTHESIS

You can obtain an overview of the evidence that you have gathered by scanning the note cards. After reviewing the evidence, you may discover that the hypothesis is unsupportable, weak, too broad, too limited, or even inaccurate. In any of these instances you should alter, limit, or expand the hypothesis accordingly; at other times you will retain it as the thesis statement with little or no change in its wording. A review of one of the hypotheses from chapter 2 (p. 23) will illustrate the testing process:

• HYPOTHESIS

When all the states are willing to provide their share of the financing for the construction of the interstate highway system, it will be completed.

• WHAT WAS LEARNED FROM SURVEYING THE EVIDENCE

1. That many states have provided their share of money
2. That some states have misused funds
3. That partisan politics has played a part in some allocations
4. That some states have not provided their portion of money

• CONCLUSION

Whereas there are many reasons for the delay in the completion of the interstate highway system, the reluctance of specific states to share the financial responsibility stands out as one of the main factors contributing to this delay.

A test of the original hypothesis shows that it is basically sound and could stand as the thesis statement.

FORMING THE THESIS STATEMENT

Obviously, you do not draw the thesis statement out of the air at the last minute. Once the hypothesis has been thoroughly tested and possibly restated, it becomes the thesis statement.

Characteristics of the Thesis Statement

The thesis statement goes by several names, such as *central idea, controlling purpose, main idea,* and *proposition.* All these terms are accurate, but *thesis statement* is the one most widely employed. Whatever it is called, the statement possesses the following characteristics:

1. It contains the controlling purpose of the written work: the problem that is to be solved or the perplexing question that is to be answered.
2. It expresses the ideas clearly and specifically.
3. It contains no illustrative materials such as quotations or examples.
4. It contains approximately twenty to thirty words.
5. It contains a disputable fact. If it does not, it voids the body of the paper, leaving nothing to prove, no problem to solve. A statement such as "George Washington was the first president of the United States" is an indisputable fact and hence could not serve as a thesis statement. But the sentence "George Washington was the nation's best president" contains a disputable fact; therefore, it could stand as a thesis statement.

A thesis statement may have two additional characteristics:

1. It is often a complex sentence. Such a thesis statement presents the problem in the dependent clause and the solution(s) in the independent clause. The hypothesis, which could serve as a thesis statement for the proposed paper on the interstate highway system (see p. 84), illustrates the use of a complex sentence.
2. In literary studies, the thesis statement usually contains the names of the work and the author under consideration.

Uses of the Thesis Statement

Beyond its principal use as a guide for coherence, the thesis statement also stands as an integral part of the written work. Although there are rare occasions when the thesis statement is implicit and does not appear in the paper at all, it is most often a part of the introduction. Such placement assures that it will be understood at the outset.

DETERMINING THE APPROACH

Even though the major purpose of research is problem solving, it would be naïve to suggest that every research paper simply presents a specific problem and then sets out to give solutions. The truth of the matter is that there are different kinds of problems demanding a variety of approaches. The traditional approaches are as follows:

1. Comparison and/or contrast
2. Survey (cause and effect)
3. Interpretation
4. Problem solving
5. Biography

The problem set forth in the thesis statement will help guide you to the right approach. Because each thesis statement and each body of evidence are unique, it is impossible to prescribe a fixed approach or organizational pattern that will work in every case. The traditional approaches, depending on the problem and the evidence, may be varied and even combined. The following discussion will aid you in understanding the elements of these methods. Once you have this background, you can adapt the approaches and the organizational patterns they suggest to the particular requirements of your subject.

Comparison and/or Contrast

Showing similarities and/or differences, whether they pertain to persons, places, things, or ideas, can serve as the basis for a paper in most academic fields. When you take this approach, be sure that there is a true basis for, and some point to, the comparing and/or contrasting. Of course, a sound thesis statement will preclude an aimless listing of similarities and differences.

Uses. The arts offer numerous possibilities for comparing and/or contrasting historical periods, styles, individual artists, and specific works of art. In literature a study of the similarities and differences between Mark Twain's *The Adventures of Huckleberry Finn* (1884) and J. D. Salinger's *The Catcher in the Rye* (1951) would add an additional dimension to both novels. In the language field the student of Spanish could note the differences and similarities between the Spanish spoken on the United States–Mexico border, where English is so prevalent, and that spoken in the interior of Mexico, where English is less common. In the social sciences, studies employing the techniques of comparison and/or contrast could be undertaken on rural and urban education, on class structures, or on behavioral patterns in two or more groups.

Patterns of Organization. Here is a basic organizational pattern for a paper relying on comparison and/or contrast:

PART I: One by one, present the similarities between the two subjects, and discuss and explore them.

PART II: One by one, present the differences between the two subjects, and discuss and explore them.

PART III: Draw conclusions from the examination of the similarities and differences.

Depending on the subject, the organization might vary somewhat. Parts I or II could be dropped if either contrasts or comparisons were being considered exclusively. Also, instead of the conclusions being presented separately, they could be considered after each similarity or difference from which they were drawn.

This rough outline for a paper comparing and contrasting *Huckleberry Finn* and *The Catcher in the Rye* illustrates the process:

I. Similarities
   A. Youthfulness of the protagonists
   B. Search for understanding
   C. Meeting a variety of people
   D. Variety of experiences
   E. Style of writing
      1. Picaresque
      2. Humor
      3. First person
      4. Slang
II. Differences
   A. Rural (*HF*) and urban (*Catcher*) settings
   B. Noneducated (*HF*) and educated (*Catcher*) protagonists
   C. Late nineteenth-century (*HF*) and mid-twentieth-century (*Catcher*) periods

III. Conclusions
    A. Realizations about life
    B. Similarity of narrative techniques
    C. Universality of growing up

Relationships.   Establishing relationships between events or
ideas is a subtler kind of comparison. For example, if you were
doing research for a paper on the Populist party in the United
States, you might decide that this nineteenth-century movement bears a relationship to the so-called new politics of the
1970s. A paper that explored this relationship would be much
more exciting than an enumeration of bare historical facts concerning the Populist party.

When you are preparing a paper that shows relationships,
you may follow one of two methods for internal organization.
The first is to introduce all the historical facts and then relate
them to the present. The other is to organize the historical
facts into logical divisions and establish the relationships point
by point within the divisions.

Here is a rough outline that uses the first method of organization for a paper showing the relationships between the Populist party and the new politics:

I. Populist party (historical facts)
    A. Time of social unrest
    B. Cross section of people in the party
    C. Rejection of Populist proposals
    D. Role in national politics
II. New politics (current facts)
    A. Time of social unrest
    B. People in the movement
    C. Rejection of ideas by the establishment
    D. Place in national politics

If you were following the second pattern, your rough outline
would look something like this:

I. Social unrest
    A. In time of Populist party
    B. Today
II. Issues and proposals
    A. Of Populist party
    B. Of new politics

III. Members
    A. Of Populist party
    B. Of the movement in new politics
IV. National influence
    A. Of Populist party
       1. In nineteenth century
       2. Lasting influence
    B. Of new politics

Survey

The survey paper has fallen into some disfavor because it tends to be too general. No one should ever attempt, for instance, to cover in 3,000 words subjects such as "The French Revolution" or "The History of Opera." One student's plan to write a ten-page paper on English literature will illustrate the faulty approach to the survey paper. When asked what aspect he intended to cover, he answered: "All of it." Discouraged from taking this unrealistic approach, he decided to settle on "just a century or so." Further discussion led him to realize that a general survey of "just a century or so" was too ambitious and he must limit his paper to a specific aspect in the broad subject of English literature.

Uses. Avoid the general survey paper unless it is specifically assigned, as unfortunately it sometimes is. However, when limited properly, the survey approach is legitimate. For example, a paper on "Puritanism in America" might turn into nothing more than a rambling history of puritanism from the beginnings of the nation to the present time. As such, it could be a fascinating collection of facts leading to the obvious conclusion that puritanism has influenced American life—and perhaps still does. But how? That question would go unanswered. However, if the paper were focused on a specific aspect, such as "The Influences of Puritan Thought on American Art," it would result in more than an accumulation of information. Note that the subject has been limited to a single aspect of American life: art. Even the topic "The Influence of Puritan Thought on American Life" is too broad for a relatively short paper; the general term "American Life" suggests a long list of categories, including law, sex, art, business, and religion. But by singling out one aspect of American life—art, in this case—

the writer can develop the paper more exactly.

To cite another example, a survey of world theater during the past twenty-five years could turn into nothing more than a hit-and-miss discussion of some of the major playwrights and their works. On the other hand, a definite tracing of the influences of these writers and their plays on the contemporary world theater would be much more worthwhile.

In deriving influences and establishing their effects, keep in mind that the influences must be valid ones and that they must show a definite bearing on the subject. If either of these elements is missing, then the problem presented in the thesis statement was faulty initially, or it was not solved logically.

Patterns of Organization. This approach to organization is sometimes called *cause and effect.* When you use this method, you need to answer two questions in your paper: What are the major influences (cause)? How have or are these influences affecting the subject (effect)? In order to answer these questions fully, you should follow one of these patterns of organization:

PATTERN ONE

PART I: One by one, present the influences, and discuss and explore them.

PART II: Examine the ways in which these influences have affected or are affecting the subject.

PATTERN TWO

One by one, present the influences; discuss and explore them; examine their effects.

Here is a possible outline, using the first pattern, for a paper titled "The Influences of Puritan Thought on American Art":

I. Puritan thought regarding art
  A. Necessity for art to be instructive
  B. Suspicions of art for art's sake
  C. Necessity for art to be morally proper
II. Effects of these thoughts on contemporary American art
  A. Censorship
  B. Lack of support by the general public
  C. Suspicions of art and artists

Here is a rough outline that follows the second pattern:

I. Instructive necessity of art
II. Suspicions of art
III. Moral propriety of art

Under each of the main divisions, you would first discuss Puritan thought and then show how it has influenced modern thinking about art.

Of course, early in either of the proposed papers, you would need to explain what you mean by "art."

Interpretation

Interpreting and explaining a given set of facts or ideas is common to most academic areas.

In order to interpret facts or ideas meaningfully, you must understand them thoroughly and approach them objectively. The research paper differs vastly from the critical paper. The research paper depends on an investigation for its conclusions; whereas the critical paper depends more on the writer's reactions, background, and opinions.

Uses. Historians rely heavily on this method. James Truslow Adams observed "that the ripest fruit of knowledge is to *interpret* facts, to try to find out how they are related and how they influence one another."[1] But he cautions the writer: "This calls for wider background and far more concentration of thought. It is more dangerous, for one cannot prove one's interpretations by citations from 'sources.' "[2] Again, if you were assigned a paper on the Populist party, you might approach it from the interpretive rather than from the comparative standpoint. You could possibly interpret the facts concerning this political movement as indicators of the social unrest during the late nineteenth century.

Interpretation also plays a large part in writing about literature. Several of Franz Kafka's short stories, for example, could

1. James Truslow Adams, "My Methods as a Historian," *Writing for Love or Money* (New York: Longmans, Green and Co., 1949), p. 181.
2. Adams.

be interpreted in a paper on the theme of alienation. The literary paper dealing with *symbols* (concrete objects standing for abstract ideas) is also interpretive; an example is a study of the symbolic meanings of the names for the ships in Herman Melville's *Billy Budd, Foretopman* (1891).

In philosophy and religion the interpretive approach is probably taken more often than any other approach. A study of the philosophical writings of Ralph Waldo Emerson could be directed toward the interpretation of his ideas on nature. Or a paper on Saint Paul might focus on interpreting his views of truth. The interpretive paper in philosophy or religion is based primarily on the writings of the particular philosopher or theologian. Even though related works by other authors would probably be consulted, they would not be reechoed. There is an exception to the last statement: the paper that traces several interpretations of a particular person's ideas. Plato's work, for instance, has been interpreted variously through the centuries, and a study of these interpretations would be a reasonable topic.

Patterns of Organization. The methods of organizing interpretive papers are as varied as the interpretations that might result from them. However, because you are considering either a single idea and its parts or a series of related ideas and their parts, the organization should unfold naturally. The following outline will help to illustrate this point:

TOPIC: EMERSON'S IDEAS ON NATURE

  I. Nature as the reflection of the Divine
 II. Nature as the sustainer of Life
III. Nature as the giver of lessons
 IV. Nature as the source of language

Each of these main ideas would be developed through direct reference to Emerson's work and possibly through reference to books about Emerson.

If just one idea on nature were being explored, the rough outline would be on this order:

TOPIC: EMERSON'S IDEA OF NATURE AS THE REFLECTION OF
THE DIVINE (GOD)

  I. Immanence (God is everywhere.)
 II. Emanation (Nature flows out of God.)
III. Presence (God is now.)

Problem Solving

A thesis statement may set forth a clear-cut problem requiring specific solutions.

When you are writing a problem-solving paper, be sure that a problem actually exists, that its existence can be proven by documented sources, and that the proposed solutions are realistic and workable.

Uses. The problem-solving approach is frequently taken in the social and physical sciences, where the evidence is usually drawn from field studies or laboratory experiments. Topics of current interest (such as ecology, education, foreign relations, welfare, and economics) lend themselves to this approach.

Patterns of Organization. An examination of the proposed thesis statement for the study of the interstate highway system will illustrate how this kind of paper may be organized. The thesis statement is as follows:

> When all the states are willing to provide their share of the financing for the construction of the interstate highway system, it will be completed.

The dependent clause contains the problem that must be solved before the statement in the independent clause becomes a reality. The organization for such a paper, then, involves an analysis of the problem and a presentation of proposed solutions. Before giving solutions, all aspects of the problem must be analyzed in order to determine its causes. The proposed solutions represent an attempt to remove the causes, on the assumption that once the causes are eliminated, the problem will be solved.

The sample outlines on pp. 102–3 illustrate further how the problem-solving paper is organized.

Biography

The biographical paper is a common writing assignment, and it is one of the most abused. A study of an individual who has made some special mark on the world should provide more than a recounting of his birth, growing up, education or lack of it, success or failure, and death. Although these factors are relevant, there are other elements to consider in a good biography. In a brief study of an individual, it is likely that you will concentrate on only one of the following aspects: influences, accomplishments and contributions, reevaluations and corrections of previous assessments. In a book-length study, however, the biographer usually covers all three in depth.

Influences. One aspect of the biographer's task is to determine how certain experiences influenced the subject of the biography.

In his search for influences, the biographer investigates a number of possibilities. One of the most common approaches is finding out what books the subject read and how they influenced him. It is generally concluded, for instance, that John Bunyan's study of the King James Bible influenced both the content and the style of his writing.

The biographer also investigates firsthand experiences that might have played a part in molding the character of an individual and determining his work. Willa Cather once noted that she had gathered all the material for her novels *O Pioneers!* (1913) and *My Ántonia* (1918) before she was eighteen, from her experiences on the Nebraska frontier. This statement could lead the biographer into a closer examination of Miss Cather's actual frontier experience. Or a biographer of the late President Lyndon Johnson would not ignore the fact that Mr. Johnson grew up in an atmosphere of Texas politics. This approach offers numerous possibilities for biographical writing. But it should be handled honestly and accurately, with sufficient evidence, not just assumptions, to prove that the experiences actually influenced the person's life.

The biographer also examines the effects of personal relationships on the individual. Recent biographical studies of Mark Twain, for instance, have explored his wife's and William Dean Howells's combined influence on his writing.

In addition to his reading, experiences, and relationships, an individual is influenced in varying degrees by the economic, political, and cultural events of his time, commonly called his *milieu*. In treating a subject such as the development of Thomas Paine's political philosophy, the biographer would likely consider Paine's presence in the colonies at the outset of the American Revolution. The biographical subject cannot be separated from his milieu, but he should not be wedded to it so totally that the paper dwells more on background than on the individual's life.

Accomplishments and Contributions. Biographers are also concerned with the accomplishments and contributions of their subjects. For instance, a biographer of John Wesley Powell (1834–1902) an American explorer and surveyor, would cover his explorations of the Southwest and his difficulties in persuading the federal government to recognize the unique nature of the landscape, including the Grand Canyon. The biographer would also show how Powell's persistence eventually resulted in the preservation of much of the area under the National Park Service and that Powell lived to see a partial fruition of his work. Of course, recognition during the subject's lifetime is not always the case. The writing of Herman Melville, for instance, went largely unnoticed while he was living. The biographer would relate this fact and describe how his work was discovered later. He would also evaluate Melville's accomplishments in American literature and his contributions to world literature.

A person's accomplishments and contributions should be neither overestimated or underplayed. The biographer would be wise to heed James Thomas Flexner's admonition: "Complete intellectual honesty is perhaps the most important single attribute of the biographer."[3]

Reevaluations and Corrections. Another job of the biographer is to reevaluate other biographical accounts. Closely allied with this task is the correction of errors, either in fact or in judgment.

A person who exercised widespread influence during his lifetime will often be glorified in biographies written by family members or followers shortly after his death. For example, some of the early biographies of Sir Thomas More were mainly mixtures of legend and fact. Many years passed before an objective biography of him was written.

Another opportunity for reevaluation and correction arises when additional information is revealed. Such was the case with Robert Peel's *Mary Baker Eddy: The Years of Discovery* and *Mary Baker Eddy: The Years of Trial* (New York: Holt, Rinehart & Winston, 1966, 1971). Mrs. Eddy (1821–1910), who founded the Christian Science movement, had been both canonized and vilified in earlier biographical accounts. Peel, relying principally on sources previously unavailable to biographers,

3. James Thomas Flexner, "Biography Is a Juggler's Art," *Writing for Love or Money* (New York: Longmans, Green and Co., 1949), p. 172.

corrected most of the misinformation, especially some of the allegations made in the unfavorable and often-quoted biographical articles that appeared in *McClure's Magazine* at the turn of the century.

The beginning writer rarely undertakes this kind of biography, but when he does, he should be careful not to add more misinformation or make additional unsound judgments. The reevaluation and correction process should always be based on reliable evidence.

Patterns of Organization. The methods of organizing a biographical study depend on what aspect or aspects you plan to cover. In discussing influences, you would logically list the major influences and then develop them one by one. The same method would work for accomplishments and contributions. If you are engaged in reevaluation and correction, you would likely present the inaccurate and spurious matter first and then give the corrected material and newly appraised views.

In a general biographical paper, you would probably rely on the chronological method, showing the influences on the subject and his accomplishments and contributions within the structure of chronology.

Challenge of Biographical Writing. In his autobiography, Mark Twain summed up the challenge facing the biographer when he observed:

> What a wee little part of a person's life are his acts and his words! His real life is led in his head, and is known to none but himself. . . . Biographies are but the clothes and buttons of the man —the biography of the man himself cannot be written.[4]

According to Flexner, "A biography is regarded as a serious contribution in exact proportion to its dullness."[5] Taking exception to this assumption, he goes on to say that "drama is natural to biography because it is natural to the human mind."[6] He warns that draining off the excitement from the "men who have shaped events" makes the picture untrue.

4. Mark Twain, *Autobiography* (New York: Harper & Brothers, 1924), p. 2.

5. Flexner, p. 173.

6. Flexner.

MAKING THE OUTLINE

The next step in the organizational process is making the outline. Presumably, a rough outline, based on the hypothesis, was formed prior to the actual research and developed further during the investigation. If so, that outline will likely require revision and refinement, preferably being turned into a sentence outline so that it will serve as a reliable guide for writing the rough draft. If no outline has been made up to this point, the formation of one will be the logical outcome of the first two steps of organization (i.e., forming the thesis statement and determining the approach).

Purposes of the Outline

The outline—free of developmental materials such as quotations, examples, and specific details—is a series of generalizations, all relating to and stemming from the most general of statements: the thesis statement. Even though the effectiveness and value of the outline are disparaged by some students, its use will help assure organization and logic in the paper. Rare is the writer, no matter how experienced, who does not rely on some kind of outline, even if it consists of only a few key words or exists only in his mind.

The outline has three basic purposes:

1. To list all parts of a subject in a conventional form
2. To show logically equal parts of a subject
3. To provide an approximate guide for paragraphs and transition

Structure of the Outline

Here is the conventional set of symbols that constitute the basic structure of an outline:

I. ⎫ Division of logically equal
II. ⎭ parts, *first* in importance
   A. ⎫ Subdivisions of logically equal
   B. ⎭ parts, *second* in importance
      1. ⎫ Subdivisions of logically equal
      2. ⎭ parts, *third* in importance

$$\left.\begin{array}{l} \text{a.} \\ \text{b.} \end{array}\right\} \begin{array}{l} \text{Subdivisions of logically} \\ \text{equal parts, } \textit{fourth} \text{ in importance} \end{array}$$

Single division—that is, only one symbol of a particular kind —is an error in logic. Since nothing divides into only one part, there must always be two or more divisions; you can have as many divisions or subdivisions as you want, as long as the parts you list under any set of symbols are logically equal in importance. In addition to the symbols, there are two other indicators of equal value: (1) parallel sentence structure in the sentence outline and (2) the consistent use of nouns and prepositional phrases in the topic outline.

Always place the thesis statement at the beginning of the outline—an appropriate place for it because it is the determiner of what follows. Never attach meaningless terms such as "introduction" and "conclusion" to the outline.

The following specimen shows what a good outline *is not*:

There should be a)
definite title.   )————————→ OUTLINE

Meaningless label)————————→ Introduction

The thesis statement)
should be presented)————————→ Thesis Statement: Problems in
in its entirety.   )   high schools

                                              I.   Problems
Single division;   )————————→ A.   Discipline
"Problems" suggests)
more than one.   )
                                              II. Restrictions
                                                    A.   Tight schedules
Lacks equal value;)   B.   Dress codes
this would likely be)————————→ C.   No gum chewing
placed under D.   )   D.   Petty rules

                                              III. Subject matter
Not a noun; should be)————————→ A.   Not applicable
a word like *"relevance"*)   B.   Preparation
in order to be parallel)
with *"preparation"*; it)
is not indented properly.)

                                              IV. Faculty
A topic outline   )————————→ A.   Administrators are not
should not have a   )   interested in students'
sentence dropped in)   welfare.
occasionally.   )   B.   Teachers

Meaningless label)————————→ Conclusion

Formation of the Outline

In order to form the outline, analyze the thesis statement, discover its key ideas, and then develop and arrange these ideas. Even if you made a rough outline earlier, you may want to follow the same process in order to test its completeness and accuracy.

Let us take the following thesis statement as an example to illustrate the steps of the process:

Even though the modern high school may appear hopeless, the implementation of some major changes could alter this bleak picture.

Step 1. Analyze the thesis statement and then state its key ideas. Let us determine that the key ideas are as follows:

1. The modern high school may appear hopeless. (This statement suggests that there is a problem.)
2. Major changes could alter the picture. (This statement suggests that there are solutions.)

Step 2. Ask general questions about each key idea. For example:

1. What makes the modern high school appear hopeless? What are the indications of this problem?
2. What are the major changes that could solve the problem? What are the solutions to this problem?

Step 3. Answer the questions by listing as many possible answers as you can think of. Here are some possibilities for this thesis statement:

WHAT ARE THE INDICATIONS OF THIS PROBLEM?
1. Student apathy
2. Discipline
3. Narcotics
4. Dropouts
5. Destruction of school property
6. Lack of patriotism

WHAT ARE THE SOLUTIONS?
1. Better classes
2. Better teachers
3. Better buildings

    4. More money
    5. Fewer rules and regulations
    6. More concern with real life
    7. More concern with the individual
    8. More activities

Answering the questions should not be difficult because the information gathered during the research will provide sufficient background. In fact, the list of answers will probably be too long.

Step 4.   Select the ideas that you think are the most important. In the indications list, let us choose 1, 2, and 4. In the solutions list, let us select 1, 2, and 5. This selection sounds rather arbitrary, and in this case it is—for purposes of illustration. However, the selection process in an actual instance is guided primarily by the amount of material available and by your particular interests and preferences. In looking over the answers, you will be able to eliminate some immediately because they are either repetitious or would serve better as subdivisions.

Step 5.   List the ideas in rough outline form. The thesis statement in this example is worded so that it presents a problem in the dependent clause and gives solutions in the independent clause. You should therefore devote most of your paper to the solutions after you have explored the problem. With this idea in mind, you would make a rough outline something like the following one:

    I. Problems (meaning aspects of the main problem)
       A. Dropouts
       B. Discipline
       C. Apathy
   II. Better classes
  III. Better teachers
  IV. Fewer rules and regulations

Step 6.   Fill in the subdivisions of II, III, IV; that is, supply an A, B, and so on under each of the Roman numerals. Use the same method (steps 3 and 4) you used to derive the major divisions and the subdivisions under Roman numeral I. You would likely ask and answer the following questions:

II. What would improve classes?
III. What makes a good teacher? (Should administrators be included in this division?)
IV. What are the unnecessary rules and regulations?

Step 7. Arrange the main divisions in an effective order. The placement of "Problems" under Roman numeral I in this outline is already determined by the structure of the thesis statement. Obviously, you must discuss the aspects of the problem before you can offer solutions. There are three solutions, however, and you should arrange them according to the following rhetorical rules:

1. Place the second most important point at the beginning.
2. Place the least important point or points in the middle.
3. Place the most important point last.

The entire process, if followed carefully, will eventually lead to a polished topic or sentence outline.

Kinds of Outlines

The *topic outline* consists of a series of like grammatical elements, such as nouns or prepositional phrases. It is easier to construct than the *sentence outline,* which states the ideas in simple or compound sentences. But the topic outline does have a serious drawback: It is easy to jot down general words that often carry little significance once you are depending on the outline as a guide in developing the paper. For some writers the topic outline is sufficient. Usually, however, the sentence outline is preferable. The writer who understands his subject thoroughly should have no difficulty in forming a sentence outline. The seeming repetitiveness of the sentence outline is easily offset by the fact that it states the main points in a more concrete and precise manner than does the outline consisting exclusively of topics.

Here is an example of a topic outline:

CHANGES IN HIGH SCHOOLS

Thesis Statement: Even though the modern high school
may appear hopeless, the implementation of some major
changes could alter this bleak picture.

   I. Problems
      A. Discipline
      B. Dropouts
      C. Apathy

  II. Restrictions
      A. Tight schedules
      B. Dress codes
      C. Petty rules

 III. Subject matter
      A. Relevance
      B. Preparation

  IV. Faculty
      A. Administrators
      B. Teachers

In this topic outline the major parts of the subject are listed
succinctly and provide an overview of the paper. However,
when the topics are developed into sentences, the ideas take on
fuller shape, as this sentence outline shows:

CHANGES IN HIGH SCHOOLS

Thesis Statement: Even though the modern high school may
appear hopeless, the implementation of some major changes
could alter this bleak picture.

   I. The modern high school may appear hopeless.
      A. It is beset by discipline problems.
      B. A large percentage of students drop out before
         completing school.
      C. There is an air of apathy among students.

  II. Many of the unnecessary restrictions should be
     eliminated.
      A. The tight schedules should be replaced by more
         flexible ones.

B. The mode of dress and length of hair should
be left up to the individual.
C. The petty rules should be replaced by greater
emphasis on self-discipline.

III. The content of the subject matter should be improved.
A. The courses should be relevant to the students'
lives and the world around them.
B. The courses should prepare the students for the
future.
1. Preparation for college is necessary for
some students.
2. Preparation for an occupation is important
for many students.

IV. The faculty, both administrators and teachers, should
improve.
A. The administrators should be aware of the school's
overall needs.
1. The development of curriculum is important.
2. Hiring and maintaining a good faculty is
important.
3. Understanding students' needs is important.
B. The teachers should be aware of the students'
overall needs.
1. Considering individual differences is
important.
2. Understanding the characteristics of the age
group is important.
3. Presenting the subject matter effectively is
important.

The sentence outline does not make for particularly interesting reading because of its repetitive sentence structure and general nature. The writing style, however, is immaterial. What is important is the setting forth of the ideas in a logical pattern. More than an exercise in logic, though, the outline is a practical guide to writing the paper. If you rely on it, the outline will demonstrate its practicality again and again.

GETTING ORGANIZED

For some writers the organizational process is one of the most difficult tasks to carry out. But ignoring the necessity for organization and starting to write, hoping that the ideas and evidence will magically fall into place, produces more frustration than progress. Attention to the thesis statement, selection of the right approach, and formation of the outline will evolve into an effective diffusion of knowledge.

Chapter 6

Writing the Research Paper

> *The effort of research is so taxing and exhausting*
> *that whoever has gone through it feels a natural desire*
> *to exhibit the results.*
>
> Jacques Barzun and Henry F. Graff,
> *The Modern Researcher*

The concepts of *analysis* and *synthesis* are opposites, but both are essential to the writing of a research paper. Analysis (from the Greek word meaning "to break up") describes the taking apart of the ideas and the evidence and looking at all sides of them; the preparatory work has been directed toward analyzing, or breaking up, the material. On the other hand, synthesis (from the Greek word meaning "to put together") denotes the combining of all the elements. The formation of the outline was the first move toward synthesizing the ideas and evidence, and it will be a guide to the final synthesis: writing the paper.

Before looking into the putting-together process, let us retrace the analytical steps:

1. You selected a subject.
2. You formed a statement of the problem that you isolated from the general subject.
3. You made a preliminary investigation of the evidence.
4. You formed a hypothesis based on the statement of the problem and the investigation of the evidence.
5. You gathered the evidence, guided by the hypothesis.
6. You tested the hypothesis by surveying the evidence you had gathered.
7. You formed the thesis statement, basing it on the hypothesis.

8. You set forth in the outline the logical parts of the thesis statement.

Thus far, the movement has been analytical in nature, that is, from the general to the specific. The final step toward the specific is writing the rough draft, thereby developing the outline through a synthesis of the evidence. The following diagram traces the basic structure of the research paper as it evolves during the writing of the rough draft:

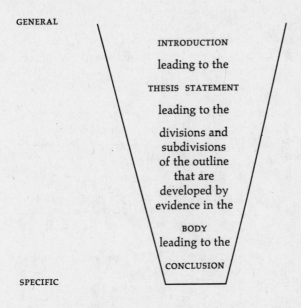

GENERAL

INTRODUCTION

leading to the

THESIS STATEMENT

leading to the

divisions and
subdivisions
of the outline
that are
developed by
evidence in the

BODY
leading to the

CONCLUSION

SPECIFIC

This diagram shows the three parts of the written work: (1) the introduction and thesis statement, (2) the body, and (3) the conclusion. The three-part structure is basic to all expository writing. It assures a *beginning* (introduction and thesis statement), a *middle* (body), and an *end* (conclusion). Although the introduction and conclusion are not mentioned specifically in the outline, which determines only the middle of the paper, they will grow out of it logically as the beginning and end.

The plan of the paper is clear, but the question remains: How does this logical, well-organized, and fully developed paper evolve from an outline and a stack of note cards? The answer to this question is in five parts:

1. Organize the *evidence* on the note cards according to the outline.
2. Understand the kinds of evidence and their derivatives: the developmental materials.
3. Use the evidence effectively by writing a *rough draft*.
4. Give credit to the sources of the evidence through *documentation*.
5. Turn the rough draft into a *finished paper*.

THE EVIDENCE

The evidence, quoted directly, paraphrased, or summarized on the note cards, consists of the facts drawn from the sources.

Organization

On a mechanical level, you should begin the organization of the evidence by finding a place where you can spread out your note cards and bibliography cards for easy access. It is helpful to post the outline on the wall above the writing area.

Sort the note cards into stacks according to their relationship to the Roman numerals on the outline. That is, all the note cards bearing the designation "I" should be placed in one stack; all those bearing "II," in a second stack; and so on. If you labeled the note cards with descriptive terms or with the outline symbols (as suggested in chapter 3), the sorting will be simple; if you did not, you will need to scan each note card in order to determine the outline heading under which it belongs.

Use and Kinds of Evidence

The basic use of the evidence is to develop the generalizations contained in the outline. From the raw evidence, the following kinds of *developmental materials* are refined:

Details
Examples
Direct quotations
Statistics
Definitions
Analogies
Rhetorical questions

These developmental materials, drawn from the evidence on the note cards, bring to life the basic structure of your paper. The successful writer employs as wide a variety of developmental materials as his subject will permit.

Details. In the broadest sense, all developmental materials are details. Specifically, however, details are used for explanation, analysis, and elaboration of a general statement.

The series of details on the following note card is drawn into a paragraph that explains the development of pantomime in Ancient Rome.

Note card for the paragraph

> I. B.
>
> Pantomime started in Rome in 22 B.C. Pylades, tragic dancer, and Bathyllus, comic dancer, gave it style. Comic pantomime on love in, and travesties on, Olympic society was short-lived. Tragic pantomime outlived Roman Empire. Subjects included Medea, Phaedra, Pentheus, Hercules, Oedipus. Latter had orchestra and chorus.
>
> Nagler, p. 28

Paragraph based on the note card

Pantomime as a recognized art form made its official Roman debut in 22 B.C. The tragic dancer, Pylades, and the comic dancer, Bathyllus, seem to have been instrumental in giving the new genre its definite style. The comic pantomime, featuring the amorous aspects of Olympic society and outright travesties, was rather short-lived, while tragic pantomime, supported by orchestral music and choral singing and dealing with such subjects as Medea, Phaedra, Pentheus, Hercules, and Oedipus, outlived the Roman Empire.[1]

This example is developed through historical details, one of the most common methods. However, details may also be used to explain theories, to describe processes, and to form the basis of a series of reasons for a particular occurrence or development.

1. A. M. Nagler, *A Source Book in Theatrical History* (New York: Dover, 1959), p. 28. (Quoted directly.)

Here is an example of a paragraph that relies on details to tell how something works:

Another of the busiest exhibitors, almost lost among the big-company displays, was a new, young New York firm, Retention Communication Systems, Inc., whose "book-size" microfiche reader attracted exceptional attention because it is small enough (10 inches high, 8½ inches wide, and 3 inches deep) to fit into an attaché case, and weighs only 3½ pounds. Its optical head can be removed from the viewing screen and snapped onto a larger screen, or even projected on a wall. RCS was also displaying a rear-projection cartridge viewer that promises to be revolutionary. This small machine, designed for either home or office, employs a cartridge-carrying sound film, in motion or stills. Its potential for entertainment and education was remarked by many of the delegates.[2]

Details are the easiest of the developmental materials to use, but a written work developed entirely by details lacks variety and depth, especially when examples or other stronger materials would add vitality to the paper.

Examples.   When you are listening to a speaker and he says "for example," you probably tune him in. This fact holds true in written work as well. One of the most arresting ways to develop ideas is by *examples,* or specific illustrations of your point.

Sustained or long examples develop general statements effectively, as illustrated in the paragraph following the note cards.

NOTE CARDS FOR THE PARAGRAPH

I. C.

"Einstein once believed that if he could only get two per cent of the population to disavow war he might succeed in abolishing it. How deeply ironic that this very man should have been the one to write the letter of introduction to President Roosevelt for a group of physicists, whose visit to the President initiated the whole process that finally gave us the hydrogen bomb."

Niebuhr, p. 6

2. John Tebbel, "Micrographics: A Growing Industry," *Saturday Review,* 10 July 1971, p. 49.

I.c.

"The late Professor Einstein came to the despairing conclusion that if he had to live his life again he would want to be a plumber or a peddler and not a scientist."

Niebuhr, p. 6

Paragraph Based on the Note Cards

Generalization

Although many scientists are aware of the direction that science is taking, they have, ironically, become a part of the very thing they loathe. Einstein, for example, once thought that if he might persuade only two percent of the people to renounce war, he could see it abolished. It was this same man who wrote the letter of introduction for a group of scientists to visit President Roosevelt. And this visit was the first step in the process that ultimately led to the hydrogen bomb. No wonder he reached "the despairing conclusion that if he had to live his life again he would want to be a plumber or a peddler and not a scientist."[3]

Development by example based on evidence from the research (paraphrased)

(direct quotation)

The material on these note cards is quoted directly, but the paragraph is based partially on a paraphrase of the material and partially on a direct quotation. It is not suggested that the paraphrase is better, but a paper should not contain an excess of quoted material. Generally speaking, put the evidence into your own words whenever possible, but always be sure to cite the source of a paraphrase.

The following illustrations of two series of short examples are both quoted directly. If you discovered such material in your research, you would probably summarize the details that make up the short examples, rather than copying them in their entirety. However, in their original forms they illustrate how you

3. Reinhold Niebuhr, "Einstein and the World Situation," *Messenger*, 14 Dec. 1954, p. 6.

might use such a series of examples in writing.

The first writer states a problem and then proves its existence by citing three specific examples:

Statement of the problem

Assuming that the spenders work a standard forty-hour week, $1-million worth of tax money is now being spent for construction of new sewage facilities in the United States every hour.

Practically none of this money is buying what most taxpayers think they are paying for.

Series of three examples

Disease-carrying viruses are not being removed from waste water the new facilities are pouring into our streams, lakes, and oceans.

Nitrogenous contents of sewage are being converted into nitrates hazardous to health.

Organic substances known to provoke cancer are being dumped into waterways that subsequently become sources of drinking water for homes and public places.[4]

In this selection, the writer cites four short examples and then draws a conclusion from them:

Series of four short examples

The superhighway that wasn't built . . .

The Everglades Jetport that is still wilderness . . .

The SST that didn't get off the ground . . .

The hundreds of Black councilmen, legislators, sheriffs, mayors in that South which, 10 years ago, was driving Blacks with dogs, cattleprods, and guns . . .

Conclusion drawn from examples

These are the witnesses that the system not only can be beaten but *has been beaten*—by working within it.[5]

Examples, whether sustained, abbreviated, or in a series, should be based on concrete evidence. Examples from personal experiences are more commonly employed in the informal essay than in the research paper. Hypothetical examples (ones that

4. John Lear, "Environment Repair: The U.S. Army Engineers' New Assignment," *Saturday Review*, 1 May 1971, p. 47.

5. Robert Claiborne, "Turning America Around," *The Village Voice*, 22 Apr. 1971, p. 50.

are drawn from imaginary situations) usually lack the drama and immediacy that characterize concrete and specific material.

Direct Quotations. Although indispensable as developmental materials, *direct quotations* should not be strung like beads on a necklace with flimsy introductory statements providing their support. They must be an integral part of the text. The writer who constructs a paper consisting of nothing more than a series of direct quotations has omitted one of the most important aspects of research: synthesis. The advice that Bronson Alcott gave in *Table Talk* is appropriate: "One must be a wise reader to quote wisely and well."

In order to determine the use of a direct quotation, follow this principle: If the original wording is so concise, or dramatic, or totally right that paraphrasing it would destroy its meaning and effectiveness, then quote it directly; otherwise paraphrase or summarize it.

Papers on literary subjects probably use more direct quotations than other papers do. This example shows how a quotation from the work under consideration helps to support and develop a generalization:

Generalization

When a character in a play by Jean Anouilh accepts life as it is, he takes on a hollowness, exchanging the essence of his manhood for security. Witness Jason in the play *Medea:*

Support through a quotation

I want to accept now. . . . I want to be humble. I want the world, the chaos where you led me by the hand—I want it to take shape at last. You are probably right in saying there is no reason, no light, no resting place, that we always have to search with blood-stained hands, strangle and throw away all that we have torn apart. . . . I answer the appalling contradictions, the abysses, the wounds by the simplest gesture man has invented in order to live: I discard them.[6]

Quotations used sparingly and wisely are valuable developmental materials that lend authority and variety to a written

6. Jean Anouilh, *Medea*, English version by Luce and Arthur Klein. (Garden City, N.Y.: Doubleday & Co., 1957), pp. 204–205.

work. Employed excessively and presented awkwardly, quotations turn the research paper into a collection of note cards typed onto 8½-by-11-inch sheets of paper.

The correct use of quotations in a written work presents many problems regarding punctuation, omissions, additions, and other matters. (For a complete guide to these details, see chapter 9, pp. 226–31.)

Statistics.   Reliable numerical facts and data, known as *statistics,* have a limited but respected place as a developmental material. Often statistics are presented in tables (as discussed in chapter 8). They are also frequently included within the text of the paper, but it is a deadly practice to present a list of statistics that has not been absorbed into the flow of the text.

The bare statistics on this note card were taken from the highly readable paragraph that follows it:

NOTE CARD FROM PARAGRAPH

Distribution of wealth in Mexico

1956 — 60% ill-fed, −housed, & −clothed; 40% illiterate; 46% children not in school; cost of living rose 5 times since 1939; 89% families, according to 1950 census, reported income of 600 pesos per month ($69 in 1950, $48 in 1960; 12.50 pesos per dollar).

Lewis, p. xxix.

ORIGINAL PARAGRAPH

Despite the increased production and the apparent prosperity, the uneven distribution of the growing national wealth has made the disparity between the incomes of the rich and the poor more striking than ever before. And despite some rise in the standard of living for the general population, in 1956 over 60 percent of the population were still ill fed, ill housed, and ill clothed, 40 percent were illiterate, and 46 percent of the nation's children were not going to school. A chronic inflation since 1940 has squeezed the real income of the poor, and the cost of living for workers in Mexico City has risen over five times since 1939. According to the census of 1950 (published in 1955), 89 percent of all Mexican families reporting income earned less than 600 *pesos* a month, or $69 at the 1950 rate of exchange and $48 at the 1960 rate. (There are 12.50 *pesos* to the dollar.)[7]

Statistics play an important role in the development of papers concerned with current issues, such as education, prison reform, political scandals, and welfare irregularities. Statistical information is also appropriate for the development of topics in other fields, including history, linguistics, and literature. A study of the American Civil War, for example, might call for citing numbers of casualties, prisoners of war, and troops.

Definitions. In a research paper, *definitions* usually contain more than specific meanings of words. Through details, examples, or quotations, definitions clarify the unfamiliar or specify the familiar.

This definition of molecular biology opens with a statement that gives an overall view of the science, and the following sentences expand the definition through more specific details.

In its broadest context, molecular biology is that part of biology which attempts to interpret biological events in terms of the molecules of the cell. The subject matter merges indistinguishably with older more traditional areas of biology, such as biochemistry and genetics. In a general way molecular biology may be described as that subject which grew out of the merging of biochemistry and genetics, since in this discipline special emphasis is placed on the molecular basis of genetics and of macromolecular replication. This field has been an important activity since about 1945, during which time increasing attention has been focused on the role of nucleic acids in biological systems.[8]

Another approach to defining molecular biology is taken in the following paragraphs. Here the writer, who is directing his definition to a general audience, does not define the term specifically; instead he is more concerned with explaining its implications.

We are going to hear a lot more, in the decades ahead, about the

7. Oscar Lewis, *The Children of Sanchez* (New York: Random House, 1961), p. xxix.

8. *McGraw-Hill Encyclopedia of Science and Technology* (New York: McGraw-Hill, 1971), vol. 8, 632.

prospects of improving the human species by inducing changes in the submicroscopic components of the body cells. "Molecular biology," a much-pursued study today, holds out the expectation that eventually men will succeed in altering the genetic codes which determine the makeup and behavior of body cells—spotting and correcting (or even improving?) the function of the cell's chemical machinery.

Biologists raise distant hopes that, through this altering, more durable humans could result, with disease strains eradicated or fortified against, even as fungus-resistant wheat is developed by genetically trained horticulturists.[9]

Specifying the familiar is the other function of the definition. Because a familiar word often has no single meaning, it is necessary to tell the reader how it is going to be used in a particular context, as in this definition of "truth":

> I am very excited by the possibilities for Truth, in the sense of the Greek word for Truth, *aletheia*, which etymologically means unveiling or unmasking. . . .[10]

Here is another example of a definition that specifies a familiar term:

> Science is a form of human activity through pursuit of which mankind acquires an increasingly fuller and more accurate knowledge and understanding of nature, past, present and future, and an increasing capacity to adapt itself to and to change its environment and to modify its own characteristics.[11]

In defining a word, always consider the levels of definition suggested by the word's *denotation* and *connotation*. The denotation is its primary or exact definition; the connotation is its secondary or implied meaning. Sometimes a particular word will have several different connotations. The word "heart," for instance, in its denotative meaning, is defined as "a hollow, muscular organ that by rhythmic contractions and relaxations keeps the blood in circulation throughout the body." But here are a few of its many connotations: love, affection, spirit, courage, enthusiasm, compassion, and mercy.

9. William H. Stringer, "Do Genes Build Men?" *Christian Science Monitor*, 1 Nov. 1967, p. 16.

10. James Alvin Sanders, "The Vitality of the Old Testament," *Union Seminary Quarterly Review* (Jan. 1966), p. 179.

11. Paul Freedman, *The Principles of Scientific Research* (New York: Pergamon Press, 1960), p. 3.

Keep in mind, too, that some words are *abstract* and others are *concrete*. Abstract words are more difficult to define because they stand for qualities, concepts, and ideas—intangibles such as love, truth, life, loyalty, and virtue. Concrete words stand for persons, places, and things—tangibles such as books, cities, cars, and research papers. Defining abstract terms is a more common practice in research papers than defining concrete words unless you are using a concrete word in a special sense (e.g., heart).

Without doubt, the poorest method of definition is the one most commonly used by inexperienced writers. It opens with such phrases as "according to Webster" or "the dictionary says"; after this deadly introduction appears a sterile definition, lifted directly from the dictionary. Although there may be rare cases when this kind of definition is sufficient, there are so many better approaches that this one could be retired without leaving a void. Three possibilities have already been illustrated. In defining "molecular biology," the first writer employed specific details, and the second used an analogy as well as details. In defining "truth," the writer turned to *etymology*, a study that is concerned with the history of words, tracing them to their original roots and meanings. Such details often enrich and broaden the development of a definition. A good source for the etymology of words is the *Oxford English Dictionary*.

Another way to define a word is to tell what it does not mean; this is essentially an act of contrasting. John Dewey takes this approach in the following sentence:

> The phrase "progressive education" is one, if not of protest, at least of contrast, of contrast with an education which was predominantly static in subject-matter, authoritarian in methods, and mainly passive and receptive from the side of the young.[12]

Examples will also expand a definition. Here, the writer employs a series of short examples in an elaboration on his original definition of "truth":

> "What is truth?" asked Pilate of our Lord. And he did not answer, for Truth is judgment, divine judgment; it is judgment of the condemned on the accuser, of the oppressed on the oppressor, of

12. John Dewey, "The Need for a Philosophy of Education," *The New Era in Home and School*, 15 (1934), 211.

tomorrow's discovery on today's ignorance. It is the saving judgment of the Ultimate on all our penultima: it is the silence of God's Christ in the presence of our Pilate.[13]

In order to define a term in a research paper, you may begin with the dictionary, but do not stop there. Keep in mind that the dictionary definition is available to the reader; your purpose and duty are to explain and describe the term so thoroughly that its meaning becomes richer, fuller, and clearer.

Analogies. Analogies are striking explanatory devices that show the similarities between two things, usually one familiar and the other unfamiliar. By comparing the unfamiliar with the familiar, you can often clarify a complex idea or stress a strong point. In the analogy that follows, the writer compares the workings of genes (unfamiliar) to a factory computer program (familiar):

> These genes, myriad in number, are said to be what determine a cell's growth and performance, whether in muscle or brain—even as a computer program determines, say, the successive operations at Ford Motor which fashion a finished engine block from a blank piece of steel.[14]

Because nearly everyone has some idea of a computer program, the comparison serves to clarify the theory of genes.

This analogy makes two rather complex ideas seem deceptively simple:

> Free will and determinism, I was told, are like a game of cards. The hand that is dealt you represents determinism. The way you play your hand represents free will.[15]

Stressing a strong point is the purpose of this analogy:

> Both Milgrim [High School] and Hartsburgh [High School] are valid examples—though of very different aspects—of American democracy in action. And in neither could a student learn as much about civil liberty as a Missouri mule knows at birth.[16]

During your research you will probably discover analogies

13. Sanders, "The Vitality," p. 182.

14. Stringer, "Genes," p. 16.

15. Norman Cousins, "A Game of Cards," in *This I Believe* (New York: Simon & Schuster, 1952), p. 175.

16. Edgar Z. Friedenberg, "The Modern High School: A Profile," in *Crisis* (New York: Harcourt, Brace and World, 1969), p. 134.

that seem to clarify or stress ideas so perfectly that you may want to use them in your paper. Or original analogies might emerge in your own thinking as you analyze the evidence.

Before you use an analogy, be sure, first, that there is a basis for comparison and, second, that the analogy sheds light on the subject and does not muddle it all the more.

Rhetorical Questions. The much-abused rhetorical questions should be used only for dramatic emphasis and should be provocative in nature. Stringer, in his essay on the uses of molecular biology, opened with the question: "How shall mankind build a nobler race of human beings?"[17] This question has a dramatic and provocative tone that would probably lead the reader to pursue the idea further. But if he had started with the question, "Have you ever wondered what 'molecular biology' is all about?," it is doubtful if the reader would have gotten past that first question. Later in the same essay, the writer proposes some more questions:

Can virtue and truth—or superior intelligence—be implanted chemically in man? Is this the way to produce either pugilists or poets? And if this proves possible, who is to say which should be ordered up?[18]

Excellent as they are for introductory and transitional purposes, rhetorical questions should not be overused. When you do employ them, see that they are purposeful, provocative, and even startling.

THE ROUGH DRAFT

In preparing the research paper, it seems that one exerts endless energy in hypothesizing, analyzing, synthesizing, and proposing, but it does all lead to a single objective: writing the paper.

The writing begins with the rough draft. How the rough draft is written from a mechanical standpoint depends largely on the individual. Some writers compose the first draft quickly, just getting the ideas down and not concerning themselves with diction and style. Others work in an opposite manner and assem-

17. Stringer, "Genes," p. 16.
18. Stringer.

ble the first draft slowly and meticulously, thus avoiding extensive revision. Through experimentation, you will find the system
that best suits your abilities.

Parts of the Rough Draft

The three parts of the rough draft are the introduction and
thesis statement, the body, and the conclusion. Whether or not
you compose the parts in this order does not matter.

Introduction and Thesis Statement.   The introduction presents the paper to the reader. In doing so, its prime function is to
catch the reader's interest. Once this has been accomplished, the
introduction should then lead into the thesis statement. It is unwise to eliminate the introduction and open directly with the
thesis statement. By its complex and abstract nature, the thesis
statement usually demands some preliminary explanation.

The length of the introduction is determined by the overall
length of the paper. Accordingly, in a ten-page paper, the introduction might cover less than one page, whereas in a fifty-page
paper, it may extend four or five pages.

Introductions are as varied as the material they introduce, but
there are some basic techniques that are usually successful.

One method is *to tell what is not going to be discussed*. After
some of the main aspects of a subject are eliminated, the aspect
to be discussed is set forth, as in this example:

> The unfamiliarity of Kafka's method as a novelist offers the
> literary critic an opportunity for discussing quite a wide range of
> subject-matter with some show of relevance. The sound critic of
> impeccable orthodoxy can run through his mental card-index where,
> somewhere among Tragedy, the Lyric, and the Epic, he will find a
> neglected but still serviceable dossier on the Allegory. . . . Those
> more fully equipped with modern conveniences can pass many a
> pleasant hour tracking to earth Kafka's castration complex or super-
> ego fixation. Or if everything else fails, it is always possible to analyze
> one of Shakespeare's plays in detail. . . .
> The most obvious of the temptations that offer themselves is
> a discussion of Kafka's philosophy. . . . Our concern is with his
> success in recreating from a sympathetic and consistent standpoint
> the complexity of the individual problem in its wider and profounder
> implications.[19]

19. R. O. C. Winkler, "The Novels," in *Kafka: A Collection of
Critical Essays* (Englewood Cliffs, N.J.: Prentice-Hall, 1965), pp. 45–46.

Another method is *to summarize opposing ideas*. Once they have been summarized and, in a sense, disposed of, the particular idea to be discussed emerges. This approach makes a good opening for a study that intends to prove a new idea or to correct or reevaluate an existing one. The following example summarizes two opposing ideas and then contradicts them:

It is hardly fair to dismiss much of Conrad Richter's work as nothing more than historical fiction, which, after all, does not rank very prominently in literature. His novels are more than "period pieces," those books that recreate past society so exactingly and whose characters live their lives so unrealistically. Nor can they be described as "historical romances" because they are not full of the grand exploits of equally grand people. Rising above the level of ordinary historical fiction, his novels of the frontier are distinctive; for, through his technique, he shapes his material into a design that is part of the overall pattern of history.

A review of the developmental materials will suggest other methods of introduction. The sustained example easily leads into the thesis, just as the series of short examples does. Also, statistics of a surprising nature create interest and act effectively as an introduction to the thesis statement. Rhetorical questions, if dramatic and provocative, are sometimes appropriate. Historical facts are another basis for introductory material.

Quotations, both indirect and direct, often serve effectively; both kinds are employed successfully by the writer of the following introductory paragraph:

At the turn of the seventeenth century, John Donne realized that no man is an island and that the bell tolls for us all. Picturesque as those images are, they were too parochial for so contemporary a man as Adlai Stevenson. In his last speech before the United Nations Economic and Social Council just a few days before his death, Stevenson said,

> *We travel together, passengers of a little spaceship, dependent on its vulnerable reserves of air and soil; all committed for our safety to its security and peace; preserved from annihilation only by the care, the work, and I will say, the love we give our fragile craft.*[20]

This introduction uses an indirect and a direct quotation. Steven-

20. Rene J. Dubos, "The Human Landscape," *Department of State Bulletin*, 60 (10 February 1969), 128.

son's view is an extension of Donne's, both showing the inescapable unity of mankind.

Studying the opening paragraphs of articles by skilled writers is the best instruction in the art of writing introductions. By applying the ideas gained from other writers and by reviewing the basic introductory techniques, you should experiment with several approaches until you discover the one that best suits your topic. Some writers wait until they have finished writing the body of the paper before turning to the introduction. This practice is acceptable and sometimes advisable because ideas for the introduction may surface during the sifting and organizing of the evidence.

In order to make a favorable first impression on the reader, the introduction must be lively, provocative, and above all, engaging. These qualities will be gained in proportion to your setting aside those practices that promise only dullness. One such practice is restating the thesis statement a half-dozen different ways before revealing the real thing. Another is asking meaningless rhetorical questions that would probably stop the reader after the second question mark. And beginning the introduction with "Webster says" or "according to the dictionary" is a practice that will probably discourage the bravest of readers.

Body.   The body—the major part of the paper—develops the outline. It progresses logically from one idea to another, substantiating the generalizations on the outline with specific developmental materials such as details, examples, and quotations.

Many writers find it difficult to achieve flow in the body of the paper, that is, to connect and relate the ideas, the generalizations, and the evidence. Basically, though, they face this problem because they do not use *transition* to bridge the various parts. Defined as the movement from one subject to another, transition depends on customary connecting words and special expressions. Samuel Taylor Coleridge once commented that the effective use of connectives (transitional words and devices) was the mark of an educated man. The importance that such a comment seems to place on the use of transition is justifiable.

The three purposes of transition are to connect the parts of the subject, to show the relationships between such parts, and to add emphasis. Although the parts of the subject are labeled on the outline with the conventional symbols, these outline designations rarely appear in the text. Instead, the connecting words and special expressions called *transitional devices* take the place of the symbols. (A list of the main transitional devices, with an explanation of their uses, is provided in chapter 9, pp. 218–22.)

An example showing how to develop the body of the paper appears in the section entitled "Development of the Rough Draft," p. 123. You should also study the model term paper (p. 135) that illustrates the developmental process.

Conclusion. The content of the conclusion logically depends on the material that has preceded it. In tying this material together, the conclusion can perform one of three functions: (1) recapitulate the ideas, (2) extend a challenge, or (3) draw inferences.

The conclusion that recapitulates the ideas of the paper in terms of the thesis statement returns to the first paragraph or so and ties up both ends neatly. The following conclusion (the introduction to the same paper was cited on p. 119 illustrates the method of recapitulation:

> The universality of mankind, the uniqueness of each person, and the need for social integration are three determinants of human life that must be reconciled in order to achieve individual freedom, social health, and the diversity of civilizations.[21]

The conclusion that extends a challenge is usually reserved for the problem-solving paper. Such a conclusion may call on the reader himself to help effect the solutions by telling him what he can do, as in the concluding paragraph from an editorial on the invasion of privacy:

> The historic American qualities of independence and contentiousness reinforce a healthy suspicion of imperious bureaucracies. There is no reason why they should not be applied for the purpose of harassing the local snoop if he comes around. Privacy, like clean air and water, can be polluted until none is left. Then we will have Big Brother.[22]

Such a conclusion, by suggesting that the ideas presented in the body of the paper have not been shelved, gives a feeling of

21. Dubos, "Landscape," p. 128.
22. Peter Schrag, "Dossier Dictatorship," *Saturday Review*, 17 Apr. 1971, p. 25.

continuity and immediacy to what has gone before.

If opposing ideas have been presented, the conclusion may challenge the reader to accept one or the other of the ideas or at least to consider their relative value. In the conclusion to the essay on the manipulation of genes, the writer suggests specifically that scientists question themselves regarding the conflict between a biological and a spiritual solution to man's problems, but the statement could be interpreted on a broader level to include anyone who thinks that science has all the answers.

> In this confrontation, the researchers should ask themselves whether they should not look—for reality—well beyond that which is visible to the micro-electronic eye.[23]

A conclusion may draw inferences from the preceding evidence and sometimes issue a warning based on the evidence and its implications, as in this example:

> But then America will be deceiving itself further. If Rap Brown is jailed, SNCC will find another leader who will sound the same tones, not because he will have taken his cue from some foreign ideology, but because he has gone through an American experience and come out of it a revolutionary. The black guerrillas have become convinced that it is impossible to achieve decent human values within this system and that it must therefore be overthrown. If America in its arrogance refuses to confront this elemental fact, then the revolutionaries will have had the last laugh. For if it merely tries to purge itself of what it considers a foreign element in its midst, America will have lost its last chance to understand the horrors of ghetto life that produce black revolutionaries. And it is that failure of understanding which produces the Detroits in the first place.[24]

Probably the most difficult of the three kinds of conclusions to write, the inference-warning conclusion is most often used in papers concerned with controversial problems.

As with the introduction, the length of the conclusion is determined by the overall length of the paper.

Remember that a feeble conclusion can easily mar the total effectiveness of the paper. Several factors make for weak conclusions. One is the sense that the writer is anxious to wrap up

23. Stringer, "Genes," p. 16.

24. Sol Stern, "America's Black Guerrillas," in *Crisis* (New York: Harcourt, Brace and World, 1969), p. 94.

the paper and get the whole thing over with. Obviousness is another factor; seldom is "in conclusion" or any of its relatives necessary in the concluding paragraphs. Exceptions to this rule do exist, but logically the content of the conclusion and its position at the end of the paper make it clear to the reader that he is at the end of the discussion.

Moralizing, apologizing, and congratulating weaken the conclusion, too. Phrases like "this paper having tried to prove," "having shown," "hopefully given you a better understanding," or "hopefully inspiring you" are inappropriate and usually insulting to the reader's intelligence.

Nor do meaningless rhetorical questions elicit a favorable response from the reader. Ending with a banal question such as "What are you going to do about it?" would more likely offend than inspire.

The use of a direct quotation can confuse the reader. After all, the purpose of the conclusion is to summarize your ideas, not to depend on someone else to do the work for you. In order to give added emphasis, you may use a brief quotation within the conclusion, but for the most part the conclusion should be original.

Probably the greatest error in forming a conclusion is the introduction of new ideas. Never include new ideas in the conclusion because there is no place for them to go from there. They are left dangling, and so is the reader.

In order to learn how to write effective conclusions, (1) study the final paragraphs of good writing, (2) understand the basic kinds of conclusions, and (3) practice.

Development of the Rough Draft

The full procedure for developing the rough draft may be demonstrated by using the sentence outline on p. 102 as the basis for a hypothetical paper. (Let us assume for the moment that you actually conducted the research on the problems in secondary schools.)

Your first step is to sort the note cards into four stacks, according to the four main points on the outline. With the outline before you and the note cards sorted, you are ready to begin writing.

Introduction. You may have uncovered some evidence during the research that would be appropriate for the introduction, or perhaps some ideas came to you as you surveyed the evidence. In either case, review the evidence or ideas and study the thesis statement and outline before beginning the introduction. Once you have a good idea what you are going to introduce, your next step is to determine how to introduce it. While you were conducting the research, you may have discovered several problems and solutions concerning secondary education with which you disagreed. These ideas could lead to an introduction that tells what is *not* going to be discussed:

Newspapers from almost any part of the country give the impression that the greatest problem in secondary education is a financial one. Dire predictions of "cutting back" and "tightening the belt" are all too frequent. Or there is the narcotics scare. It seems to be fashionable to equate the problems of the high school with the use of drugs. Certainly not to be forgotten are the racial problems. Integration, or the lack of it, is often exposed as the real demon behind the difficulties in high schools. And then there are the groups who believe that the students are being indoctrinated with Communism by left-wing teachers and textbooks. To them the problem is one of subversion. But are these the real problems? Actually, they are symptoms of other more deep-rooted problems that could be solved, not by higher taxes, crash programs, federal rulings, or increased patriotism, but from within the schools. Even though the modern high school may appear hopeless, the implementation of some major changes could alter this bleak picture.

This introduction opens with a series of examples that summarizes what many people seem to believe are the major problems in secondary education: (1) finances, (2) narcotics, (3) integration, (4) subversion. The rhetorical question asks if these are the real problems after all. The next sentence is a preliminary to the thesis statement. By the time the thesis statement appears, it is clear that this paper is going to take a different approach from the aspects just mentioned. (Because of the general nature of the information in the series of examples, it is not necessary to document the sources from which the examples were drawn.)

Body. Let us assume that the assignment calls for approximately 4,000 words. The fairly short introduction contains about 200 words, and the conclusion will probably have about the same number. That leaves 3,600 words for the body, or 900 words for each of the four divisions of the outline. Always consider the length of the assignment in order to distribute the words somewhat equally. Otherwise you may spend all the allotted words on the first division or have too many left when you approach the last division. In both cases, you will be faced with extensive revision, either in cutting or expanding.

The outline for the first division of the body is as follows:

I. The modern high school has many problems.
   A. It is beset by discipline problems.
   B. A large percentage of students drop out before completing school.
   C. There is an air of apathy among students.

You do not have to follow the outline rigorously; sometimes you will find that it is too ambitious, too vague, or too limited. In such cases, adjust the outline accordingly—shifting the order of points, eliminating them, or altering them as necessary. Before you stray from the outline's original plan, though, give it a fair chance; if it was formed thoughtfully, it should serve with minimum alteration.

Using the outline (not revised in this instance) as a guide, sort the note cards from the "I" stack into additional stacks to provide for the development of the first Roman numeral and the letters A, B, and C.

You should have enough material to divide this part of the outline into four paragraphs:

Paragraph 1: general discussion of the problems (development of I)
Paragraph 2: discussion of discipline problems (development of A)
Paragraph 3: discussion of dropouts (development of B)
Paragraph 4: discussion of apathy (development of C).

Discipline problems might cover two paragraphs or apathy might be combined with the paragraph on dropouts. It is difficult to say exactly when to paragraph because this depends on the amount of evidence, the overall organizational pattern, the relation to other parts, and the length of the paper.

Keep in mind that the *paragraph* is a unit of thought which develops one idea and its related parts through specific evidence and that this development may require ten words or two hundred. For the most part, however, research papers should contain fairly long paragraphs; excessive paragraphing is usually an indication of poor organization and scanty development.

Next, select and analyze the evidence you will use in developing the generalizations in the outline. At this point you might find it necessary to eliminate some of the note cards. Do this with no regrets. It is better to be in a position to choose among pieces of evidence than to discover that there is not enough evidence available to develop your outline.

After you have completed the selection and analysis of the evidence, set up a plan for writing the first division. Here is what the plan might look like:

PARAGRAPH 1
   I. The modern high school has many problems.
     Developmental materials
     1. Direct quotation from an authority on education
     2. Example of a serious problem

PARAGRAPH 2
   A. It is beset by discipline problems.
     Developmental materials
     1. Series of short examples covering the major kinds of discipline problems
     2. Direct quotation from a school principal
     3. Details on methods of handling discipline problems

PARAGRAPH 3
   B. A large percentage of students drop out before completing school.
     Developmental materials
     1. Details giving reasons for dropping out
     2. Direct quotation from a dropout
     3. Statistics regarding dropouts

PARAGRAPH 4
   C. There is an air of apathy among students.
     Developmental materials
     1. Definition of apathy developed by an analogy and a list of what the school does not offer
     2. Example of a typical classroom
     3. Direct quotations from several apathetic students

Point by point, then, the first division takes shape. Following the same procedure, you will develop each major division down to its final subdivision.

Transition. The symbols on the outline are guides to transition; almost every paragraph should be connected by sentences using transitional words in place of the outline symbols. The need for transition is especially apparent at the opening of each paragraph that introduces a main division. The paragraphs that follow are subdivisions of the idea expressed in the opening paragraph, as the topic outline shows:

I. Problems (main idea)
   A. Discipline ⎫
   B. Dropouts ⎬ the specific problems, the subdivisions of the main idea
   C. Apathy   ⎭

The following sentence, based on Roman numeral I in the above outline, opens the first paragraph:

First, before proposing solutions, it is necessary to examine the major problems that beset high schools. (The transitional word is "First"; it shows the number of the division.)

Here are transitional statements for the openings of paragraphs A, B, and C:

A. For one thing, discipline, a lack of it or too much of it, is a constant problem in every high school.
("For one thing" is the transitional device; it shows that discipline is one aspect of the larger problem.)
B. In addition, the students who simply give up and drop out pose a real problem to school authorities.
("In addition" is the transitional device; it shows that here is another idea of equal importance.)
C. Perhaps the most elusive problem and yet the most enduring manifests itself in the students' general apathy.
("Perhaps the most" provides emphasis and suggests that here is the main problem; "and yet" shows that the two characteristics of the problems—elusive and enduring—must be considered equally.)

In these examples the transitional statements elaborate the simple sentences from the outline; seldom do you transfer a sentence verbatim from the outline into the body of the paper.

There are two other uses for transition. (1) Transitional devices bridge the gaps between the major parts of the paper (the beginning, middle, and end). (2) Transitional devices are sometimes necessary within a paragraph to connect its various parts.

Above all, remember that the ultimate purpose of transition is to assure clarity; thus, the transition itself must be clear.

Conclusion.   The topic under consideration could be concluded by any one of the three methods (recapitulation of ideas, extending of a challenge, drawing of inferences). Examine the preceding parts of the paper, and then determine which kind of conclusion would best serve as a final statement. You might want to experiment with all three approaches in order to find the one that is right for your particular material.

Here is an example of a conclusion that employs the method of recapitulation to summarize the main ideas in the paper:

The modern high school is not hopeless after all. And the solutions to its problems need not be dramatic or drastic. The lack of discipline, the plight of dropouts, and the air of apathy would disappear if some changes—changes from within—took place. Regard for the individual and opportunities for self-discipline should supersede the restrictions that turn the student into a second-class citizen. Irrelevant and often useless curriculum should evolve into a meaningful and practical experience. Both administrators and teachers should become accountable for the real needs of the students they guide, counsel, and teach. When all aspects of these three proposals become realities, the modern high school will emerge from its present foreboding condition into one full of hope.

DOCUMENTATION OF EVIDENCE

Another aspect involved in writing the rough draft is acknowledging the sources of the evidence by making specific documentary notes.

The main purpose for documentation is to give credit where credit is due in the name of honesty and courtesy. Careful documentation also provides the reader with information to judge your conclusions by checking the reliability of your sources and the accuracy of your research. Or he may even want to explore the sources more fully in order to obtain additional information on an aspect of your subject.

The writer who publishes material from sources that he does not credit could be sued for plagiarism; whereas the student who is caught plagiarizing will probably receive a failing grade.

Although you may be convinced of the necessity for documentation, you will probably still ask these questions:

How many documentary notes are necessary?
Exactly what requires documentation?
How is a source documented?

There are no definite answers to the first two questions, only guidelines; however, the third question can be answered more specifically by pointing to the various systems of documentation.

HOW MANY DOCUMENTARY NOTES ARE NECESSARY? There is no mathematical formula for the number of notes; it all depends on the nature of the subject and the method of development. Some papers will require very few notes, and others, which rely heavily on source material, may require a large number. The answer to the next question will help to clarify this.

EXACTLY WHAT REQUIRES DOCUMENTATION? The beginning writer who is overly conscientious or totally confused will probably make an excessive number of notes. Application of the following principles will eliminate this mistake in judgment:

1. Document all direct quotations.

2. Document any idea that is not your own. For instance, if you use a specific idea from a philosophical work such as *I and Thou*, you would document it because the idea is original on the part of the author.

3. Document all facts that are not generally known. This principle is somewhat flexible, depending largely on the material and its particular uses. For instance, if you told how Turgenev was led to write *Nest of Gentlefolk*, you would document the facts because they have not been widely circulated; but the fact that Turgenev was a nineteenth-century Russian writer need not be documented because this is general knowledge.

4. Document at the end of a series of sentences based on a single source. For instance, if you took statistics from a book such as *Crisis in the Classroom* and used them in a single paragraph, you would document at the end of the paragraph. There is, however, an exception to this rule: If the facts came

from several different parts of the book and you used them in a single paragraph, you would document them separately according to the different page numbers.

5. Document all indirect quotations and paraphrases. Sometimes you will use the essence of a person's statement without quoting him directly; that is, you will make use of an indirect quotation or paraphrasing. For instance, you could base an indirect quotation on the following statement:

> In order to bring about this great vision and hope, the university would have to be reorganized.[25]

An indirect quotation based on this statement might read as follows:

> Becker said that reorganization of the university would have to take place in order to realize this vision.

Or a paraphrase might read:

> The university must be reorganized if this hope and dream is to be fulfilled.

Keep in mind, however, when you are documenting, that the research paper is more than a compilation of sources on which it is based. If the material has been synthesized, original observations will be made, and conclusions will be drawn. To an extent, then, overdocumentation is a symptom of undersynthesis.

HOW IS A SOURCE DOCUMENTED? This question may be answered by pointing to a dozen or more systems of documentation. But that raises another question: Which system is the best? In some cases the instructor might make the choice for you by requiring that you follow a specific form. Many colleges and universities or individual departments publish style sheets designating specific forms of documentation. The more recent style sheets have eliminated the complex method employing the Latin abbreviations and are leaning toward the simpler approach contained in *The MLA* [*Modern Language Association*] *Style Sheet*. (The system in appendix D, "Form for Documentary Notes," p. 273, is based on *The MLA Style Sheet*.)

25. Ernest Becker, *Beyond Alienation* (New York: George Braziller, 1967), p. 17.

Basic Documentary Notes

Although basic documentary information is essential in the rough draft, it is not necessary to make formal documentary notes while you are writing it. All you have to include at this point are the names of the authors, the page numbers, and in some cases, the titles of the sources. Once you have finished the first draft, you can complete the notes.

As you are writing and use material that requires documentation, record the author's name and the page number in parentheses. Circle it if you want to make it stand out from the text. Include the title of the source when you are using several books by the same author or books by authors with the same last name. If a book has two or more authors, identify it by the name of the first author listed; identify anonymous works by their titles.

If you numbered the note cards to correspond with the numbers on the bibliography cards (see p. 51), simply identify the source by the code number in the rough draft.

Later, when you are making the documentary notes, this information (consisting either of authors' names and sometimes titles or of code numbers) will direct you to the bibliography cards that contain the complete details.

Recording documentary notes on a separate page, although sometimes suggested, seems to be a risky practice. It might be difficult to match up the material and the documentary information later, especially after possible revision may have led to changes in the order of the text.

Here is a sample from a rough draft that includes basic documentary information:

---

and for its gambling, Nevada is still one of the most

sparsely settled states. At the very first, the barren

land and inadequate water discouraged settlers. From 1829

to 1840, men trapped the few streams for several months

each year, but they did not remain. They did, however, tell

the rest of the world something about Nevada, namely, "how

> dry and poor the soil was, how hot the climate was, and how
> miserable the Indians looked." (Mack, p. 55)[4]
>
>   It was not until 1851 that a few ranchers came to the
> area, later known as the Carson Valley, and established the
> first permanent settlement at Mormon Station, renamed
> Genoa in 1856. ("Comstock Country," p. 35)[5]   Perhaps the

If you were using numbers to identify the sources, place the source numbers, rather than the writer's name or the source's title, in parentheses. Of course, you always include the page number or numbers.

Complete Documentary Notes

Once you have finished writing the rough draft, you then must form complete documentary notes based on the partial notes that you included within the text.

Number each partial note consecutively from the beginning to the end of the paper. Be sure to number the notes accurately because if you miss a note, you will have to go back and change all the numbers that follow it.

First, refer to the bibliography cards to obtain the complete bibliographical information. Then, in order to construct the documentary notes correctly, follow the form for documentation as outlined in appendix D (p. 273) or an alternative required by your instructor.

Either record the completed notes on the back of the rough-draft pages on which they occur or place them on a separate sheet of paper. Earlier you were warned not to use a separate sheet of paper for recording the partial notes, but when you are listing complete notes, the danger of separation and the resulting confusion do not exist.

An illustration of a portion of a rough draft containing partial documentary notes appeared above. Here is what those two notes would look like as formal documentary notes:

---

[4]Effie Mona Mack and Byrd Wall Sawyer, <u>Our State</u>:. <u>Nevada</u> (Caldwell, Idaho, 1940), p. 55.*

[5]"Comstock Country," <u>The American West</u>, 7 (Sept. 1970), 35.

---

* The name of the publisher does not appear in the note because it is given in the bibliography.

Parenthetical Notes

In some research papers, especially literary ones, you may quote extensively from a single source. You can then use parenthetical notes for that particular work. When the work is first cited, place a complete first-citation note at the bottom of the page and follow the note with the statement: "All subsequent references to this work will be noted parenthetically." Thereafter, place only the page number in parentheses after the quoted material or references to the material. Do not number these notes. Place parenthetical notes after the quotation marks and before the period when the quotations are part of the sentence (see line 15 in the illustration). If the quotations are separated from the text, put the notes after the period (see line 24 in the illustration).

The following sample text illustrates the use of parenthetical notes:

The stark and terrifying beauty of the summer electrical

storm, a commonplace-enough subject, takes on a new

significance:

> Half the sky was chequered with black thunder-
> heads, but all the west was luminous and clear:
> in the lightning flashes it looked like deep
> blue water, with the sheen of moonlight on it;
> and the mottled part of the sky was like marble
> pavement.[1]

In an area that undergoes severe winters, the coming of

spring is exciting; and Miss Cather captures the excitement:
"There was only--lovely spring itself; the throb of it, the
light restlessness, the vital essence of it everywhere; in
the sky, in the swift clouds, in the pale sunshine, . . . "
(p. 79). If cornfields were to disappear from the Midwest,
this description would preserve the picture of them for
later generations:

> July came on with that breathless, brilliant heat
> which makes the plains of Kansas and Nebraska the
> best corn country in the world. It seemed as if
> we could hear the corn growing in the night; under
> stars one caught a faint crackling in the dewy,
> heavy-odoured cornfields where the feathered stalk
> stood so juicy and green. (p. 90)

----

[1]Willa Cather, <u>My Ántonia</u> (Boston, 1918), p. 92.
All subsequent references to this work will be noted
parenthetically.*

* The publisher (Houghton Mifflin) is not given in the documentary
note.

When using parenthetical notes for a much-quoted source,
follow the regular procedure for documenting the other sources.

REVISION OF THE ROUGH DRAFT

No writer skips over the revising process; usually the more
experienced the writer is, the more time he spends on revising
his first draft. As you revise, focus your attention on these two
factors:

Development of the ideas
Exactness of expression

Development of the Ideas

In order to determine how effectively you have developed
the ideas and achieved coherence, ask yourself these questions:

Does the paper solve the problem set forth in the thesis statement?

Does it develop each point of the outline?

Does it employ a variety of developmental materials?

Is there an excess of quoted matter?

Are the parts connected by transitional devices?

Will the introduction catch the reader's interest?

Does the conclusion bring the paper to a logical end?

If you cannot answer all these questions as they should be, then your paper will require some revision before it achieves coherence.

Exactness of Expression

Outstanding organization and evidence are of little account if the ideas and their supporting materials are obscured by poor word choice, awkward or incorrect sentences, spelling and punctuation errors, and dullness. (See chapter 9, p. 206, for a discussion of these matters.)

THE FINAL PAPER

The preparation of the final version is, in some ways, the most important step of all. Lack of attention to mechanical details can void the effort you have expended on researching and planning, on writing and revising. (See chapter 9, p. 234, for detailed instructions on preparing the paper in its final form.)

MODEL RESEARCH PAPER

There is really no such thing as a model research paper (or even a typical paper, for that matter), but the one that follows illustrates techniques of organization and development and could serve as a guide in preparing a paper on almost any subject. The analysis of the text and other parts may prove helpful in understanding how the paper was conceived, researched, organized, developed, and documented.

THE MUSICAL PLAY

AS A RITUAL

BY
ANNE A. STUDENT

English 221.2
June 2, 1973

Analysis of Thesis Statement and Outline. The field of theater is broad; the field of musical theater is somewhat more limited but still too vast for a short paper. Therefore, the writer limited her study to a single aspect: the musical theater as a ritual. Because this idea is expressed in a complex sentence, the outline unfolds in a natural organization: Roman numeral I develops the dependent clause ("as the American musical play has developed"), and II, III, and IV develop the ideas suggested by the independent clause ("it has taken on the characteristics of a ritual"). The subdivisions under each Roman numeral are logical parts of the larger idea.

THE MUSICAL PLAY AS A RITUAL

Thesis Statement: As the American musical play has devel-
     oped, it has taken on the characteristics of a ritual.

I.   The development of the musical play is significant.
     A. The early plays paved the way.
     B. Pal Joey was ahead of its time.
     C. Oklahoma! set the precedents for the musical play's
        ritualistic form.

II. The plot is one aspect of the ritualistic form.
     A. The plot follows a basic pattern.
     B. The plot from Oklahoma! illustrates the basic pattern.
     C. The plot usually comes from another source.

III. The visual presentation is another aspect of the ritual-
     istic form.
     A. The setting and stage effects serve a purpose.
     B. The costumes serve a purpose.

IV. The ritual itself has a purpose.
     A. The purpose is partly to entertain.
     B. The purpose is mainly to reaffirm the perfectibility
        of life.

Analysis of the Text.   The introductory paragraph opens with
two negative views concerning the contemporary musical theater. But these two views are contradicted by the transitional
sentence that leads into the thesis statement. The transitional
word "for" has been added to the thesis statement to connect it
to the previous sentence. Following the thesis statement, ritual
is defined: first by details, then by three instances ("religious
worship" and so on), finally by descriptive words ("safe" and
so forth). The last sentence links the idea of ritual and musical
comedy. Developmental materials in this paragraph include an
indirect quotation, a direct quotation, and a definition.

The second paragraph opens the body of the paper with a
major transitional statement ("it would be well first"). Most
of the material that follows consists of historical details. The
definition of burlesque is necessary because the meaning of the

A critic suggested recently that the songs in the current Broadway musicals could easily be interchanged because
they all sounded alike, sticking as they do to what he called
a "melodic formula."[1] To another reviewer, the musicals
appeared "manufactured, manipulated, and found wanting" in
their faithful adherence to "a preordained, long since stale,
commercial formula."[2] But it is this very likeness, brought
on by the formula, that seems to be the secret of the musical theater's success. For as the American musical play has
developed, it has taken on the characteristics of a ritual.
The established and prescribed procedure that is a ritual is
basic to man's experience, whether it governs his religious
worship, his fraternal organization, or his daily activities.
The ritual is safe, familiar, tried, and secure. And so are
the products of the contemporary musical theater.

In order to understand the ritualism of the modern musical play, it would be well first to trace its development.
The New World's premier musical production took place in

word has changed since the early nineteenth century; it is not necessary, however, to define ballad opera and minstrel show because these terms are generally known. Note that the titles of the plays are underlined and that the names of the month and state are written out. A documentary designation (3) appears at the end of the paragraph, denoting that the historical facts were taken from a specific source.

The third paragraph continues the historical survey of the musical theater in America. Again a title and date are mentioned to illustrate the general description "melodramatic spectacle," thus making the survey more specific. The transitional words are "a new kind of musical."

This paragraph opens with a transitional phrase showing the passage of time and presents more historical details that bring the historical survey up through the 1930s. These paragraphs illustrate how the survey may be used to supply background material.

2

Charleston, South Carolina, February 8, 1735, when a group
of colonials saw an English ballad opera called _Flora_. Almost a century passed, however, before the appearance of an
original American musical, a burlesque treatment of _Hamlet_,
in 1828. In its original form, the burlesque parodied famous
serious plays through song, dance, pantomime, and dialogue.
The year 1847 marked the beginning of the minstrel show in
Virginia, an entertainment that retained its popularity until recent years; significantly, these shows were the first
for which important popular music was written.[3]

A new kind of musical play, a melodramatic spectacle
called _The Black Crook_, opened in New York in 1866. Its
elaborate staging, ornate production numbers, ballets, and
immense cast caught the audience's imagination in spite of
its impossible plot. Running for 400 performances, this
play by Charles M. Barras is usually considered to be the
real beginning of musical theater in the United States.[4]
But it was not until 1874 that the term "musical comedy" was
introduced, in this instance to describe a burlesque of
Evangeline.[5]

In the years that followed, comic operas such as Ed
Harrigan's and Tony Hart's _The Mulligan Guard_ (1879) and
operettas like Harry B. Smith's and Reginald de Koven's
Robin Hood (1890) gained theatrical favor.[6] From the end of
the nineteenth century until the early 1920's, the musical

Opening with a strong transitional phrase ("the next significant step"), this paragraph presents historical details of an
important event in the development of the musical theater. Note
how the final sentence leads into the next paragraph with the
words "another musical"; this idea is picked up in the opening
of the following paragraph: "That was *Oklahoma!*."

Historical details and a direct quotation develop this paragraph. The final sentence is an important one because it states
the main quality of the new musical, a fact that is basic to the
remainder of the paper.

3

theater flourished, taking no particular direction and developing no new forms; but during the twenties it did gradually give birth to revues and vaudeville that remained popular through the 1930's.

The next significant step in the development of the musical theater came in 1940 with the production of Richard Rodgers' and Lorenz Hart's Pal Joey, described by Wolcott Gibbs as "a song-and-dance production with living, 3-dimensional figures, talking and behaving like human beings"[7] and condemned by Brooks Atkinson, who asked: "Although it is expertly done, can you draw sweet water from a foul well?"[8] Based on several of John O'Hara's short stories, the play followed the adventures of a New York con man and portrayed his tawdry world and sleazy companions. Because it broke the traditions of the orthodox musical comedy, which always created a fanciful realm, Pal Joey did not enjoy a successful run in 1940; but upon its revival in 1952, the critics hailed it as a "masterpiece" and "classic," admiring the way its text, music, lyrics, dancing, and humor formed a carefully built-up composition.[9] But during the twelve years between Pal Joey's cool reception and its wide acceptance, which led it into 542 performances, another musical had paved the way.

That was Oklahoma! by Richard Rodgers and Oscar Hammerstein II. In 1943 this production, based on Lynn Riggs' comedy Green Grow the Lilacs, set the precedents for the new

The word "though" in the first sentence of this paragraph suggests transition, and that is the paragraph's basic function: to provide transition from the first point to the second, doing so through a summary of the historical details.

The opening transitional sentence is a clear statement of the idea to be developed in the subsequent paragraphs. Analytical details are used to introduce the idea of plot.

This paragraph is developed through comparison. By stating "are almost as strict as," the writer introduces the idea of the similarities of Greek drama and musical theater and then backs up this generalization with specific analyses of the conventions governing the two kinds of theater. The first analysis is documented because it is borrowed from a source, but the second one is original on the part of the writer and is not documented.

4

musical play, precedents for plot, characters, dancing, music, and production.[10] In reviewing <u>Oklahoma!</u>, one critic noted that the music was "well built into the production," that the singing was natural, and that the dancing was "an integral part of the show," not an "interpolation."[11] His obsewvations summed up the special quality of the new musical production: an integration of all the elements.

<u>Oklahoma!</u> did not just happen, though; it evolved from the burlesques, operettas, comic operas, minstrels, extravaganzas, vaudeville, and revues, finally tying all the loose strands together into a form that became the basis for the ritual of today's musical play.

The first aspect of this form is the plot. On the simplest level, the story line follows this pattern: boy and girl meet; boy and girl are separated; boy and girl are united. Around this structure the musical play revolves, sometimes adding comic lovers or following several sets of lovers and throwing all varieties of obstacles in their paths.

The conventions dictating plot development are almost as strict as those governing the ancient Greek drama; and in some ways the two forms are similar. The structure of Greek tragedy includes the following parts:

1. Prologue: action before entrance of chorus
2. Parodos: entering dance of the chorus

The transitional words "other distinguishing characteristics" announce the paragraph's purpose. Note that the first statement contains four characteristics as well as the transitional words. The second sentence adds three additional characteristics.

The preceding paragraphs discuss and describe the plot structure; now, an analytical plot summary of *Oklahoma!* illustrates the structure. The first sentence states this fact clearly. Literary papers often rely on plot summaries for analytical and illustrative purposes; but such summaries must be handled carefully because they can degenerate into a pointless retelling of the story. The two-page summary in this paper attempts to show how the plot integrates dialogue, songs, and dances into a single form. Ordinarily the plot summary would not be this long; it becomes more detailed through inclusion of song titles and dance sequences. None of this material is documented because nothing is quoted directly from the play. Bibliographical data are provided in the appendix, however. If there were no appendix, a documentary note could be placed at the end of the summary.

5

    3. Episodes: action between choral odes
    4. Stasima: choral odes
    5. Exodos: action after last stasimon [12]

The plot of the musical comedy unfolds in this manner:

    1. Short dialogue (prologue)
    2. Opening production number (parodos)
    3. Series of scenes with action and dialogue (episodes)
       that lead into musical and dancing numbers (choral
       odes) which further develop the plot
    4. Final production number (exodus)

The musical play, always in two acts, has other distinguishing characteristics, including a dance sequence near the end of Act 1, a production number at the opening of Act 2, and duets by the two lovers. The first act runs somewhat longer than the second act, which does not usually introduce more than three or four new musical numbers but depends mainly on reprises (repetitions of songs already introduced) from Act 1.

The plot, musical numbers, and dancing from Oklahoma! effectively illustrate this structure. Set in Oklahoma at the turn of the century, the play opens with Curly asking Aunt Eller about Laurey, the girl he loves. Because it is a fine morning on the frontier and Curly is in a good mood, he breaks into "Oh, What a Beautiful Mornin'." Laurey then enters and pretends to ignore Curly. In an effort to persuade her to attend the box social with him, he sings "The Surrey with the Fringe on Top." After some additional dialogue, in which Laurey still refuses Curly's invitation, Will Parker and the cowhands arrive; Will has just returned from Kansas City and

6

tells about his trip in a song called "Kansas City," which evolves into a dance routine. Following this sequence, Will and Ado Annie, the comic lovers, converse, Will accusing her of infidelity, the accusation leading Ado Annie into "I Cain't Say No."

In the next dialogue episode, a Persian peddler sells Laurey a bottle of "Egyptian Elixir," a potion that will bring her dreams concerning her future. The chorus girls, who are on their way to the box social, then appear and perform a dance routine. At this point, Curly and Laurey are "separated" because Curly pays too much attention to one of the other girls. In anger, Laurey agrees to go to the social with Jud, a disreputable farmhand; and to show her indifference to Curly, she sings "Many a New Day." But as the scene ends, Laurey regrets her haste and joins Curly in singing "People Will Say We're in Love."

Next Jud and Curly meet and exchange warnings and threats regarding Laurey's attentions, ending the scene with the song "Pore Jud," a description of people's reactions to a dead Jud. In this scene it becomes apparent that Curly is the hero and Jud the villain.

The act ends with a dream sequence, brought on by the potion, in which Laurey sings "Out of My Dreams" and the chorus performs a ballet depicting a struggle between Curly and Jud, with Curly emerging as the victor. Awakening from her

This short transitional paragraph ties the summary of *Oklahoma!* to the plot structure of the musical plays since 1943.

The opening sentence presents "one other characteristic." To develop this characteristic, the writer gives four specific instances of how musical plays have borrowed from varied sources

7

dream, Laurey unhappily leaves with Jud for the social.

Act 2 opens at the box social with a production number, including the song "The Farmer and the Cowman" and a lively square dance. The conflict between Jud and Curly over Laurey's affections develops further, and after Curly saves Laurey from Jud, the two of them break into a reprise of their earlier duet, "People Will Say We're in Love."

The comic lovers appear again and sing "All 'er Nuthin'," a humorous song about what their marriage would be like.

The final scene, three weeks later, takes place immediately after Curly and Laurey's marriage. Someone mentions that Oklahoma has just become a state, a fact that produces the title song, "Oklahoma!" Before the play ends, however, the various strands of the plot are tied together. Jud reappears, tries to murder Curly, who kills him in self-defense and is immediately acquitted. The entire cast then reprises "Oklahoma!" after wheeling on a surrey with a fringe on top and setting the newly married Laurey and Curly in it. Love and goodness have triumphed, and all is well.

These are the rites that the musical play follows. An analysis of almost any successful musical's plot since 1943 would follow a similar outline.

Regarding the plot, one other characteristic stands out: Rare is the musical that is original. Oklahoma was based on a stage play; and since then the major musical plays have for their plots. The second part of the paragraph shows how familiarity with the story seems to enhance the audience's reaction to the play; this generalization is developed by comparing the musical theater with English medieval drama.

This paragraph opens the discussion of Roman numeral III and tells the reader so with a definite transitional statement. First, the writer defines "visual effects" by stating their functions. Then she compares the visual presentation of the musical theater with that of the English medieval theater, developing this idea through the use of a direct quotation from a medieval document.

8

been drawn from books, such as <u>Mame</u>, from Patrick Dennis's
<u>Auntie Mame</u>; from spoken plays, such as <u>My Fair Lady</u>, from
George Bernard Shaw's <u>Pygmalion</u>; from legends, such as <u>Damn</u>·
<u>Yankees,</u> from the Faust legend. The fact that the audience
is often familiar with the story does not seem to detract from
the play's appeal; on the contrary, it often enhances it. In
this respect, the musical play bears a resemblance to the English medieval drama, which retold the familiar biblical accounts of the Creation, the Fall, the Flood, prophecies, Christ's
life, and the final judgment. Everyone knew the stories already,
so one of the main reasons for attending the plays was to see
how the material would be handled. And, like the musical comedies, the same plays were performed year after year.[13]

Another element of the ritual, in addition to plot, is its
visual presentation. Certainly the musical theater in America
has a tradition of extravagant production, and many of the
earlier shows relied almost exclusively on elaborate settings,
costumes, and stage effects. But in the modern musical play,
the visual effects serve a distinct purpose that may be divided
into three interrelated functions: clarification of the plot,
intensification of the action, and identification of setting
and characters.[14] The musical theater may once more be compared with the English medieval drama, which had its roots in
the church. Once it left the sanctuary, however, and told its
story in the streets, the medieval play relied more and more

Three specific instances develop the general statement in the first sentence regarding "traditions" in scenery. By returning to the introductory idea that the songs could be interchanged, the writer makes an interesting point in the last sentence in the paragraph; however, the idea is not developed or supported in any way, a weakness in the paper at this point, it would seem.

This paragraph first generalizes about the "set form" of the costumes and then becomes specific by using the costuming in *Hello, Dolly!* as an example.

9

on spectacle. Witness these directions by an anonymous med-

ieval producer:

Let Paradise be set up in a somewhat lofty place; let there be
put about it curtains and silken hangings, at such an height
that those persons who shall be in Paradise can be seen from
the shoulders upward; let there be planted sweet-smelling
flowers and foliage; let divers trees be therein, and fruits
hanging upon them, so that it may seem a most delectable place.[15]

This description might well fit the scenic specifications for

a modern musical play requiring a paradise.

    The scenic aspects of the musical play have taken on cer-

tain traditions, such as the elegant interiors used in the ball-

room scene in My Fair Lady, the divided sets in Mame, and the

colorful exterior settings in West Side Story. To a certain

extent, the scenery in the various plays could be interchanged

almost as easily as the songs.

    Similarly, the costumes receive careful attention because

they, too, help to clarify, intensify, and identify. Because

of their specific functions, the costumes follow a set form.

The leading characters are dressed most elaborately; the sup-

porting characters, a little less so; and the chorus, most

simply. For instance, the chorus members in Hello, Dolly!

were costumed in carefully coordinated turn-of-the-century

dresses and suits, but not nearly as elaborately as Dolly and

Vandergelder were. In turn, the complexity of the supporting

characters' costumes lay somewhere between the ones worn by

the chorus and those worn by the leads.

The opening sentence summarizes the ideas in Roman numerals II ("a set form") and III ("spectacular visual effects") and introduces IV ("purpose"); the key word "ritual" is also included. "At first consideration, though" suggests that entertainment, although important, is not the only purpose. The statistics are an interesting way to develop the idea in addition to the general details in the final sentence.

Relying on the previous paragraph as a point of reference, the first sentence suggests that there is another purpose; and this purpose is stated at the end of the second sentence, developed further in the third sentence, and then specified through the direct quotation regarding *Hello, Dolly!*.

10

The ritual of the musical theater is thus governed by a set form that relies on spectacular visual effects to achieve its purpose. At first consideration, though, it might seem that the only purpose of the musical theater is to entertain; and the statistics on long-running shows prove that they have fulfilled this function. Oklahoma! set a record on Broadway when it played 2,248 performances, later topped by My Fair Lady, which ran 2,717 performances. Some of the musicals passing the 1,000 mark in Broadway performances include South Pacific, 1,925; The Sound of Music, 1,443; The King and I, 1,246; and Guys and Dolls, 1,200.[16] Each of these plays later became a film, played on the road, and continues to be performed in professional, educational, and civic theaters all over the world.

But the lasting popularity of the musical theater productions suggests that they offer something more than boy-meets-girl stories, songs, dance routines, and spectacular stage effects. Just as any ritual clothes its message in form and visual design that are pleasing to the viewer and will engage his attention, the musical theater tells a story that contains a message. The entire production suggests this message, and its specifics are carried out to some extent in the dialogue but more fully in the songs. One critic observed that the success of Hello, Dolly! grew from the fact that the audience wanted the nostalgic message that with patience and

The final paragraph may appear at first to violate the rule forbidding the introduction of new ideas in the conclusion. However, the discussion of the rock musical simply reaffirms the permanence of the form, a fact that is stressed again through the analogy of the traditional and rock musicals and the similar masses. The last sentence ties all the ideas together.

11

faith, the good things in life will come true.[17] He observed

that "watching the show is a little like catching a glimpse

of Old Glory fluttering in the breeze when the mere sight of

the flag could muster sweet American dreams of perfectibility."[18]

The musical theater continues to flourish, playing out

its ritual, in spite of the demands of many critics and some

theatergoers for change and revitalization. Many people

believed that the revolution had come in 1967 when Hair, the

first rock musical, opened; but once the novelty had worn off

and the shouting had died away, most critics and viewers

agreed with Robert Brustein that Hair was "too closely linked

to the meretricious conventions of American musicals" to

change anything much.[20] After Hair's immense success,

numerous other rock musicals have appeared, each imitating

Hair, which patterned itself according to the form set

down in Oklahoma! The rock musical, then, compared with the

traditional musical is a little like the rock mass and the

traditional mass, a new way of saying the same thing. Thus,

until man no longer needs to reaffirm the perfectibility

of life, or until he discovers a new form to provide

this reaffirmation, the ritual of the American musical

is safe.

Analysis of Documentation.   The first four pages rely heavily on documented sources (notes 1 to 12). The rest of the paper offers more original observations on the part of the writer, based mainly on her reading and viewing of the various musical plays she mentions. As stated previously in the discussion on documenting sources, the number of notes depends entirely on the nature of the paper.

The writer, however, did not rely on any one source extensively for information. Even though Ewen's book supplied most of the historical facts, the other thirteen sources (containing a good balance of specific works, general studies, and periodical articles) provided a basis for additional facts, views, and ideas.

NOTES

[1]Harold C. Schonberg, "The Broadway Musical: Getting Away with Murder," Harper's, July 1970, p. 106.

[2]Catharine R. Hughes, "Decline and Fall of the Broadway Musical," America, 6 Feb. 1971, pp. 124–125.

[3]David Ewen, The Story of America's Musical Theater (New York, 1968), pp. 1–2.

[4]Ewen, pp. 4–5.

[5]Ewen, p. 6.

[6]Ewen, pp. 9–10.

[7]Stanley Green, The World of Musical Comedy (New York, 1968), p. 161.

[8]Green.

[9]Edward Weeks, "The Peripatetic Reviewer," Atlantic Monthly, July 1967, p. 108.

[10]Abe Laufe, Broadway's Greatest Musicals (New York, 1969), p. 67.

[11]Robert A. Simon, "Musical Events," New Yorker, 29 May 1943, p. 61.

[12]Meyer Reinhold, Classical Drama: Greek and Roman (Great Neck, N.Y., 1955), p. 11.

[13]William Moody and Robert Lovett, A History of English Literature (New York, 1964), pp. 91–92.

[14]H. D. Albright et al., <u>Principles of Theatre Art</u> (Boston, 1968), pp. 226-233.

[15]A. M. Nagler, <u>A Source Book in Theatrical History</u> (New York, 1952), p. 45.

[16]Laufe, <u>Broadway's Greatest Musicals</u>, pp. 391-397.

[17]Robert Kotlowitz, "From the Fourth Row: American Types," <u>Harper's</u>, Apr. 1968, p. 112.

[18]Kotlowitz.

[19]Robert Brustein, "From Hair to Hamlet," <u>New Republic</u>, 18 Nov. 1967, p. 38.

Analysis of Appendix. The appendix in this paper (not lettered appendix A because there is only one) provides bibliographical and other information on the plays mentioned in the text. All this information is significant and related, but including it within the paper would have cluttered the text.

APPENDIX

BIBLIOGRAPHY OF MAJOR MUSICAL PLAYS SINCE 1940

MENTIONED IN THE TEXT

<u>Damn Yankees</u>

    Book: George Abbott and Douglass Wallop
    Music and Lyrics: Richard Adler and Jerry Ross
    Publisher: New York, Random House, 1956
    Original Cast Recording: RCA Victor LOC/LSO 1021
    Sources: Douglass Wallop's novel <u>The Year the Yankees Lost the Pennant</u> and the Faust legend

<u>Guys and Dolls</u>

    Book: Abe Burrows and Jo Swerling
    Music and Lyrics: Frank Loesser
    Publisher: <u>The Modern Theatre</u> (Vol. 4), Ed. Eric Bentley, New York, Doubleday, 1960
    Original Cast Recording: Decca DL (7) 9023
    Source: Damon Runyon's short stories

<u>Hair</u>

    Book and Lyrics: Gerome Ragni and James Rado
    Music: Galt MacDermot

Publisher: New York, Pocket Books, 1969
Original Cast Recording: RCA LOC/LSO 1150
Source: Original

Hello, Dolly!

Book: Michael Stewart
Music and Lyrics: Jerry Herman
Publisher: New York, DBS Publications, 1964
Original Cast Recording: RCA Victor LOCD/LSOD 1087
Source: Thornton Wilder's play The Matchmaker

The King and I

Book and Lyrics: Oscar Hammerstein II
Music: Richard Rodgers
Publisher: New York, Random House, 1951
Original Cast Recording: Decca DL (7) 9008
Source: Margaret Landon's fictionalized biography Anna
        and the King of Siam

Mame

Book: Jerome Lawrence and Robert E. Lee
Music and Lyrics: Jerry Herman
Publisher: New York, Random House, 1967
Original Cast Recording: Columbia KOL 6600/KDS 3000
Sources: Patrick Dennis's novel Auntie Mame and
          Lawrence and Lee's play Auntie Mame

My Fair Lady

Book and Lyrics: Alan Jay Lerner
Music: Frederick Loewe
Publisher: New York; Coward-McCann, 1956
Original Cast Recording: Columbia OL 5090/OS 2015
Sources: George Bernard Shaw's play Pygmalion and the
          Pygmalion legend

Oklahoma!

Book and Lyrics: Oscar Hammerstein II
Music: Richard Rodgers
Publisher: Six Plays by Rodgers and Hammerstein, New
          York, Random House, 1955
Original Cast Recording: Decca DL (7) 9017
Source: Lynn Riggs' play Green Grow the Lilacs

Pal Joey

Book: John O'Hara
Lyrics: Lorenz Hart
Music: Richard Rodgers
Publisher: New York, Random House, 1952
Film Version Recording: Capitol (D) W 912 (original cast
                          recording no longer listed)

Source: John O'Hara's short stories

The Sound of Music

Book: Howard Lindsay and Russel Crouse
Lyrics: Oscar Hammerstein II
Music: Richard Rodgers
Publisher: New York, Random House, 1960
Original Cast Recording: Columbia KOL 5450/KOS 2020
Source: Maria Augusta Trapp's book The Trapp Family
        Singers

South Pacific

Book: Joshua Logan
Lyrics: Oscar Hammerstein II
Music: Richard Rodgers
Publisher: Six Plays by Rodgers and Hammerstein, New
        York, Random House, 1955
Original Cast Recording: Columbia OL 4180/OS 2040
Source: James A. Michener's short stories Tales of the
        South Pacific

West Side Story

Book: Arthur Laurents
Lyrics: Stephen Sondheim
Music: Leonard Bernstein
Publisher: New York, Random House, 1958
Original Cast Recording: Columbia OL 5230/OS 2001
Source: Original

BIBLIOGRAPHY

Albright, H. D.; Halstead, William P.; and Mitchell, Lee.
   Principles of Theatre Art. Boston: Houghton Mifflin,
   1968.

Brustein, Robert. "From Hair to Hamlet." The New Republic,
   18 Nov. 1967, pp. 38-39.

Ewen, David. The Story of America's Musical Theater. New
   York: Chilton Book Co., 1968.

Green, Stanley. The World of Musical Comedy. New York:
   A. S. Barnes & Company, 1968.

Hughes, Catharine R. "Decline and Fall of the Broadway
   Musical." America, 6 Feb. 1971, pp. 124-125.

Kotlowitz, Robert. "From the Fourth Row: American Types."
   Harper's, Apr. 1968, p. 112.

Laufe, Abe. <u>Broadway's Greatest Musicals</u>. New York:
    Funk & Wagnalls, 1969.

Moody, William Vaughn, and Robert Morss Lovett. <u>A History of
    English Literature</u>. Rev. by Fred B. Millett. New York:
    Scribner's, 1964.

Nagler, A. M. <u>A Source Book in Theatrical History</u>. New York:
    Dover, 1952.

Reinhold, Meyer. <u>Classical Drama: Greek and Roman</u>. Great
    Neck, N.Y.: Barron's Educational Series, Inc., 1955.

Schonberg, Harold C. "The Broadway Musical: Getting Away
    with Murder." <u>Harper's</u>, July 1970, pp. 106, 108.

Simon, Robert A. "Musical Events." <u>New Yorker</u>, 29 May 1943,
    pp. 61-62.

Weeks, Edward. "The Peripatetic Reviewer." <u>The Atlantic
    Monthly</u>, July 1967, pp. 108-110.

EXHIBITING THE RESULTS

The desire to share the results of your research with others
is a natural one. But to realize this ambition, you must assume
the responsibility of exhibiting your research in an acceptable
form—not for the sake of form, but for the sake of communication. That is what analysis and synthesis are all about. You do
not just hand your reader the raw evidence. Instead you first
take it apart (analysis) and then reconstruct it (synthesis). When
this is completed, the evidence is ready to go on exhibit.

Chapter 7

Organizing and Writing Reports

*It follows that the ability to express himself well
is a decisive factor in the career of the professional
technologist or scientist.*
George C. Harwell, *Technical Communication*

In the scientific, technological, and business fields, written reports are extremely important. Without them, proposals to seek answers through original research or to provide services could not be set forth. The state of a project could not be reported to the interested persons; the results of research could not be transmitted to a wider audience.

Reports summarize written material, propose projects, record the progress of such projects, and reveal their findings. The major kinds of reports are:

Abstracts
Proposals
Progress reports
Research reports

The writing requirements of reports in specialized fields are the same as those of the research paper: coherence and clarity. In commenting on scientific writing specifically, Robert Sommer pointed out that "writing is writing and must be treated as such. Scientific writing is not unique or mysterious in any way."[1]

Essentially, report writing falls into two categories: (1) that

1. Robert Sommer, *Expertland* (Garden City, NY: Doubleday, 1963), p. 69.

which is aimed toward people in its field and (2) that which is directed toward the general public. Obviously, the first kind of writing can include more technical details and specialized vocabulary. Popular report writing, such as an article in a general publication, requires fuller explanations and less technical language. In either case, however, you are obligated to inform the reader of your research plans or results, not to impress him with your erudition.

Report writing, with the exception of highly personal articles for popular magazines, remains in the third person, avoids slang, and maintains an objective viewpoint.

ABSTRACTS

An *abstract* is a condensation of the major ideas in a report, a paper, an article, or a book. The length of an abstract varies from one sentence to several paragraphs, depending on its purpose and the material being condensed. It may be merely a description of the thesis and subsequent points covered in the work. Or, in addition to the descriptive elements, it may include detailed information on the major points.

Although it bears some similarity to the summary, the synopsis, and the abridgment, the abstract is different from these devices. The summary, usually a part of the total report or paper, recapitulates the main points from the body of the work. Although it performs the same function, the synopsis is often in outline form, thus presenting the gist of the work in a way that allows it to be grasped at a glance. The abridgment retains the original wording but reduces the length of the original work by deleting certain passages.

It is also important to distinguish between the abstract and the review. Whereas the review may incorporate an abstract of the work, the abstract does not include other features of the review. The abstract is not a critical work; therefore, it does not offer opinions or evaluations. It is limited to the summation of the major points.

Uses

One of the main uses of the abstract is to digest information from the vast amount of published material. It would be impossible for anyone to read all the literature appearing in a particular field, but by depending on abstracts, it is possible to survey the articles and books and then read only those that are of immediate interest. With scores of abstract services available, covering world publications that range from literature to medicine, the abstract plays an important role in research. Efforts toward organizing and centralizing the numerous abstract services are under way, and it is likely that in the near future abstracts will be stored extensively on, and made immediately available through, electronic equipment. A fairly exhaustive list of abstract services has been compiled in a new reference work: *Encyclopedia of Information Systems and Services* (Ann Arbor, Mich.: Edwards Brothers, 1971). Discovering specific sources for abstracts is a natural part of becoming familiar with reference materials in a particular field.

Another place for the abstract is at the beginning of a long research work (such as a thesis or dissertation) or an article. This practice enables the reader to determine quickly whether the content of the work will meet his particular needs.

Organization and Writing

In order to write an abstract of someone else's work, you must read the material with intelligence, discover the main ideas with accuracy, plan your writing with care, and then write, knowing that in the process you will rewrite and expand or condense as necessary. Preparing an abstract of your own work should be easier because you already have the major points in mind and understand the scope of what you have written.

If you are assigned to write an abstract, you will find it helpful to check one of the abstract volumes in your field and then, after studying a specific abstract, go to the original to see exactly how the professional abstractor carried out his assignment.

Read the Material and Discover the Main Ideas. A well-written work will lend itself to easy abstracting. Most often the central idea appears near the beginning and transitional devices identify the secondary ideas. In many cases, too, subheadings within the body act as a guide. Of course, the abstract consists of more than a lifting and listing of the thesis and topic statements, but these sentences will prove helpful in grasping the author's main ideas and intent.

Once you have the author's plan in mind, you should then

read the material more carefully, sifting out the main ideas and determining the proper emphasis. By gliding over a major point and stressing a minor one, it is possible to shift the meaning of the entire work. Such a procedure is analogous to that of an artist who draws a cathedral and makes the door larger than the main bell tower.

If the material lacks organization and transitional aids, then your work will be more difficult. You will need to make a careful analysis in order to determine the exact purpose of the writer and to understand the development of his work.

Plan the Writing. As you read and reread, you should form a plan to direct the actual writing of the abstract. The order of the points is logically determined by the original's sequence of development. However, the inclusion of the right material is determined by your understanding of the work. Whenever possible, it is wise to check or underline significant sentences in the original. It can also be to your advantage to make a rough topic outline from your reading.

Write. Once you understand the material and have a plan in mind, your next step is obvious: begin writing. The first draft may turn out to be much too long, even though it includes only the major points. It is time then to cut the verbiage, combine sentences, and eliminate extraneous details.

Stylistically, the abstract should be distinguished by absolute clarity. Lacking this quality, it defeats its purpose. For the most part, the wording should be original. Again, an abstract is not a collection of an article's lead sentences, nor is it a series of sentence fragments or telegraphic phrases. The abstract stands as a complete and coherent written unit.

In certain cases, it is permissible to employ incomplete predications. A bibliographical annotation (the abstract at its briefest) often uses this method, as in the following example:

Encyclopedia Canadiana. 10 vols. Ottawa: Canadiana Co., 1960. Provides vast store of information on Canadian persons, places, things, and words. Illustrations, maps, index.

However, in most abstract writing, it is preferable to use complete sentences in order to assure understandability and accuracy. Easily recognizable abbreviations are sometimes employed. Their use naturally depends on the requirements of the specific writing assignment.

Although no set length prevails, generally the abstract should be approximately 1 to 3 percent of the length of the original. If it is too short, it does not provide enough information to reveal the original work's content; if it is too long, it turns into nothing more than a paraphrase of the original.

Final Form

The nature of the assignment should dictate the specifics of form. However, the abstract always includes complete bibliographical information on the work abstracted. Often a brief note on the author's background is added; the number of references is noted; and supplementary materials such as indexes and appendixes are described.

A well-structured abstract of a scientific article would read something like this one from *Chemical Abstracts* (Vol. 76, No. 9, p. 269, Abstract No. 44712g, 28 Feb. 1972. Reprinted by permission.):

Edible protein products from Cruciferae seed meals. Sims, R.P.A. (Food Res. Inst., Canada Dep. Agric., Ottawa, Ont.). *J. Amer. Oil Chem. Soc.* 1971, 48(11), 733–6 (Eng.).

Rape, crambe, and mustard seed are compared with respect to properties of the fixed oil, nature of the mustard oils, and properties of the seed protein. Rapeseed (*Brassica campestris* and *B. napus*) has benefitted greatly from plant breeding; the erucic acid content of the fixed oil and the level of glucosinolates can now be selected. Crambe seed (*Crambe abyssinica*), however, is still high in erucic acid and in glucosinolates. The glucosinolate patterns of the mustards are naturally simple. Procedures for prepg. edible flours and isolates from rape, crambe, and mustard seed are described. With mustard (*B. hirta, B. juncea* and *B. nigra*), the glucosinolate hydrolysis products are volatile and steam-stripping yields a bland flour. With rape and crambe seeds, the intact glucosinolates must be removed; aq. extn. is practicable. The phys., chem., and nutritional properties of some of the meals, flours, and isolates prepd. from crucifer seeds are described. 24 refs.

Here is an example of a well-executed abstract of a book-length work from *Sociological Abstracts* (Vol. 20, p. 308, Abstract No. F4473, Jan.–Apr. 1972. Copyright by *Sociological Abstracts*, reprinted by permission.):

Westley, William A. (McGill U, Montreal Quebec), VIOLENCE AND THE POLICE: A SOCIOLOGICAL STUDY OF LAW, CUS-

TOM, AND MORALITY. Cambridge, Mass.: The MIT Press, 1970,
xxi+222 pp, $8.95.

A book in 6 Chpt's, with a Foreword & a Preface, which reports
res done 20 yrs ago into the municipal police force of a small mid-
western city, which examines the nature of police activities, how the
police are org'ed, & how they function, the kind of men they employ,
& the ways in which they build a special occup'al culture that defines
the police self & role in society. Preface—comments on the study from
the res'ers' present viewpoint, emphasizing the hostility of the
police's occup'al audience & its effect on them. (1) Introduction—
sets forth the purpose of the study, identifies the police as a public
service agency, discussing the police att toward the juvenile court,
the need of the police to guard against criticism, & the necessity for
maintaining respect for police authority in the community. The major
res objectives are listed, the method of res is described, law, custom,
& morality are discussed. (2) Within the Department—describes police
duties in general & dirty work, investigates the community background, examines the role of the Chief of Police, a pol'al appointee,
breaks down the operations of the dept, focusing on the detective
division, considers police work as a way of life, & analyzes the
choice of the occup & the selection of the members by the occup.
(3) The Public as Enemy—presents illustrations of the public's att
toward the police, an account of the major types of occup'al experience
to which the policeman is subjected, a survey of the policeman's
interpretation of the public's att toward himself, & a description of
various categories into which the police divide the public. (4) The
Morality of Secrecy and Violence—indicates that the police in this
city possess the characteristics of a soc group in having as collective
ends the maintenance of secrecy about public affairs & the maintenance of respect for the police by the people of the community; in
having a consensus on these ends, developed through a community
of experience & discourse resulting from the occup'al experiences; in
having a set of norms that guide conduct & sanctions to enforce the
norms represented in the rule of silence and the use of the silent
treatment for offenders, the rule of maintaining respect for the
police and the use of ridicule to punish offenders, & in the rule that
the means justify the ends in the apprehension of the felon, a rule
maintained by the reward of prestige; & finally in their possession
of org'ed action bodies as represented by the Fraternal Order of
Police. Secrecy among the police is traced to the soc definition of
their occup as corrupt & brutal, & may be seen as a protective
mechanism against this attack. (5) On Becoming a Policeman—describes 4 mechanisms responsible for the rookie's acceptance of the
rules of the group: (i) expediency, or the need for a way to act in

view of the uselessness of previous definitions & the acceptance of the safest & most available channels of action—imitation of what the rookie sees around him; (ii) categorical reaction, or the response to being stereotyped, which involves the knowledge on the part of those involved that their chances lie with those of the group, & which leads to their upholding the values of the group on this basis; (iii) application of sanctions, which refers to the system of the rewards & punishments provided by the group that guide the newcomer's behavior & structure & his perspectives on the basis of a hedonistic response; & (iv) the maintenance of personal integrity, or the tendency toward self-consistency, in which the individual tries to maintain a homogeneous generalized other, in which he has self-esteem. (6) Postscript 1970: A Shared Fate—stresses the importance of training, high pay, & SS, & most of all of full democratic participation of the police in the life of the community. Appendices: (A) Interview Sample, Interview Structure & Data Gathering; (B) Interview Face Sheet; (C) Social & Attitudinal Backgrounds. A Bibliog & joint name & subject index. M. Duke.

PROPOSALS

A *proposal* is a written description of a project that has not yet been undertaken. It describes the nature of the project, sets forth the plans for carrying it out, and estimates its requirements for equipment, finances, and possibly personnel. The ultimate purpose of the proposal is to gain authorization to proceed with the project.

Even though the proposal writer is usually attempting to convince his readers to accept his idea, he should avoid hard-sell tactics such as exaggerating the advantages and ignoring or minimizing the disadvantages. The ideal proposal analyzes the project in a detached, honest, and objective manner.

Uses

The proposal is used in a variety of situations. The student makes a proposal for a research project and presents it to faculty members for evaluation and approval. In a large corporation, a manager prepares a proposal affecting some aspect of his department (e.g., needed personnel) and presents it to his superiors. A business concern, such as an engineering firm, offers a proposal outlining specific services to a potential client. A researcher

—say, in the physical or social sciences—prepares a project proposal and submits it to the board of directors of a college or foundation.

Organization and Writing

The proposal's actual form is dictated by the specific requirements of the individual or agency to which it is directed. The content, however, does not vary extensively. Essentially you are telling what you are going to do, why you can do it, and how you are going to do it. The following parts are included in most proposals. In the event that one or more are not applicable to your proposal, you should eliminate it (or them) rather than manipulate the content to fit a set form.

Summary. State the substance of the project in a few clear sentences. This summation will give the reader a general idea of what you intend to do and will prepare him for the specific details that follow.

Statement of the Problem. Proving that a problem actually exists and that a solution to this problem will be advantageous is the heart of the proposal. If fruitless or partially successful attempts to solve the problem have already been made, mention these efforts and, at the same time, stress the reasons why your project will succeed where others have failed.

At this point try to approach the project with total objectivity and judge its possible flaws as well as its merits. You may not wish to list the faults in the final proposal, but considering them will prepare you to defend your project and will also aid you in defining the merits more clearly. One of the purposes of this section is to demonstrate the advantages of the project.

Procedures. Describe the exact procedures that you plan to employ in carrying out the project. The amount of detail in this section depends on how comprehensive the proposal is, but in any case you should prove that you do possess the knowledge and ability to handle the project and to complete it successfully.

Facilities and/or Materials. First, list the facilities and/or materials (equipment, library sources, supplies, and so forth) that are available. Second, if some of the necessary materials are not readily available, list them and note the difficulty and cost of securing them. Frequently if costs are extensive, a detailed tabulation of them will be submitted separately.

Schedule and Progress Reports. State the approximate amount of time you expect to spend and how you will spend it. The issuing of reports would likely follow the completion of various steps of the project. At this point indicate the number and nature of progress reports.

Personnel. If the project involves assistance in laboratory work, fieldwork, or clerical duties, indicate the number, cost, and availability of the required helpers.

Qualifications and References. Often the approval of the proposal hinges on your qualifications. In a forthright and honest manner, state the details concerning your past experience, education, and related background. List the names of responsible persons who are familiar with your work, thus adding further credibility to this section. In a business proposal, the firm will usually list other concerns for which they have provided similar services or products.

Conclusion. The conclusion can usually be omitted. You have already summarized the proposal in the opening paragraph, thereby eliminating the necessity of repeating that material. Gentle pleading or polite phrases do not carry much weight in proposals; thus, those possibilities are ruled out. Unless a conclusion seems absolutely necessary, avoid it. If it does seem essential, it should be in the form of a brief and forceful statement on the project's merits.

Visual Aids. For some proposals, the inclusion of diagrams or other visual materials adds interest and clarity. Depending on the circumstances, they would probably be included within the text of a short proposal and placed in appendixes at the end of a long proposal.

Final Form

Specific requirements, length, and nature of the proposal will for the most part determine its final form. The sample that follows is typical of a short, relatively uncomplicated proposal. A proposal that covers the project in detail is similar to this in form but is usually presented in the same form as a research paper, including title page, table of contents, and so forth. Sometimes the proposal is in the form of a letter addressed to a specific person who has the authority to approve the proposal or who represents an agency or group that has this power.

Because the proposal is usually directed to a limited audience (possibly only one person), you can generally assume that the readers are conversant with the subject. You will therefore gear the style and vocabulary accordingly.

Here is an example of a proposal for a scientific project. Note that the areas of qualifications and references and personnel were omitted from this proposal because they were obviously not applicable.

MODEL PROPOSAL

TO: Dr. S. S. Jones

    Chairman, Biology Department

FROM: John Jones

SUBJECT: Proposal for dissertation research project

SUMMARY

Because of expanded laboratory research with the cereal leaf beetle, Oulema melanopa (Linnaeus), the demand for large numbers in all life stages has increased. The successful implementation of this project would enable the mass rearing of these beetles.

STATEMENT OF THE PROBLEM

Extensive research with the cereal leaf beetle is under way; however, the supply of these beetles is limited. Procedures for laboratory production of eggs, larvae, pupae, and adult beetles would fulfill research needs and eliminate dependence on field collections.

T. R. Castro experimented with rearing the cereal leaf beetle and was able to produce limited numbers of beetles by using covered lamp chimneys over 4-inch pots of oats for adult feeding and oviposition and uncaged 6-inch pots of oats for larval feeding. However, the results were inconsistent, and numerous beetles were injured by handling when being transferred from pot to pot. (Castro, T. R. Natural History of the Cereal Leaf Beetle, Oulema Melanopa [Linnaeus], and Its Behavior Under Controlled Environmental Conditions. [Unpublished doctor's dissertation, Michigan State University].)

This project will eliminate the handling problem, provide for rearing larger numbers, and produce the beetles in varied life stages.

PROCEDURE

1. The rearing facility will consist of a windowless room with a 16-hour photoperiod and a 300-foot candlelight intensity at plant height. The temperature will remain constant at 78° during the light period and at 74° during the 8-hour dark period. The humidity will remain constant at 60%.

2. Approximately 200 unsexed ovipositing adults will be placed in a cage that has proper ventilation and contains seedling plants (oats or barley) about 5 inches high. The pots in which the eggs will be laid will be changed at intervals to provide eggs of suitable ages.

3. After the pots containing the eggs are removed from the cages, they will be placed on trays. It will take four to seven days for the eggs to hatch. The larvae will then be permitted to feed on the plants until the larvae reaches the second instar.

4. The plants containing the larvae will be cut and laid

over trays of oat or barley seedlings. The soil will be covered with plaster of paris and one-half inch of sand. When
the prepupae attempt to enter the soil, they will be unable to
do so and will be forced to pupate in the sand from which they
may be easily recovered.

   5. The pupae will be placed on trays with 4-inch pots of
seedling barley or oats and put into cages where the adults
will emerge from the pupal cells and may be collected.

FACILITIES AND MATERIALS

   The following facilities and materials will be necessary
to conduct this project:

   1. One windowless room lighted and heated according to
       specifications set forth under "Procedure"

   2. Cage

   3. Cereal leaf beetles

   4. Oat or barley seedlings

   5. Pots

   6. Trays

   7. Plaster of paris

   8. Sand and soil

   All the materials and facilities are available except for
the beetles, which may be purchased for a nominal sum through
a laboratory service that stores frozen beetles collected during the summer months.

SCHEDULE AND PROGRESS REPORTS

   The project will cover a six-month period. The first
month will be spent in obtaining and setting up the equipment.
The next five months will entail following several cycles

> through the process described under "Procedure" and perfecting
> this process.
>
>   Progress reports will be issued every month: (1) the
> first report will cover the acquisition, preparation, and com-
> pletion of the materials and facilities; (2) subsequent reports
> will cover the stages of research.

It is possible that this brief proposal might create interest but that those in authority who hold the stamp of approval may want more details. If so, the preliminary proposal would be expanded accordingly and would probably be put into the form of a research paper. For a proposal to go through several drafts is not at all unusual, considering the demands of the people to whom the proposal is directed and the possible revisions in procedure, adjustments in cost, and deletion or addition of materials and personnel—to name but a few changes that might be required.

PROGRESS REPORTS

A *progress report* contains information regarding the work done during a project. It may cover a number of areas such as accomplishments, problems, solutions to these problems, and the need for revising plans. Issued as necessary or as required by those to whom it is submitted, such a report is sometimes made in the form of a letter. The length and form depend on the complexity of the project, the requirements of the report's recipients, and the time intervals between reports.

A few examples of persons who would prepare progress reports are a contractor informing his client of the progress of a building project, a student assuring a professor that his research is nearing completion, and a scientist advising the foundation financing him that his work is progressing satisfactorily.

No set form applies to all progress reports. If the recipient does not require a certain form, the following example would be appropriate:

PROGRESS REPORT NO. 2

March 15, 1973

TO: Dr. S. S. Smith

FROM: John Jones

SUBJECT: Research project on the effects of underground irrigation on soil

PROGRESS: Soil samples have been gathered from several fields that have been irrigated by underground methods over a period of years. These samples are being tested to determine the amount of chemicals deposited in the soil. Currently, samples of soil from fields that are irrigated by aboveground methods are being gathered. One problem that has arisen concerns the variations in actual underground irrigation systems. Therefore, it has been necessary to consider this factor in evaluating the soil condition.

Another kind of progress report is the *periodic report,* which as the name implies is issued at regular intervals, possibly monthly or yearly. Examples of such reports include a supervisor's monthly report regarding the status of his department and a corporation's annual report concerning the financial condition of the organization. A periodic report may be a one-page typewritten sheet or an elaborately printed and illustrated booklet.

RESEARCH REPORTS

The researcher is usually required to state the results of his work in a written report and to present it to whoever sponsored or assigned the project. In addition, he may submit it to a journal or periodical or read it to colleagues at a meeting.

Recording the results of original research is the main function of a research report. However, it may contain or be devoted exclusively to directions, descriptions, compilation and review of literature, or recommendations.

Record of Original Research

Simply to state that one purpose of the report is to record original research does not indicate the various areas that such a work may cover. The following list summarizes the major purposes of this kind of report writing:

1. To establish priority on a phase of a project
2. To report on an aspect of a problem and to give a possible solution
3. To assist other workers in the same field
4. To name and to describe new species or to add recognition features to species already named
5. To prove or disprove existing but not very well substantiated theories or beliefs

Organization. The uses of the research report are so varied that it does not follow any consistent form. Your department or agency will probably provide a style book covering the specifics of report preparation and presentation. If not, you should refer to published reports in your own field.

Particular requirements notwithstanding, the report follows the pattern of any coherent written research work: title, introduction, thesis statement, body, conclusion, bibliography. (For detailed discussion of these matters, see chapter 5.)

TITLE. The title of a technical report should describe the content concisely, clearly, and exactly. Ambiguous words, clever or pretentious phrases, and obvious declarations, such as "studies," "contributions," and "investigations," have no place. The purposes of the title are to enable others to locate the material easily, to avoid burying valuable information, and to aid nontechnically trained library personnel in cataloging and classifying the information accurately.

INTRODUCTION. Depending on the nature of your subject, the introduction may carry out one or more of the following functions: limiting the scope of the subject, defining unfamiliar terms, reviewing other literature on the subject.

THESIS STATEMENT. Near the end of the introduction, you should state the reason for writing the report. In other words, express in one or two sentences what you have discovered and what you are going to prove. This statement of purpose is the thesis statement, which is the core of your report.

BODY. The body of the paper contains descriptions of the materials used in the research, discussions of the methods for obtaining information, and/or accounts of the experiments conducted.

Once you have laid this groundwork, you then present the results of the research.

CONCLUSION. From these results, you derive principles, show causal relations, and draw generalizations. This section is the most original part of the report. It should state your contribution in a logical and clear manner in order to allow your reader to examine the principles, relationships, and generalizations.

Do not confuse the conclusion with the summary (or abstract) of the report that is often required. The summary (or abstract) is a concise statement of the important points in the entire report, including methods, results, and conclusions. It may appear at the end of the report or at the beginning, but the latter procedure seems to be gaining in favor.

VISUAL MATERIALS. Research reports may often benefit from the use of visual materials such as tables, graphs, and illustrations. These materials are usually placed within the text if they are closely related to, and illustrative of, the written matter. If supplementary in nature, they are grouped separately at the end of the text. (See chapter 8 for discussion of visual materials.)

BIBLIOGRAPHY. Although the main source for the report is original research, it is likely that you will refer to other literature in the field, notably accounts of similar research. A report with no bibliography will lead the reader to suspect that you have written your report in a vacuum, without examining related materials. In addition to giving the necessary credit to the sources you have used, the bibliography should direct the reader to other records of research in the same or closely related areas.

Final Form. The title page, preface (if there is one), the table of contents, and so on, follow the form given in chapter 9 (p. 235). The parts of the text—introduction, thesis statement, methods, results, and conclusion—are usually labeled and often numbered I, II, III, and so on. The back matter is handled as it is in a research paper.

Directions and Descriptions

Material telling how to operate a mechanism or how to carry out a process may cover only a few lines or comprise a complete manual. Similarly, material that describes how a mechanism operates or how a process works will vary in length and complexity. Writing directions or descriptions is one of the most difficult tasks a writer will face. Careful organization, forthright sentence structure, and exact diction are basic requirements. Visual materials usually play a strong part in such reports.

Compilation and Review of Literature

Someone proposing a study in a particular field may compile a list of articles and books on various aspects of the subject and review them in order to show what work has been done, how well it has been done, and what is left to do. This kind of study resembles an annotated bibliography. Conclusions would be drawn regarding the availability, quality, and completeness of the literature.

Recommendations

Research is often conducted for the sole reason of discovering ways to solve a problem. Based on the results of the research, recommendations are made with the idea that their implementation will lead to a satisfactory solution. Recommendations are often included in a separate section of the research report or they may be part of the conclusion. Sometimes separate reports are issued containing only recommendations.

AN ACT OF SHARING

Scientific investigation is an expression of man's innate curiosity. It is the seeking of answers to some of his basic questions. Man investigates his world and his universe all through his life. When the investigation ceases, so does the man. At certain phases of his continuing exploration, man stops and takes stock and shares what he has learned. The culmination of knowledge in one man's search is perhaps the beginning in another's quest.

Chapter 8

Using Visual Materials

Since the day when man first began scratching pictographic ideographs on his cave walls some 25,000 or more years ago, he has been refining his methods of recording and diffusing ideas.

Paul B. Horton,
"Does History Show Long-Time Trends?"

The fact that visual materials were the first means of, and are still valuable in, "recording and diffusing ideas" is sometimes overlooked by researchers who have become dependent entirely on the written word. But in the presentation of evidence, visual materials can often clarify or specify details that any number of words may leave obscure.

Popular publications make extensive use of such materials, often to spur interest in the written matter. However, to include illustrations in a research work for this reason alone is not advisable. They should be used only when they definitely aid in making the text clearer and more specific. It should be remembered that visual materials are essentially another kind of developmental material serving the same function as an example or a direct quotation.

The main kinds of visual materials are:

Illustrations
Maps and map graphs
Tables
Graphs

Generally, these materials are used more often in reports than in documented research papers, but this fact should not make you hesitate to include them in the latter when they are appropriate.

ILLUSTRATIONS

Regarding the description of human physiology, Leonardo da Vinci pointed out that "it is necessary to draw *and* to describe" because the more minute the description, the more it restricts the mind of the reader.[1] This observation, stressing the need for illustrations, holds true in other fields as well. Since Leonardo's time, of course, the photograph has augmented the drawing as an illustrative device.

The two kinds of illustrations are photographs and drawings, with some variations within these two classifications.

Photographs

Photographs may be either current or historical. Current photographs can add dramatic evidence to a paper concerned with a specific problem such as the need for urban renewal. Similarly, historical photographs will sometimes bring a past event to life more quickly than words can. Or studies of the visual arts can gain vitality through pictures of the subjects, such as individual pieces of sculpture or striking examples of architecture.

Drawings

Drawings may be fully representative, that is, an exact picture of the device, organism, plant, or whatever. Or they may take the form of diagrams that explain rather than represent. Two other kinds of explanatory drawings are pictographs and flow charts.

Representative Drawings. Used extensively in the natural sciences, *representative drawings* make the textual matter visible and decrease the likelihood of its misinterpretation. In many cases, the numerous minute details that characterize scientific study can be recorded and explained accurately only through drawings, as this biological illustration demonstrates:

1. David Bland, *A History of Book Illustration* (Berkeley: Univ. of California Press, 1969), p. 15.

Scientific illustration. Red-legged grasshopper, adult male, enlarged. Reprinted by permission from J. R. Parker and R. V. Connin, *Grasshoppers: Their Habits and Damage,* Information Bulletin No. 287 (Washington, D.C.: Department of Agriculture, Nov. 1964), p. 9.

But such drawings are not limited to the natural sciences. They may also be used effectively to illustrate research works in the humanities, the arts, and the social sciences.

Diagrams. The purpose of *diagrams* is explanatory. The diagram in this example explains how a device works:

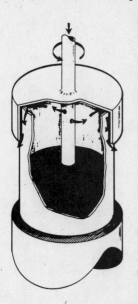
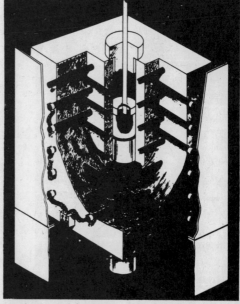

Diagrams. The glass-making furnace, besides heating the glass mixture to a high temperature, allows the glass to be stirred and permits various gases to be introduced, as shown in the top diagram. Reprinted by permission of the editor from A. D. Pearson and W. G. French, "Low-Loss Glass Fibers," *Bell Laboratories Record,* 50 (April 1972), 107. Copyright 1972, Bell Telephone Laboratories, Incorporated.

In addition to depicting mechanical devices, diagrams have numerous other uses. They may, for example, give floor plans, explain the structure of an organism, or show geographical phenomena.

Pictographs. Also explanatory in nature, *pictographs* are simple figures or cartoons that help to clarify the meaning of complex ideas. They should be used with discrimination, however, because they can tend toward oversimplification or cuteness. Here is an example of an effective use of pictographs:

Pictographs. Reprinted by permission from City of San Diego, Public Relations Department, *City of San Diego Fiscal 1971: Budget in Brief* (1971).

Flow Charts. As their name indicates, *flow charts* depict movement of various kinds, such as the flowing of a liquid or current through a mechanical device or the shipment of a commodity from a central place to other parts of the country or world. They may also show the steps of a process, such as the exposure, development, and printing of film. Organizational flow charts depict the channels of authority or divisions of responsibility.

Here is a flow chart that follows the movement of a current through a mechanical device:

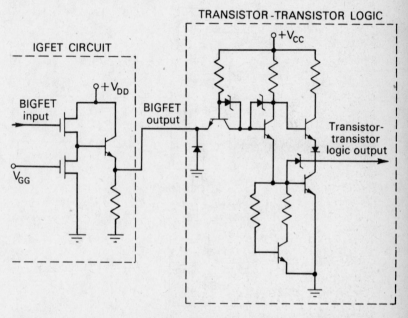

Flow chart (mechanism). A BIGFET output stage is connected to a transistor-transistor-logic circuit. Both circuits require a 5-volt supply voltage ($V_{CC} = V_{DD}$). When the IGFET portion (upper left) is conducting, the output portion of the BIGFET rises to approximately 4 volts—a logic "1" (or ON) state. When the input IGFET is turned off, the output voltage falls to within a few tenths of a volt—a logic "0" (or OFF) state. (Reprinted by permission of the editor from G. T. Cheney and G. Marr, "BIGFET Makes IGFET More Versatile," *Bell Laboratories Record*, 50 (June-July 1972), 198. Copyright 1972, Bell Telephone Laboratories, Incorporated.

This flow chart shows how a process is carried out:

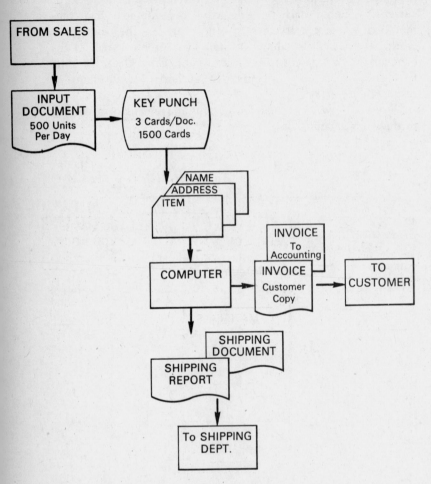

Flow chart (process). Sales invoice flow chart.

The channels of authority in a specific department are set forth in this flow chart:

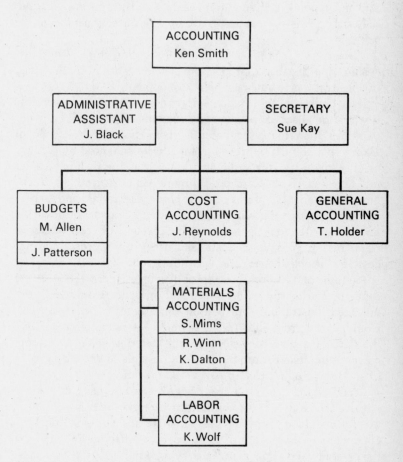

Flow chart (organization). Department 4-C, Office of the Controller.

Uses of Illustrations

Illustrations add most to the texts of papers in the visual arts and reports in the natural sciences and technical fields, but they may be used, if appropriate, for the development of other subjects.

Visual Arts. Studies in painting, architecture, sculpture, design, and theatrical production are some of those that may use illustrations to advance their development.

In a paper on the French impressionist school of painting, it would be wiser to include reproductions of some of the major paintings than to try to describe them. Similarly, a study of Victorian architecture in America might be enhanced by pictures or drawings of Victorian landmarks such as the Bishop's Palace in Galveston, Texas, and the Biltmore Mansion near Asheville, North Carolina. Diagrams of floor plans, elevations, and elaborate woodwork or masonry might also be included. Through the text, the writer could present the background of such buildings (their history, designers, costs, and uses), but words could not describe the actual structures very effectively.

A study of the French sculptor Auguste Rodin (1840–1917) concerned primarily with his life and influence would probably not need illustrations, but one on some aspect of his sculpture would profit from illustrative material. It is possible to give the date of a piece of sculpture, its materials, and the events surrounding its creation; but it is not possible to describe a work of art—say, Rodin's *Call to Arms* (1879)—fully.

In a research work on the design of a famous landscaping effort, such as Butchart's Gardens in Victoria, British Columbia, the text could contain the factual material, but only pictures could convey the beauty of the gardens. A diagram might show the overall landscape plan, specifying kinds of shrubs, trees, and flowers used in various sections.

A study on the literary aspects of theater would probably not need illustrations; for instance, in a paper on the songs in Bertolt Brecht's *Mother Courage*, pictures of the play in production would be superfluous. However, in considering a subject such as "Design Problems in *Mother Courage*," the writer could make use of pictures and diagrams to show how some designers did or did not overcome the problems or to reveal his own plans for surmounting the difficulties of design.

Science. Scientific reports rely heavily on illustrations because science is in large part a discipline of observation and description. Scientific illustrating is characterized by clarity, exactness, and simplicity. Its purposes, like those of most scientific writing, are to describe, to elucidate, and to explain, not to interpret. In the words of scientific illustrator Charles S. Papp, "The illustrator is morally obligated to record exactly what he sees, omitting any impressions whatsoever. . . . The 'scientific illustrator' may not allow himself any deviation from factual truth."[2]

In reporting on a botanic study concerned with leaf characteristics in diseased maple trees, the researcher could include drawings of the leaves, showing the appearance they take on when the tree becomes diseased. For contrast, he might include a drawing of a healthy leaf. Similarly, the geologist studying the formation of the Baja California area could rely on photographs, as well as on drawings, to present his findings. Diagrams are also useful in scientific reports. In a report on soil conditions, for instance, a diagram showing the content and makeup of the soil on various levels would contribute to a clear understanding of the text.

MAPS

"The earliest maps were simple because life itself was simple,"[3] Lloyd Brown observes in his book on the history of map making (a science known as *cartography*). But as life grew in complexity, man's increasing knowledge of, and his desire to know more about, his world led to the demand for more elaborate maps to represent geography and for map graphs to show natural and cultural distributions.

Geographical Maps

Maps, in their most basic forms, represent specific geographical areas and show one or more natural features, such as topography, vegetation, or bodies of water. Next in complexity

2. Charles E. Papp, *Scientific Illustration* (Dubuque, Iowa: William C. Brown, Publishers, 1968), p. vii.

3. Lloyd A. Brown, *Map Making: The Art that Became a Science* (Boston: Little, Brown and Company, 1960), p. 3.

are maps representing man's additions to the landscape (such as roads, cities, and monuments) and man's political divisions (such as nations, states, counties, and cities).

Maps showing only natural features may be included in scientific reports such as studies on reforestation projects, water conservation, or erosion control. On the other hand, papers on subjects such as politics, literature, or history might contain maps representing man-made features and political boundaries. A study of the political situation in Southeast Asia, for instance, would be clearer if it included a map showing the area's political boundaries, population centers, and major roads. Similarly, a paper on the geographic locales of Shakespeare's historical plays would benefit from a map showing the settings of the various plays; a historical study of Europe before World War I might include a map designating the national boundaries at that time.

Map Graphs

Map graphs show distribution of natural and cultural phenomena through symbols or shading on *base maps* (simple representations of geographic areas). Keys to the symbols or shading appear at the bottom of the map graphs.

Examples of map graphs showing natural distribution are weather maps, which give visual information on weather conditions in specific areas, and vegetation maps, which show what types of plants grow in certain places. The map graph on the facing page depicts world weather conditions.

Map graphs presenting cultural distribution may be political in nature (e.g., showing the areas in the United States where a political party predominates), or economically, religiously, or educationally oriented. A map graph showing distribution of one religious denomination in the United States appears on the facing page.

Through depicting distribution, map graphs may also suggest contrasts and comparisons. For instance, the weather map illustrated on p. 193 provides information that enables the viewer to compare the amount of rainfall in Africa with that in the British Isles or any other area.

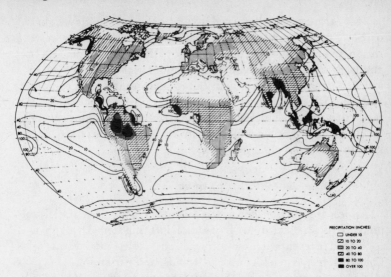

Map graph (weather). General pattern of annual world precipitation (inches). Reprinted by permission from *Climates of the World* (Washington, D.C.: Department of Commerce, Jan. 1969), p. 4.

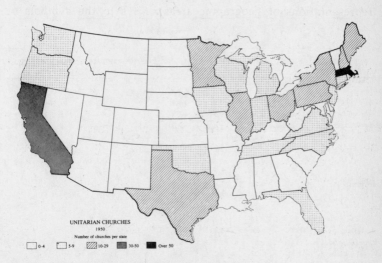

Map graph (cultural distribution). Reprinted by permission from Edwin Scott Gaustad, *Historical Atlas of Religion in America* (New York: Harper & Row, 1962), p. 128.

Map graphs may be used extensively in the development of both reports and research papers, especially those relying for their approach on comparative methods. A report, for example, stressing the advantages of industrial development in a specific area might use a distribution map graph that compared and contrasted the chosen area and other possible locations. Or a research paper on educational spending in a specific locality could include a map graph comparing this area with other parts of the state or country.

TABLES

Tables are condensed arrangements, usually in parallel columns, of statistical or other factual information. Through this organized presentation of information, tables may show relationships, frequencies, contrasts, trends, and variations.

Here is an example of statistical data presented in a table:

INCREASES IN AVERAGE HOURLY EARNINGS

Industry	SIC #	1970	Percent Changes					
			1967/1966	1968/1967	1969/1968	1970/1969	1971e/1970	1972e/1971e
Textile mills	22	$2.45	+5.1	+7.3	+5.9	+5.3	+ 5.0	+ 5.8
Apparel	23	2.39	+7.4	+8.9	+5.9	+3.9	+ 4.6	+ 6.4
Lumber and wood products	24	2.93	+5.3	+8.4	+6.6	+6.9	+ 8.1	+ 7.5
Furniture and fixtures	25	2.77	+5.4	+6.0	+6.1	+5.7	+ 5.4	+ 6.2
Paper and products	26	3.44	+4.4	+6.3	+6.2	+6.3	+ 7.3	+ 7.0
Basic chemicals	281	4.08	+3.6	+4.9	+6.1	+6.3	+ 6.5	+ 6.5
Drugs	283	3.54	+4.3	+4.5	+9.3	+7.3	+ 7.0	+ 7.0
Petroleum	29	4.27	+5.0	+4.7	+6.7	+6.8	+ 6.0	+ 6.0
Rubber and plastics	30	3.20	+2.6	+6.6	+5.1	+4.2	+ 6.0	+ 6.0
Leather	31	2.49	+6.7	+7.7	+5.8	+5.5	+ 5.5	+ 5.5
Stone, clay, glass	32	3.40	+3.7	+6.0	+6.7	+6.6	+ 6.5	+ 6.0
Primary iron and steel	331	4.16	+1.1	+5.3	+6.9	+3.5	+ 9.6	+12.5
Primary nonferrous metals	333	3.83	+3.6	+6.3	+6.2	+6.4	+ 7.3	+14.0
Fabricated metal products	34	3.53	+3.5	+6.0	+5.7	+5.7	+ 6.5	+ 5.3
Motor vehicles and parts	371	4.22	+3.2	+9.9	+5.1	+2.9	+14.9	+ 7.4
Aircraft	372	4.12	+4.2	+4.9	+6.9	+6.5	+ 5.8	+ 6.9
Instruments	38	3.34	+4.4	+4.6	+5.7	+6.0	+ 6.0	+ 6.0

Table using statistical data. Reprinted by permission from Gary M. Wenglowski, "Industry Profit Forecasting," *Business Economics*, 7 (Jan. 1972), 61–66.

This table presents other factual information:

RANKING OF INDUSTRIES BY ESTIMATED IMPACT OF CHANGES
IN HOURLY EARNINGS ON INDUSTRY PROFITS*

Instruments
Primary nonferrous metals
Paper and products
Lumber and wood products
Autos and parts
Electrical machinery
Fabricated metal products
Primary iron and steel
Textile mills
Petroleum
Basic chemicals
Rubber and plastics
Stone, clay and glass
Nonelectrical machinery
Drugs
Furniture and fixtures
Aircraft
Leather
Apparel

* Ranking based on
c coefficient in basic equation ÷ average industry sales

Table with factual information. Reprinted by permission from Gary M. Wenglowski, "Industry Profit Forecasting," *Business Economics*, 7 (Jan. 1972), 61–66.

One advantage of the table is that its formation does not require any special artistic ability. The graph, which is essentially a visual form of the table, demands considerably more care in its preparation.

Tables containing factual information advance the development of research works because they focus the details in a concentrated manner. A language paper, for example, might include a table showing word variants in the major dialects of a specific language. Such a procedure would probably be preferable to presenting this information within the text.

Tables consisting of statistical information should not be overused because they tend to become uninteresting to the reader, and if they are too complicated, they can even confuse him. It is preferable, whenever possible, to put the information into graphic form.

GRAPHS

Graphs present numerical data in visual forms in order to show comparisons, make analyses, and forecast events or trends. Well-designed graphs explain, emphasize, and visualize statistical information in a more simple and forthright manner than can be accomplished through listing the information within the text or even in tables.

Kinds of Graphs

The field of graphic presentation is reasonably standard in the forms it uses for presentation of information. In 1915 the American Society of Engineers appointed a committee to investigate whether "simple and convenient standards [for graphs] can be found and made generally known."[4] The society's desire for standardization was realized, as was its prediction that such standardization would lead to "a more universal use of graphic methods, with a consequent gain to mankind because of the greater speed and accuracy with which complex information may be imparted and interpreted."[5]

The major kinds of graphs fulfilling these functions are line graphs, bar graphs, and circle graphs.

Line Graphs. *Line graphs,* which are the basis of all other graphs, are especially effective in showing one or more relationships between two factors, frequency distributions, and variations in trends. One factor is presented on the bottom horizontal line and the other is presented on the left-hand vertical line. A single line (if only one aspect is shown) and multiple lines (if two or more aspects are shown) appear inside the rectangle and connect the various factors.

4. Herbert Arkin and Raymond R. Colton, *Graphs: How to Make and Use Them* (New York: Harper and Brothers, 1940), p. 2.
5. Arkin and Colton.

Here is an example of a line graph that shows relationships:

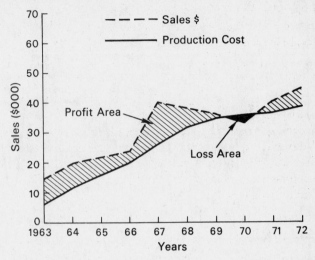

Line graph (relationships). Ten-year analysis of sales-to-production cost.

This line graph shows frequency distribution:

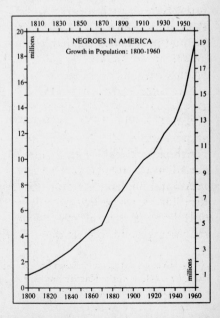

Line graph (distribution). Reprinted by permission from Edwin Scott Gaustad, *Historical Atlas of Religion in America* (New York: Harper & Row, 1962), p. 148.

Variations in a trend are shown in this line graph:

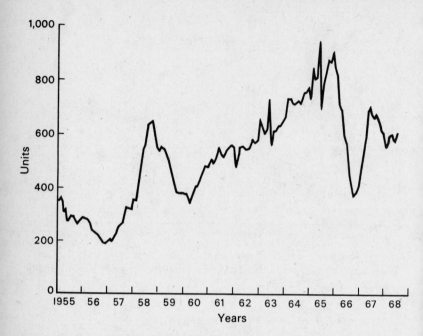

Line graph (variations). Reprinted by permission from President's Committee on Urban Housing, *A Decent Home* (Washington, D.C.: Government Printing Office, 1968), p. 129.

Bar Graphs. Bar graphs are popular because they are more easily read and appear less statistical than line graphs do. It is not always possible, however, to substitute bar graphs for line graphs because bar graphs are somewhat more limited in the kinds of information they can present.

The main purpose of a *vertical-bar graph* (opposite) is to depict numerical values of a given item over a period of time.

A *horizontal-bar graph* (opposite) is especially useful in comparing different items in a specified time.

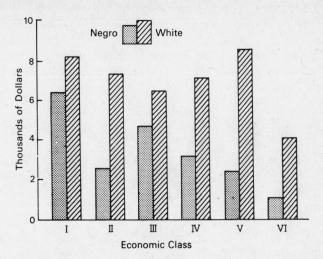

Vertical-bar graph. Average loan size by race and economic class. Reprinted by permission from Commission on Civil Rights, *Equal Opportunity in Farm Programs* (Washington, D.C.: Government Printing Office, 1965), p. 69.

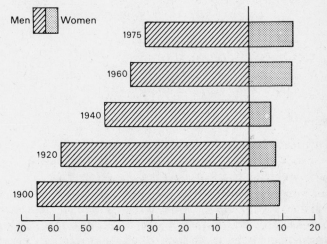

Horizontal-bar graph. Percentage of aged 65 and over in the labor force: male and female, 1900–1975. Reprinted by permission from President's Council on Aging, *The Older American* (Washington, D.C.: Government Printing Office, 1963), p. 21.

Circle Graphs. Also called a *pie* or a *sector graph*, a *circle graph* consists of a circle, the area of which is divided into parts. Through this division, circle graphs compare the parts and show their relation to the whole. Sometimes two or more circle graphs may be used together to show comparisons between various factors:

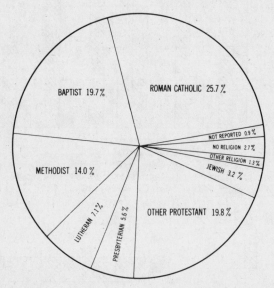

Circle graph. Religious preferences in America: 1957. Reprinted by permission from Edwin Scott Gaustad, *Historical Atlas of Religion in America* (New York: Harper & Row, 1962), p. 163.

Uses of Graphs

Because of the many subjects they can depict, graphs may be used in a variety of research works. For instance, a paper on racial problems might use a graph to present a comparison of how effectively integration has been carried out in the South and the North during the past twenty years. Or a study of economic problems in farming could take advantage of a graph to show the up-and-down trend of prices the farmer has received since 1900. Or a sociological study might use a line graph to show the relationship between family income and juvenile delinquency. Mathematical reports would also make extensive use of the various graphs in presenting material.

PREPARATION AND DOCUMENTATION OF VISUAL MATERIALS

The writer will generally prepare his own visual materials when they are a presentation of the evidence he has gathered. In other cases, visual matter may be copied from sources if the information presented in them is directly applicable. Illustrations for research papers are usually borrowed, although nothing prohibits the use of original artwork or photographs. (The main sources for visual materials are discussed in chapter 3, p. 40.)

If preparing original materials is out of the writer's scope, he may call on someone else for assistance, always of course giving full credit to the illustrator. When visual matter of any kind is borrowed, it should be as fully documented as possible.

This discussion has been limited to a description of the kinds of visual materials and suggestions on their uses; it has not attempted to give instructions on how to prepare them. That detailed subject is fully examined in several excellent books. (A selected bibliography of some of the major works in the field appears in appendix C.)

PLACEMENT OF VISUAL MATERIALS

Visual materials may be placed within the text of the research work or at the end of the text. The first procedure is preferable if the illustrations or maps or whatever relate directly to the text. Telling the reader to see Figure 16 on page 129 when he is reading page 11 tends to interrupt his concentration on the text. But if the visual materials are supplementary to the text (much like an appendix), they should be placed at the end of the written matter.

Several forms govern the listing and numbering of graphic materials used in a research work. In a short work that includes only a few visual aids, it is usually unnecessary to list and number them. In a long work, you should follow the simplified form given in chapter 9 (p. 246), or consult a book in your field in order to find the proper form for handling the materials.

The visual materials in this chapter are not numbered "Figure 1," "Figure 2," and so forth because they are so closely related to the text that they are introduced within it, thus forming an integral part of the text. However, if they had been distributed throughout the chapter, they would have been numbered and referred to within the text as "Figure 1," "Figure 2," and so on.

VISUAL REPORTS

Visual reports consist either of photographs with captions or of slides or movies with narration. They may present a specific problem, describe a process, report an activity, or illustrate an aspect of the fine arts.

These useful pamphlets covering the preparation of photographic reports are available through the Eastman Kodak Company:

Photo Reports Make It Happen (AT–5)
Slide Showmanship (AA–6)
Showmanship in Home-Movie Projection (AO–43)

Free copies may be obtained by writing to Photo Information, Department 841, Eastman Kodak Company, 343 State Street, Rochester, New York 14650.

Preparation

Although a visual report is not a highly academic procedure, it should consist of more than a haphazard collection of photographs, slides, or movies. Just as in a written report, the need for planning is paramount. You should begin with a statement of the problem and then determine the aspects of the problem. This planning will guide you in taking or selecting the pictures and will help to determine the content of the captions or narration. It also might be necessary at this point to consult some printed sources for background information.

A photographic report should have a beginning (introduction and central idea), middle (body), and end (conclusion). In order to introduce the photographic report, you should use either a picture or a written introduction. The body will contain the main pictures and captions or narration that develop the central idea set forth in the introduction. The captions could in some instances be only phrases, but generally complete sentences are preferable. In either case, the captions should be more than just obvious labels for the pictures.

The conclusion may rely on a striking picture that sums up what has gone before, a written statement, or possibly a combination of the two elements.

Here are two sample plans for visual reports:

PRESENTATION OF A SPECIFIC PROBLEM

Introduction and central idea. The deterioration of the downtown section of [name of city] must be stopped before it is too late. This idea could be introduced by a picture that emphasizes the deterioration of the downtown section.

Body. The body might consist of a series of pictures showing specifics such as vacant buildings, ugly signs, dirty streets and sidewalks, and unattractive business establishments. The captions or narration should be simple and concise, containing just enough material to emphasize the problems.

Conclusion. The conclusion could contain a picture of the efforts of one or more business places to halt the deterioration. The conclusion should state a possible solution and perhaps extend a challenge.

DESCRIPTION OF A PROCESS

Introduction and central idea. Weight lifting is an effective means of body improvement. This idea could be illustrated by a picture of several people working out with weights.

Body. The body would consist of a series of pictures showing some of the basic exercises with dumbbells and barbells. The captions would include the name and purpose of each exercise, such as the "seated single-arm curl for the building of biceps."

Conclusion. The concluding photograph might be a picture of a successful weight lifter, or even better, two pictures showing the before-and-after appearance of someone who has worked out on weights for a year.

Presentation

In order to present a series of photographs, mount them on heavy paper and type the captions beneath or at the sides of the pictures. The arrangement of the pictures will depend on their size, but appearance and clarity should always be prime considerations.

In order to show slides in a meaningful way, arrange them in consecutive order and never dwell on a single slide for too long. Plan the narration carefully, writing it out if necessary, so that it is coordinated with the pictures. The narration should serve to explain them, not to distract from them. Successful movie presentation depends even more on exact narration.

RECORDING AND DIFFUSING IDEAS

Although it has been predicted, it is unlikely that the printed word will be made obsolete by reliance on visual materials. Significantly, the pictographs etched on the cave walls 25,000 years ago led eventually to the alphabet, the ultimate refinement for recording and diffusing ideas. Illustrations, maps and map graphs, tables, and graphs will probably continue to visualize, emphasize, and clarify the written matter upon which they are often dependent for their meaning.

Chapter 9

Writing with Exactness

> *Reading maketh a full man, conference a ready man, and writing an exact man.*
>
> Francis Bacon, "Of Studies"

In research writing the emphasis lies on exactness. But there is no single formula that leads to this quality; exact writing is the sum total of several considerations. How a writer handles diction, sentence structure, transition, and punctuation leads to what is called *style*. The writer's attitude toward his subject and his reader enters into the picture, too; the result is *tone*. And the strictness of research writing demands something additional from the writer: adherence to *form*.

The development of a style and tone and the observance of form does produce exactness—both in the writing and in the writer.

STYLE

The development of a style that is vital as well as exact comes from understanding the elements of writing and from practice in applying that knowledge.

The following presentation is an abbreviated one, intended primarily as a guide to revision. If you have further questions on any of these matters, refer to one of the books listed in appendix C under "Writing."

Diction

Diction is the choice of words, and the difference between the wrong choice and the right choice is like the contrast between a plastic rose and a freshly picked one. Let your choice of words be governed by variety and preciseness.

Variety. Sometimes a word is not actually wrong from the standpoint of definition, but because it has been overused in a particular context, it is incorrect in the sense that it lacks variety. Somewhere a rule exists stating that a writer should never use the same noun, verb, or modifier twice in one paragraph. Such a rule cannot be followed rigidly, but attempting to follow it helps to achieve varied diction.

The revision of the following paragraph shows how replacing an overused word with synonyms improves the flow of ideas:

> It is hardly fair to dismiss many of Conrad Richter's
>
> novels as nothing more than historical ~~novels~~ *fiction*, which, after
>
> all, ~~do~~ *does* not rank very prominently in literature. The ~~novels~~ *works*
>
> are indisputably more than "period pieces," those ~~novels~~ *books*
>
> that recreate past society so tediously and whose characters
>
> live so unrealistically. Rising above the level of ordinary
>
> historical ~~novels~~ *fiction*, his novels of the frontier are distinctive.

Four of the six uses of the word "novels" are changed to other words, thus strengthening the placement of "novels" at the beginning and end of the paragraph.

Roget's *Thesaurus* or one of the similar dictionaries of synonyms and antonyms will often direct you to a word that you can employ in place of an overused one. Remember, however, that these books can lead to words that mean almost the same thing—but not quite. Thus, before seizing a synonym, be sure that you understand it thoroughly.

In some instances, of course, you have to use the same word repeatedly because no other word will serve as well. At times, too, the repetition of a key word adds emphasis.

Variety is important, but exactness is even more so; therefore, never use *slang expressions, archaic words,* or *trite words and expressions* simply to achieve variety. Although slang is not to be disparaged for conversational use or even for informal writing, its use in a research work is not advisable because such expressions usually lack exactness, formality, and permanence.

Similarly, use of words that are archaic or that have gone out of style can confuse or distract the reader. Some examples of words that once were acceptable but now have an old-fashioned and possibly unfamiliar ring to them are "solons" for legislators, "savants" for scholars, and "divers" for several.

Trite words such as "incredible," "great," "fabulous," and "stunning," which have been overused to such an extent that they have lost their original meanings, do not add exactness to the writing, nor do tired combinations of words, known as *clichés* or *hackneyed expressions.* Such phrases may have been colorful once but have been dimmed through overuse; a few examples are "immortal Bard" for Shakespeare, "tripping the light fantastic" for dancing, and "venture in celluloid" for film making.

Probably the soundest advice on word variety came from Alexander Pope, who admonished the would-be writer: "Be not the first by whom the new are tried, /Nor yet the last to lay the old aside."[1]

Preciseness. A foreign student struggling with the vagaries of the English language once observed that there always seemed to be a dozen English words for everything, but only one of them was ever right in a particular instance. To some degree all writers face this problem: the search for the precise word, the one that helps to express the total idea exactly.

One way to discover a precise word is to settle on a general word first. As you revise the material and think about the word

1. Alexander Pope, "An Essay on Criticism," pt. II, ll. 134–135.

you want, sometimes the right word will evolve from the general word. Or you could look up the general word in the *Thesaurus* or a dictionary and then analyze its synonyms; one of them may be the exact word for which you are searching.

In the revision of this paragraph, precise words have replaced the general ones:

---

                    to dismiss
    It is hardly fair ~~to say that~~ many of Conrad Richter's

novels as nothing more than historical fiction, which, after

                 prominently   indis-
all, does not rank very ~~highly~~ in literature. They are ~~cert~~

putably
~~tainly~~ more than "period pieces," those books which ~~tell about~~
                                          recreate

      society tediously   so unrealistically.
past ~~times~~ so ~~fully~~ and whose characters live ~~in such an unreal~~

~~way.~~ Nor can they be described as "historical romances," be-

                       exploits of heroic people.
cause they are not full of the ~~grand adventures of grand people~~.

In some instances the preciseness of a word is lost through its misuse. The confusion of words that sound alike (such as "proceed"–"precede," "eminent,"–"imminent," and "moral"–"morale") may be a good device for humor, but it does not have a place in research writing. Whenever you are unsure of the meaning of a word, check its definition in the dictionary.

Another factor that lessens preciseness is modifying weak nouns and verbs with adjectives and adverbs. Almost without exception, a strong noun or verb with no modifiers is preferable. For example, "tell fully" may be replaced with "depict," "re-create," or "distinguish"; "a devoted group" could be called "fans," "devotees," "admirers," "followers," or "disciples," depending on the context. In research writing, then, consider each adjective or adverb in order to determine its strength before you use it.

Economy of Words

The use of ten words to say what could be expressed in three words is sometimes the outcome of assignments calling for a specific number of words. It may also be the result of laziness; it is often more difficult to write economically. Sometimes, too, lack of understanding causes long, roundabout sentences full of words that do not focus on a single idea.

Always check your sentences for wordiness, and when you can express an idea in fewer words and still retain its full meaning, use the shorter version. Emphasis on economy in writing does not imply that you should trim each sentence to its absolute essentials, but it does mean that you should eliminate words that clutter the sentence, make it awkward, or obscure it. The following example shows how the same idea can be expressed with increased clarity and ease by eliminating fifteen words:

Wordy: The overall emphasis of this particular course in Shakespeare's major comedies, tragedies, and histories is to study them in relationship to the physical, the metaphysical, and the sociopolitical aspects of the Renaissance period. (33 words)
Economical: This course considers Shakespeare's major plays in relation to the physical, metaphysical, and sociopolitical aspects of the Renaissance. (18 words)

Punctuation

Punctuation, the placing of symbols within and at the end of sentences for clarity and emphasis, is at best an imperfect science. Often, the use of a particular punctuation mark is determined by the individual writer or the style sheet he is following. But some writers use punctuation almost creatively, breaking or altering rules to good advantage.

Four aspects of punctuation use that often cause problems in writing are summarized in the paragraphs that follow.

Separating Independent Clauses. Separate independent clauses with a period, semicolon, or conjunction. Otherwise you have a run-on sentence, as in this example:

Although old and tired, the man followed the same routine that had guided his life for years, it seemed that each day became more difficult.

The run-on sentence may be corrected by putting a period in place of the comma, thus separating the ideas in the two clauses; by adding a conjunction, thus connecting the two ideas; or by using a semicolon, thus relating the two ideas.

    Period: Although old and tired, the man followed the same routine that had guided his life for years. It seemed that each day became more difficult.

    Semicolon: Although old and tired, the man followed the same routine that had guided his life for years; it seemed that each day became more difficult.

    Conjunction: Although old and tired, the man followed the same routine that had guided his life for years, but it seemed that each day became more difficult.

Use a comma before the conjunction if the two clauses are fairly short and do not have extensive internal punctuation; use a semicolon if the opposite is true.

    Separating Parts of a Series. Separate by commas the parts of a series of adjectives, nouns, or phrases. (The comma is sometimes omitted before "and" and "or"; however, in order to assure clarity, it is better to include the comma unless directed to do otherwise.)

    Setting off Modifiers. Set off with commas each word, phrase, or clause that is not absolutely essential to the word it identifies or limits. That is, if the word, phrase, or clause can be omitted and the sentence is still clear, it must be set off by commas; but if its omission obscures the meaning of the sentence, then it should not be set off.

    In the following sentences, the italicized expressions are not absolutely necessary to identify or limit the words to which they refer; thus, they are set off by commas:

    The dedicatory address, *a rambling series of anecdotes,* lasted far too long.

    San Francisco, *its charm known the world over,* has always been a favorite among travelers.

    The 1970 edition, *which was edited by Lewis Norwell,* contains several new features.

    Setting off Introductory Elements. Place a comma after a long introductory phrase or dependent clause. You may omit the comma after a short phrase or clause unless you want to add special emphasis.

Here is a long introductory phrase, set off by a comma:

Upon learning about his family's background, he gained new appreciation for the courage of his ancestors.

Here is a short introductory phrase that does not need to be set off:

Through reading you can become a better writer.

This long introductory clause is set off by a comma:

Since he had not visited his home for many years and had experienced a new way of life in the meantime, he was not sure how he would react to his family and former acquaintances.

This short introductory clause does not need a comma:

Since he had left home his life had changed.

One simple way to help determine the use of commas within sentences is to read the rough draft aloud. If there is a natural pause within a sentence, you can be almost certain that a comma is needed for clarity or emphasis.

Grammar

Grammatical errors do not always obscure the meaning of a sentence, but they do distract considerably from its total effectiveness. The dangers of grammatical mistakes hinge in large part on these five elements: agreement, reference, placement of modifiers, reference of opening words and phrases, and complete sentences.

Agreement. The subject and predicate must agree in number; that is, a singular subject takes a singular predicate and a plural subject takes a plural predicate. Many agreement errors result from the separation of the subject by phrases or clauses, as in this example:

Inability to apply the principles of aerodynamics and advanced mathematics were cited in his dismissal notice.

Correction: "Inability," a singular idea, is the subject; thus the predicate would be "was cited." The phrase "principles of aerodynamics and advanced mathematics" does not affect the predicate in any way; it modifies the singular subject, "inability."

Use of compound subjects also causes agreement errors, as in this example:

The poem and the essay, both written when he was a young man, contains his thoughts about love.

Correction: "The poem and the essay" are two separate works, thus the verb must be plural: "contain."

Reference.   The reference of a pronoun to a preceding noun or phrase must be clear and consistent.

CLARITY.   Since a pronoun stands for a noun or phrase, it must have a definite point of reference. Never use a pronoun in such a way that it could refer to any number of preceding words or phrases, as in this example:

The necessity for understanding, the demand for decision making, and the insistence on honesty were obvious to him, but he still had trouble with it.

Correction: It is not clear whether "it" refers to all three phrases, two of them, or one. The sentence could be rewritten a number of ways, depending on what "it" stands for. Here are two possibilities:

The necessity for understanding, the demand for decision making, and the insistence on honesty were obvious to him, but he still had trouble with them.

The necessity for understanding, the demand for decision making, and the insistence on honesty were obvious to him, but he still had trouble making decisions.

Another use of pronouns that produces unclear writing is referring to vague forces as "they," as in this example:

It was apparent that they should do something about the conditions at the hospital.

Correction: Assuming that "they" had no point of reference in the preceding sentence or sentences, the reader would not know whether "they" referred to the staff, board of directors, patients, or taxpayers. The sentence could be worded more clearly: It is apparent that the board of directors should take some action to improve the hospital's conditions.

CONSISTENCY.   A pronoun must be consistent in number (plural or singular) with the word or phrase for which it stands.

Here is an example of a sentence with a singular noun referred to by a plural pronoun:

Every student should pick up their registration cards in the main office today.

Correction: "Student" is singular and "their" is plural; this sentence may be corrected in two ways:

All students should pick up their registration cards in the main office today.

Every student should pick up his registration cards in the main office today.

Placement of Modifiers. Related words or phrases must be kept together. Carelessly scattering through the sentence words or phrases that modify a single idea can lead to muddled thoughts. For example:

He learned that she had died from an individual at the railroad station.

Correction: "From an individual at the railroad station" should be placed after "learned"; otherwise "from . . . station" seems to modify "died."

Opening Words and Phrases. Words or phrases at the beginning of a sentence must refer directly to the subject they precede. Here is an example of a disastrous sentence, in which the opening phrase does not refer to the subject:

Blooming luxuriantly, he walked through the flowers.

Correction: Obviously "blooming luxuriantly" refers to the flowers; corrected, the sentence would read: He walked through the luxuriantly blooming flowers.

Complete Sentences. All sentences must be complete, containing both a subject and a verb. Granted that experienced authors often employ sentence fragments to good effect, it is still advisable for most writers to rely on complete sentences to express their ideas.

Kinds of Sentences

Incorporating the four kinds of sentences (simple, compound, complex, and compound-complex) into your writing is one way to assure variety and, in many cases, exactness. A series of simple and compound sentences tends to suggest elementary thinking; a string of complex and compound-complex sentences may confuse or exhaust the reader. As you revise your paper, then, take into consideration the various constructions and try not to rely too heavily on any one of them.

Simple Sentence. The simple sentence consists of one or more subjects and one or more verbs, with or without modifiers. Here is a simple sentence, first in its basic form and then in its more elaborate forms:

> The city fell.
> The ancient city fell to the conquerors.
> The city and the state fell quickly.

Compound Sentence. A compound sentence consists of two or more simple sentences connected by a conjunction. Its parts, showing opposite or equal ideas, should be balanced effectively, as in the following examples:

> He may err in the expression of them, but he knows that these things are so, like day and night, not to be disputed.[2]
> This freedom is a splendid privilege, and the first lesson of the young novelist is to learn to be worthy of it.[3]

Complex Sentence. A complex sentence consists of one or more dependent clauses and one independent clause; its structure leads to showing consequences and concessions.

Here is an example of a complex sentence containing one dependent clause and one independent clause:

> When we have new perception, we shall gladly disburden the memory of its hoarded treasures as old rubbish.[4]

This sentence consists of three dependent clauses and one independent clause:

> Once the land has been settled, once man has come to stay, once he has triumphed over nature, there is no turning back.

It is possible to achieve variety by opening the sentence with the independent clause, as in this example:

2. Ralph Waldo Emerson, "Self Reliance."
3. Henry James, "The Art of Fiction."
4. Emerson, "Self Reliance."

It is difficult to make a man miserable while he feels he is worthy of himself and claims kindred to the great God who made him.[5]

Compound-Complex Sentence. The compound-complex sentence consists of one or more dependent clauses and two or more independent clauses. This sentence begins with two independent clauses and concludes with a dependent clause:

The character inherent in the American people has done all that has been accomplished; and it would have done somewhat more, if the government had not sometimes got in its way.[6]

Sentence Length

Another way to achieve exact and vital writing is through varying the length of sentences. Avoid a series of short, choppy sentences that hamper the flow of ideas. You will find that such a series can often be corrected by combining two or more of the short sentences into a compound or complex sentence.

The following paragraph, consisting entirely of simple and compound sentences of approximately the same length, makes dull reading:

As a child, Turgenev loved to wander in the garden. He pulled the petals off rosebuds, and he tried to discover the core of them but he could not remove the inner sheaths. They were too thin and delicate. This failure always upset him, but it taught him about life. The experience seemed to influence his writing.

Revised, the paragraph gains interest:

When Turgenev was a child, he loved to wander in the garden where one of his favorite pastimes was pulling off the petals of a rosebud and trying to discover the core of it. It always upset him that the innermost sheaths were so thin and delicate that he could not remove them. One critic observed that "this practice may have taught the novelist to content himself with the exquisite epidermis of reality, which is the keynote of his novels."[7]

Sometimes when a short sentence follows a long sentence,

5. Abraham Lincoln, Address on colonization to a Negro deputation at Washington (14 Aug. 1862).
6. Henry David Thoreau, "Civil Disobedience."
7. Avraham Yarmolinsky, *Turgenev, The Man, His Art, and His Age* (New York: Orion Press, 1959), p. 105.

the contrast provides emphasis or even clinches the idea introduced in the previous sentence. The following example illustrates the use of sentences of varied lengths, the three shorter
ones stemming from and developing the longer one:

> The West of which I speak is but another name for the Wild;
> and what I have been preparing to say is, that in Wildness is the
> preservation of the World. Every tree sends its fibres forth in search
> of the Wild. The cities import it at any price. Men plow and sail
> for it.[8]

Sentence Patterns

The basic pattern of the English sentence is as follows:

> subject   verb   object or modifier

But varying this basic pattern adds emphasis, variety, and vitality to your writing. As you check your rough draft, you may
discover a disproportionate number of sentences opening with
"a," "an," or "the," followed by the subject and verb. If so, you
should rework some of the basic patterns into one of the variations described in the following paragraphs.

Dependent Clause.   Open the sentence with a dependent
clause.

> Basic Pattern: He gained perspective and wider knowledge of
> human nature because he lived for considerable periods in countries
> other than his own.
> Variation: Because he lived for considerable periods in countries
> other than his own, he gained perspective and wider knowledge of
> human nature.

Prepositional Phrase.   Open the sentence with a prepositional
phrase.

> Basic Pattern: Biography is often considered the most interesting
> of the many kinds of nonfiction.
> Variation: Of the many kinds of nonfiction, biography is often
> considered the most interesting.

Absolute Expression.   Open the sentence with an absolute
expression, one that modifies the sentence as a whole.

8. Henry David Thoreau, "Walking."

Basic Pattern: The writer was relieved once the facts were verified.

Variation: The facts verified, the writer felt a sense of relief.

Adverb. Open the sentence with an adverb or adverbs.

Basic Pattern: The writer approached the revising process apprehensively.

Variation: Apprehensively, the writer approached the revising process.

Adjective. Open the sentence with an adjective or adjectives.

Basic Pattern: The thoroughly seasoned and broadly traveled newspaper reporter related a series of fascinating stories.

Variation: Thoroughly seasoned and broadly traveled, the newspaper reporter related a series of fascinating stories.

Participial Phrase. Open the sentence with a participial phrase.

Basic Pattern: The writer proceeded to revise his work with great care.

Variation: Proceeding with great care, the writer revised his work.

Appositive. Open the sentence with an appositive.

Basic Pattern: The scientist, an authority on molecular biology, spoke to the members of the symposium.

Variation: An authority on molecular biology, the scientist spoke to the members of the symposium.

Parallel Structure

An experienced teacher and writer once commented that when you have learned how to use parallel structure, you have learned how to write. There is validity in this statement that gives so much credit to the effectiveness of *parallelism,* a structure that expresses two or more equal ideas in like grammatical form.

The three main ways that parallel structure can add to a paper's exactness are through combining ideas, correcting awkward sentences, and balancing separate parts.

Combining Ideas. Use parallel structure to combine the ideas expressed in two or more short sentences.

Short sentences: The writer accomplishes several things through careful revision. One is to correct errors in punctuation and grammar. Another is to improve diction. The elimination of wordiness and the variation of sentence patterns are also reasons for revising.

Restated in a parallel sentence: Through careful revision, the writer corrects punctuation and grammatical errors, improves diction, eliminates wordiness, and varies sentence patterns.

Comment: The one parallel sentence expresses all the ideas from the four short sentences in a clearer and more economical style. The grammatical form is a verb-object structure.

Correcting Awkward Sentences. Use parallel structure to correct awkward sentences.

Awkward sentence: They blamed the difficulties on lack of understanding and refusing new ideas.

Restated in a parallel sentence: They blamed the difficulties on lack of understanding and refusal of new ideas.

Comment: The second sentence makes use of two prepositional phrases, replacing the nonparallel prepositional phrase and gerund phrase in the first sentence. Also note that in the second prepositional phrase, but not in the first phrase, an adjective modifies the noun. This variation is permissible, in fact, preferable to an obvious and unnecessary balancing within the grammatical form (e.g., "lack of basic understanding and refusal of new ideas").

Balancing Sentence Parts. Use parallel structure to balance sentence parts followed by the correlative conjunctions: "both" . . . "and," "either" . . . "or," "neither" . . . "nor," "not only" . . . "but also."

Not balanced: He celebrated in his poetry both the beauty of truth and enjoying life.

Balanced in a parallel sentence: He celebrated in his poetry both the beauty of truth and the joy of life.

Not balanced: During his performance as Othello, it became evident that not only was he bringing a fresh interpretation to the role but also he conveyed it to the audience.

Balanced in a parallel sentence: During his performance as Othello, it became evident that not only was he bringing a fresh interpretation to the role but also that he was conveying this interpretation to the audience.

If parallel structure is overused or expresses unequal ideas, it loses its effectiveness. But if used properly, parallel structure strengthens the writing through its classic symmetry and balance.

Point of View

In research writing it is always desirable to adopt and carry through a consistent grammatical point of view. The three points of view from which you can write are:

1. First person: "I" or "we"
2. Second person: "you," singular or plural
3. Third person: "he," "she," "it," or "they"

For the most part research writing uses the third-person point of view, which is the most detached and objective of the three possibilities. Rarely is "I" used and certainly never the editorial "we." You will see "this writer" employed at times, but such a practice is not generally advisable because of its pretentious ring.

Remember that since you are the author of the paper, it is obvious to the reader that the ideas in it are either your own or drawn from your documented sources. Thus, expressions such as "I think," "this writer believes," or "I am led to conclude" are superfluous.

In papers that give directions, you may employ the second person; otherwise you will fall into passive constructions and inverted sentences. But in other kinds of papers, never use the indefinite "you," which does not refer to the reader or anyone else in particular. In a study of the American Civil War, for instance, the following sentence would not refer to the reader or anyone in particular:

> After the battles were finished, you usually spent some time in searching for missing friends.

Transition

A final aspect of style is the use of transition, that is, employing connective words or phrases to bridge and connect the ideas and their parts. In order to master transition, you should understand the connecting devices, practice using them, and study authors who make good use of them. A preoccupation with transition, however, can lead to overuse and awkwardness. Keep in mind, too, that transition should serve its purpose without calling attention to itself.

Here is a list of the major transitional devices classified according to their uses:

A. To connect the parts of a subject
   1. To show equal parts
      "also"
      "and"
      "another"
      "at the same time"
      "both" . . . "and"
      "in addition"
      "just as"
      "moreover"
      "similar"
      "similarly"
      "still"
   2. To enumerate parts
      "first," "second," "third," and so forth (never use "firstly," "secondly," and so on)
      "in the first place," "in the second place," and so forth
      "once"
      "twice"
   3. To introduce illustrative evidence
      "for example"
      "for instance"
      "for one thing"
      "in some cases"
      "often"
      "many times"
      "sometimes"
   4. To show reference to a noun or noun clause in the preceding sentence
      "it"
      "such a"

"these"
"they"
"this"

B. To show relationships
1. To show opposites or contrasts
"but"
"by contrast"
"conversely"
"different from"
"on the contrary"
"on the other hand"
"other"
"otherwise"
"whereas"
2. To show alternatives
"however"
"or"
"not only" . . . "but also"
3. To make concessions
"although"
"even"
"even though"
"granted"
"in spite of the fact"
"though"
4. To show cause and effect
"accordingly"
"as a result"
"because"
"consequently"
"for"
"hence"
"since"
"so"
"then"
"therefore"
"thus"
5. To show that opposites should be considered
"nevertheless"

   "regardless"
   "yet"
 C. To show emphasis
   "again"
   "briefly"
   "certainly"
   "especially"
   "even"
   "finally"
   "indeed" (becoming archaic)
   "in short"
   "largely"
   "no doubt"
   "on the whole"
   "specially"
   "specifically"
   "to be sure"
   "to sum up"
 D. To qualify ideas
   "in a sense"
   "in some cases"
   "in some instances"
   "often"
   "not always"
   "sometimes"

Checklist for Revision

Through extensive revision, your paper will gradually take on a style that is both exact and vital. There will probably come a time, however, in the revising process when you reach the point of no return. Knowing when you arrive at this dead end in revision is not always easy, but one sure sign is changing new words or revised constructions back to what they were originally. When you feel that further revision would hinder more than it would help, you should then appraise the condition of your final draft by asking these questions:

 Is the diction precise and varied?
 Is the punctuation correct, thus providing clarity and emphasis?

Is the sentence structure correct and varied in kind, pattern, and length?

Is the writing economical but not sterile?

Is the point of view appropriate and consistent?

Are the ideas and parts connected by transitional devices?

Does the transition make the paper flow easily and give it continuity?

And then you should take into consideration George Orwell's observation on rules:

Break any of these rules sooner than say anything outright barbarous.[9]

That should be your final consideration.

TONE

When someone reads a piece of writing, he usually gains some sort of an impression from it; maybe he can sense how the writer feels about the subject or even about the reader. This quality of writing that gives the reader an impression is called *tone*.

Although tone is usually considered more important in creative literature than in expository writing, the research paper or report does possess tone. In order to determine what that tone should be, let us examine some characteristics it should not have.

Supercilious

It is possible to write in such a supercilious manner that you seem to be looking down on your reader—like the man with the lorgnette on the cover of the *New Yorker*. Although you may know more about the subject than the reader does, your purpose is to inform him, not to insult him. Avoid expressions such as "it is obvious," "everyone should know," or "it goes without saying." It may not be obvious to the reader at all; he may not know it; and he may wish you had said what "goes without saying."

9. George Orwell, "Politics and the English Language," in *A Collection of Essays* (Garden City, N.Y.: Doubleday, 1954), p. 176.

Chatty

Taking on a chatty tone, the writer embraces the reader and engages him in a one-sided conversation. Such an approach may be appropriate for a letter or a personal essay, but not for the research paper. One writing habit that leads to chattiness is the use of "you"; avoid expressions like "you know," "you see," "you may not agree, but."

Cute

Expository writing need not be antiseptic. The best writing always conveys vitality, but it does not gain this quality through cuteness, often the result of breezy diction and clichés. Again, your purpose is to inform the reader, not to amuse him.

Preachy

To persuade and to convince are legitimate functions of expository writing, but they should be accomplished through logical arguments backed up by reliable evidence, not through preachiness or the making of pronouncements. Avoid telling your reader what to think or what conclusions to draw. Instead, let him examine your conclusions and then come to his own, based on the evidence you have given him.

Sarcastic

The research paper may include criticism of a specific subject, but criticism should not be confused with sarcasm. Since research writing has objectivity as its goal, it must be fair, open, and honest in its criticism. It realizes these qualities through reliance on evidence, not on sarcastic remarks stemming from opinions, prejudices, and half-truths.

Pedantic

The research paper is a scholarly work, but it need not advertise this fact through pedantry. In order to be sure that the writing is clear, concise, and exact, you should avoid academic jargon, elaborate qualifications, or indirect phraseology—some of the signs of pedantry.

In summary, the right tone for research writing should be knowledgeable but not supercilious, vital and alive but not chatty or cute, definite but not preachy, to the point but not sarcastic, and scholarly but not pedantic.

FORM

The third factor in exactness in research writing is attention to form. Form comprises numerous details requiring careful consideration—details of spelling, use of quotations, setting off titles, abbreviations, and division of words. A separate aspect of form concerns the materials you will need to get your paper or report into final shape.

Spelling

The poor speller often spells unfamiliar and difficult words correctly because he looks them up, but he has trouble with common words such as "develop" and "tomorrow" or homonyms such as "there" and "their." If misspelling ordinary words is your downfall, you should be alert as you write the rough draft and then check the spelling once again when revising.

The proper names of people or places may also present spelling problems. In taking notes you should be careful to record all proper names accurately, and you should be sure to transcribe the exact spelling into the documentary notes and bibliography.

Variations often occur in the spelling of foreign writers' names that have been transliterated into English. For instance, "Turgenev" is the usual English spelling of the Russian writer's name, but it does sometimes appear as "Turgenieff" or "Turgeniev." For consistent spelling of such names, check an authoritative source such as *Webster's Biographical Dictionary* or the *New York Times Index*. However, if variant spellings appear in titles, retain the variations in all documentary notes and bibliographical entries. Similarly, do not change the variant spellings in material that you quote directly.

But be careful not to create your own variations where no choices exist, as in the case of the student who wrote a lengthy study on Nathaniel Hawthorne and referred to him as "Nathanial Hawthorn" consistently throughout the paper. Granted that the spelling of the writer's name probably does not affect the quality of the ideas, but it can lead the reader to question the accuracy of the rest of the information.

The principles concerning personal names apply to the spelling of place names as well.

Another spelling problem arises when a single word has two or more acceptable spellings. Usually, one of the forms is preferable, and a good dictionary will provide this information. "Theatre" and "theater," for example, are both acceptable spellings, but generally "theater" is preferable in American English. For such a word, find its preferred spelling and then use that form consistently throughout the paper. Again, if the variant form appears in a title or direct quotation, do not change it.

Never affect British spelling by adding "-ue" here and there or ending "-or" words with "-our." However, when British spelling occurs in titles or quotations, do not change it.

Direct Quotations

The use of direct quotations as developmental material poses several problems with regard to form.

Quotations in the Text. If the quotation is three lines or less, include it within the double-spaced text of the paper. If the quotation is more than three lines, single-space it. An exception to this rule occurs when the quotation of less than three lines is unusually significant and deserves special emphasis; in such instances, the short quotation may be set off by single spacing.

Traditionally, the single-spaced quotation is indented five spaces throughout, but there is a trend toward beginning it flush with the left-hand margin, thus simplifying the typing. In either case, you indent the first line of the quotation if it is the beginning of a paragraph in the original work (ten spaces if the rest of the quotation is indented and five spaces if not).

Introduction of Quotations. One of the greatest barriers to the free flow of ideas in a paper is the awkward introduction of a direct quotation. Expressions such as "this is what John Jones has to say," "this is a quote from John Jones," or "this quote says" interrupt the development of the idea because they do not contribute to it. Another problem is the omission of any introductory comments at all, with the direct quotation simply dropped into the text and usually confusing the reader who is not prepared for the material.

When introducing a quotation, be sure to prepare the reader for the quoted material. Depending on the context, the quotation may either follow a separate introductory sentence or flow directly from the text.

A separate introductory sentence is generally used for a longer quotation set off by single spacing. The following example shows how an introductory statement can serve a twofold purpose by containing related information regarding the quotation as well as introducing it:

Introductory statement	In 1774 James Madison expressed his views on American "poetic matters" in a letter to muse-struck William Bradford:
Direct quotation	I myself use to have too great hankering after those amusing studies. Poetry, wit, and criticism, romances, plays, &tc. captivated me much; but I began to discover that they deserve but a moderate portion of a *mortal's* time and that something more substantial, more durable, more profitable befits our riper age.[10]

In the example just cited, note that a colon follows the introductory statement. Although some writers use a period after an introductory statement, the colon is still the usual punctuation mark when there is a definite break between the text and the quotation.

Incorporating the quoted material into the text and letting it flow from a sentence is the usual practice for a short quotation not set off by single spacing. This example illustrates the textual inclusion of quoted material:

Representing the patterned ethic of civilization in contrast to natural morality, West points out that "the *Indomitable* is ruled by a concept of absolute order imposed by authority."[11]

10. Fred Lewis Pattee, Introduction, *Wieland* (New York: Hafner, 1958), p. xii.

11. Ray B. West, Jr. "The Unity of *Billy Budd*," *Hudson Review*, 5 (Spring 1952), 122.

Sometimes this method may be employed for the introduction of longer quotations, as in the following example:

Introductory part of the sentence	The standard characters in the early sentimental novels seemed always to include
Remainder of the sentence developed by a direct quotation	. . . a lovely and gifted heroine, a devoted wife and mother with a brutal and vicious husband, or a vain and negligent mother, whose kind and pious spouse expires early in the first volume leaving his daughter without a protector, a heartless relative or guardian, preferably an aunt, . . . a virtuous hero, a designing villain, and one or two faithful retainers.[12]

Note that when the quotation completes the textual sentence, the colon is omitted.

Deletions from Quotations.   Sometimes you may delete part of a quotation. Depending on the specific needs, the parts of a quotation that can usually be omitted without altering its original meaning are as follows:

1. Transitional words or phrases
2. Reference to something that preceded the quotation in the original text but does not pertain to the quotation as you are using it
3. Unrelated descriptive or explanatory phrases
4. Information already presented in the text

Ellipsis points (three periods with a space between each: . . .) are used in the following ways to show that something has been left out of the original:

1. Use ellipsis points within the sentence to indicate the omission of words from within the sentence.
Original: A native literature, limited mainly to journals and diaries, began almost on the first day of settlement.
With ellipsis: A native literature . . . began almost on the first day of settlement.
Reason for omission: Let us assume that the fact that the early literature was limited mainly to journals and diaries had

12. Lillie D. Loshe, *The Early American Novel* (New York: Columbia Univ. Press, 1907), p. 5.

already been established in the text.

2. Use ellipsis points between sentences to indicate the omission of one or more sentences.

Original: A native literature, limited mainly to journals and diaries, began almost on the first day of settlement. Later, the other literary forms such as poetry and the essay appeared. However, the novel was not a part of the early literature.

With ellipsis: A native literature, limited mainly to journals and diaries, began almost on the first day of settlement. . . . However, the novel was not a part of the early literature.

Reason for omission: The study is directed toward the novel; thus, the mention of poetry and essays might be superfluous at this point.

3. Use a period and ellipsis points at the end of a sentence to indicate the omission of the final part of the sentence. Do not space before the sentence period.

Original: A native literature, limited mainly to journals and diaries, began almost on the first day of settlement. Later, the other literary forms such as poetry and the essay appeared.

With ellipsis: A native literature, limited mainly to journals and diaries, began almost on the first day. . . . Later, the other literary forms such as poetry and the essay appeared.

Reason for omission: Let us assume that the fact that this idea pertains to the "settlement" has already been established, perhaps in the sentence introducing the quotation.

4. Avoid using ellipsis at the beginning of a paragraph. Make use of introductory clauses or phrases in such instances.

Original: The first thing to consider is that a native literature, limited mainly to journals and diaries, began almost on the first day of settlement.

With ellipsis (not good form): . . . a native literature, limited mainly to journals and diaries, began almost on the first day of settlement.

With introductory phrase (acceptable form): According to most scholars, ". . . a native literature, limited mainly to journals and diaries, began almost on the first day of settlement."

Addition to Quotations. You may add words or dates within a quotation when the addition is absolutely essential to the meaning. Such additions, called *interpolations,* are enclosed in brackets ([ ]). Because most typewriters do not have these characters, you may add them by hand or by combining the slash mark and the underlining mark.

One of the main reasons for interpolating words is to specify reference, as in this example:

> He [Shakespeare] had not only read, but studied the earlier English poets; but he drew his language immediately from life itself, and he possessed a masterly skill in blending the dialogical element with the highest poetical elevation.[13]

Dates are sometimes necessary for clarification if the quotation refers to a specific event whose date is not mentioned but is related to the subject or if the quotation mentions an individual whose birth and possibly death dates are so related.

Here is an example of an interpolated first name, biographical dates, and a publication date:

> As with [Thomas] Mann's [1875–1955] other work, *Doctor Faustus* [1947] is woven of many themes, including the relationship of artist and society, the split between the Catholic and Protestant churches, and argumentation over theology.[14]

Errors in Quotations.   Some sources, especially older books, diaries, letters, and private histories, often contain spelling and/ or grammatical errors.

If the passage contains one or two misspelled words or a grammatical error that may be mistaken for a typing error, place *sic* (meaning "as in the original") in brackets after each mistake. Do not use *sic* to denote archaic words, variant but accepted spellings, colloquialisms, or abbreviations.

If the passage contains numerous spelling and/or grammatical errors, state in the introduction to the quotation that you are quoting it in its original form. An example of the trend toward eliminating *sic* from research writing appears in an early footnote in Nancy Milford's *Zelda:*

> The spelling and punctuation used by both Fitzgeralds has been reproduced exactly; no error, no matter how glaring, has been cor-

---

13. A. W. von Schlegel, "Shakespeare," in *Criticism: The Major Texts* (New York: Harcourt, Brace & World, 1952), p. 421.

14. Paul A. Bates, *Faust: Sources, Works, Criticism* (New York: Harcourt, Brace & World, 1969), p. 43.

rected. What they wrote stands as they wrote it whenever the original sources were available to me. I do not use the pedantic *sic*.[15]

Many older works, containing numerous irregularities in spelling and/or grammar, have been edited and their irregularities changed to comply with standard usage. It is often preferable to use one of these modern editions, unless recording the original spelling and/or grammar relates directly to the paper.

Setting off Titles

The titles of all works mentioned in the text or cited in the documentary notes and bibliography must be set off according to the following rules:

1. Underline (denoting italics) the titles of all books, newspapers, plays, and magazines, and poems published separately:

Vanity Fair   (novel)

Advanced Chemistry   (book)

The San Francisco Examiner   (newspaper; use this form when mentioning a newspaper in the text)

The San Francisco Examiner   (use this form when citing a newspaper in a documentary note and bibliography)

Time   (magazine)

The Ring and the Book   (long poem published separately)

2. Enclose in quotation marks the titles of poems, short stories, articles, and titled chapters that are included in a longer work:

"The Windhover"   (poem)
"The Lottery"   (short story)
"The Invasion of Privacy"   (article)
"The Middle Ages in Transition"   (titled chapter)

15. Nancy Milford, *Zelda* (New York: Harper & Row, 1970), p. 26.

Abbreviations

The use of abbreviations in the text varies somewhat from that in documentary notes and bibliography. Here are the general principles to follow.

In Text. You may use the following traditional and scholarly abbreviations in the text:

Dr.
St. (Saint—preceding a name)
A.D.
B.C.
A.M.
P.M.
e.g.   (*exempli gratia*) for example
etc.   (*et cetera*) and so forth
i.e.   (*id est*) that is

But you may not use more informal abbreviations. The following list is not complete, but it should suggest the kinds of abbreviations *not* to use.

abbreviated forms of state names (e.g., not Pa. for Pennsylvania)
Rev. (Reverend)
St. (street)
Ave. (avenue)
MS (manuscript)

When referring to an organization or government agency in the text, write out the full name and the abbreviation the first time you mention it; thereafter, you may refer to it by its abbreviation, as in this example:

First mention: Department of Health, Education, and Welfare (HEW)
Thereafter: HEW

In Documentary Notes and Bibliography. In listing bibliographical information, you may take advantage of these abbreviations:

c., ca.   (*circa*) approximate date
cf.   (*confer*) see another page, compare

ed.   (editor, edition, edited by) Ed. is capitalized in the bibliography when used to denote "editor" or "edited by."

et al.   (*et alii*) and others
ibid.   (*ibidem*) in the same place
l.   line
ll.   lines
names of states
p.   page
pp.   pages

Two other Latin abbreviations once used extensively in documentary notes but seldom used now are:

loc. cit.   (*loco citato*) in the place cited previously
op. cit.   (*opere citato*) in the work cited previously

The common practice now is to use shortened forms of previously cited references rather than these abbreviations (see appendix D).

Division of Words

Divide a word between syllables to carry it over from one line to the next. Obviously, this rule eliminates the division of one-syllable words. Never divide the last word on the page and complete it on the next page.

Dates and Numbers

Follow these basic rules in using dates and numbers in the text, documentary notes, and bibliography.

1. Spell out any number or date that begins a sentence.
2. Spell out the numbers "one" through "ninety-nine," except for dates, page numbers, and connected groups of numbers standing for dimensions, distances, sums of money, or weights.
3. Spell out references to centuries, e.g., "nineteenth-century standards do not always apply to the twentieth century."
4. Either write page numbers in their complete form: pp. 172–179; or follow the condensed form which is becoming more acceptable: pp. 172–79.

5. Remain consistent in style of date usage: (a) either "23 July 1972" or "July 23, 1972"; (b) either "July 1972" or "July, 1972"; (c) either "in 1972–73" or "from 1972 to 1973," but not "from 1972–1973."

Materials

This discussion pertains to materials for papers and reports only. Most departments have specific requirements regarding theses and dissertations.

Manuscript for Typist. If someone else is typing your manuscript, provide the typist with a final draft that is easily readable and totally correct. Generally, you should not rely on the typist to revise and correct the copy, although there are exceptions to this rule. Before you submit a manuscript that someone else has typed, proofread it carefully; and if you find mistakes, correct them whenever possible with black ink or return the pages to the typist for correction or retyping.

Handwritten Paper or Report. It is preferable (and often required) for a research paper to be typed, but in some cases handwritten papers are accepted. Use 8½-by-11-inch, white, lined paper. Write legibly on one side of the paper only, using black ink. Some instructors require that handwritten papers be double-spaced.

Typed Paper or Report. Always use white paper, 8½ by 11 inches, sixteen- to twenty-pound bond. These specifications exclude unusual colors, odd sizes, and lightweight papers. Unless you are directed otherwise, it is convenient to use the specially treated paper that makes for easy erasures.

Carbon copies are not mandatory in most instances; however, it is a good idea to keep a carbon on file in case the original is lost or is not returned by the instructor.

Pica type, which is somewhat larger than elite type, is preferable, but the smaller type is not ruled out. Unusual typefaces, such as Old English, italics, script, and all capitals, are not permissible. The type should be clean, and the ribbon should be in good condition—not new enough to smear and not old enough to make the letters indistinguishable.

Using black ink to correct a letter or two within a word is an acceptable practice; but do not take advantage of this procedure and submit a paper that is half typed and half handwritten.

Covers. The paper or report is usually enclosed in a cover with a blank sheet of paper before the title page and one after the last typed page.

In some instances you may simply secure a short paper with a paper clip and submit it without a cover, depending on the instructor's preference. But never staple a paper.

PARTS OF THE MANUSCRIPT

The inclusion of the various parts of the manuscript depends on the length and kind of research work. The average length for undergraduate and most graduate class papers or reports usually runs from ten to twenty double-spaced typewritten pages, or 3,000 to 6,000 words. Such shorter works do not generally require all the manuscript sections that longer works such as theses and dissertations do. The subject area of the research work determines the inclusion of some parts, too. For instance, even a short report in education might have a list of tables and an appendix, but such sections would be rare in a long or short philosophy or history paper.

The following parts are essential to all papers and reports:

Title page
Text
Documentary notes
Bibliographical information

In addition to these essential parts, a short research work in some fields or a long research work will include one or more of the following sections:

Preface
Table of contents
List of illustrations
Appendix
Glossary
Bibliography
Index
Subject-matter footnotes
Vita

Title Page for a Short Manuscript

A title page should carry the following information:

Title of the paper
Writer's name
Class for which the paper was written
Date of presentation

The title of the paper need not be catchy, clever, or profound; it need only to be accurate and succinct. One way to form a title is to refer to the thesis statement and summarize it in as few words as possible. But never use a complete sentence that is essentially a shorter version of the thesis statement. Avoid vague and meaningless titles, such as "High Schools" for a paper on specific problems in secondary education.

Unless you are directed otherwise, use the form on the facing page for preparing a title page for a short manuscript. (Double-space a title of two or more lines and indent in a pyramid fashion; see p. 239 for an example.)

(15 spaces)

FORMATION OF THE LAGUNA MOUNTAINS

(20 spaces)

BY

(1 space)

MARY STUDENT

(20 spaces)

Geography 202.11
May 15, 1974

Title Page for a Thesis or Dissertation

A title page for a thesis or dissertation usually includes information in addition to the basic requirements of title, name, course, and date. Subject to variations that depend on the requirements of specific graduate schools, such a title page follows a form similar to this example.

(10 spaces)

SOCIAL RESTRICTIONS

IN LOWER INCOME GROUPS

(16 spaces)

BY

(1 space)

JOHN STUDENT

(2 spaces)

Bachelor of Science, 1965

Everystate College
Middletown, Illinois

(16 spaces)

Submitted to the Faculty of the Graduate School of
Anystate University
in partial fulfillment of the requirements
for the degree of

(2 spaces)

MASTER OF SCIENCE

(1 space)

June 1974

Text

It is never necessary in a short paper or report to separate the introduction and conclusion from the body of the paper or to divide the body into chapters.

In a long work (say, forty pages or more) and in a thesis and a dissertation, the introduction and conclusion are separated, and the body is divided into chapters that have individual titles. Separated, the introduction and conclusion still retain their original characteristics and purposes; divided, the chapters are elaborate developments of the roman numerals on the outline.

First Page.   The form for the first page of the text is different from that for the subsequent pages. The typed matter begins one-third of the way down on the first page, two spaces below the title or chapter heading; the page number appears at the foot of the page. If the paper is separated into chapters, follow the first-page form for the beginning page of each chapter. (See the first page of text in the model term paper, p. 139.)

Subsequent Pages.   The subsequent pages follow the form in this illustration:

Brown, mystical of soul, meditative, and noncombative,[8] creates

in Wieland an appalling story by using three devices of terror:

the spontaneous combustion of Wieland's father, the ventrilo-

quism of Carwin, the religious mania of Wieland. In addition,

he relies on standard Gothic fixtures, including creaking doors,

shadowy nights, a mysterious closet, a haunted summerhouse, and

strange appearances and disappearances. The narrator is Wie-

land's sister, who tells the story through a series of letters,

supposedly requested by her friends. As she concludes her

letters, she spreads morals generously and lists a series of

"ifs." The entire story suggests that treachery will not over-

come virtue if virtue will stand firmly.

Brown possessed a certain skill in writing, as can be seen

in the description of the elder Wieland's death by spontaneous

combustion:

> The prelusive gleam, the blow upon his arm, the fatal
> spark, the explosion heard so far, the fiery cloud that
> environed him, without detriment to the structure, though
> composed of combustible materials, the sudden vanishing of
> this cloud at my uncle's approach, what is the inference to
> be drawn from these facts.?[9]

Although Brown's novels are not read much today, the Gothic

novel did not die with Brown. It has been conjectured that he

influenced Mrs. Shelley in her novels.

---

[8]Fred Lewis Pattee, Introduction, <u>Wieland</u> (New York,
1958), p. xi.

[9]Charles Brockden Brown, <u>Wieland</u> (New York, 1958), p. 21.

Documentary Notes

The documentary notes that you formed after you completed writing the rough draft may be included in the finished paper at the bottom of the page or on a separate note page. The traditional method—putting the notes at the bottom of the page on which the documented material appears—is being replaced gradually by the use of a note page. This method, which groups all the notes on one page (sometimes several pages) at the end of the paper, simplifies typing and lessens distraction from the text.

Unless you are specifically required to place documentary notes at the foot of the text, you will find it much easier to record them on a note page.

The illustration above contains footnotes; the model term paper in chapter 6 uses a note page (p. 159).

Bibliographical Information

The bibliography, placed at the end of the text, contains complete bibliographical information (called *entries*) for each of the sources employed in writing the research work. Some bibliographies list all the works consulted, even those not cited in the documentary notes, others include only those sources cited directly. The second method is the preferable one because a wholesale listing may result in exaggeration.

A bibliography of one or two pages, the usual length in most research papers, lists all the sources (books, periodicals, audiovisual materials, and so forth) collectively. In a longer bibliography, such as that in a thesis or a dissertation, the sources are usually listed according to categories, that is, in separate divisions labeled "Books," "Periodicals," and so on.

In order to form the bibliography, first alphabetize the bibliography cards by the authors' last names or by titles (excluding "a," "an," and "the") in the case of anonymous works. For sources by authors with the same last names, alphabetize them according to the authors' first names or initials. Place names beginning with "Mc" and "Mac" before those starting with "M." When using two or more works by one author, alphabetize the titles of the works and place the author's full name at the beginning of the first entry; thereafter, note the author's name by ten spaces of underlining, followed by a period.

In making a categorical bibliography, follow the same procedure for alphabetizing the names or titles within each division.

Next, check the form of the bibliographical entries by referring to appendix E (p. 288). If you recorded the bibliographical facts correctly when you made the bibliography cards, you will have no difficulty in transferring the information directly from the cards to the page.

Here is a bibliography containing examples of the details mentioned above:

BIBLIOGRAPHY

Alphabetized by title, excluding "the"

"The Constancy of Elegance." *Esquire*, Aug. 1971, pp. 102–108.

"Mc" precedes "M"

McMurtry, Larry. *The Last Picture Show*. New York: Dial Press, 1968.

Malamud, Bernard. *The Fixer*. New York: Farrar, Straus & Giroux, 1966.

Two authors with same last names; alphabetized by first names	Wright, Charles. "A New Day." The Best Short Stories by Negro Writers. Ed. Langston Hughes. Boston: Little, Brown, 1967. Wright, Richard. Native Son. New York: Harper & Brothers, 1940.
Additional work by previous author: alphabetized by title; underlining substituted for name	_____. Uncle Tom's Children. New York: World Publishing Co., 1943.

For another example of a bibliography, see the model term paper, p. 163.

Preface

Instructors do not often request that a preface be included in a short paper, but sometimes they do. In a long paper, thesis, or dissertation, a preface is nearly always required.

Written in the first person, a preface for a research work includes all or some of the following parts, usually in this order:

1. Reason for interest in the subject
2. Special qualifications for writing about the subject
3. Comments on the research: valuable sources, problems, techniques
4. Acknowledgment of persons who assisted in the research

Always cover parts 1 and 3 because these relate to your interest in and research on the subject.

Inclusion of part 2 will depend on whether or not you honestly believe that you have any special qualifications; sometimes appropriate specific experiences or travel may be mentioned.

You may omit part 4 if you did not receive any outside assistance, or if you agree with the realists who believe that it is the professors' and librarians' job to assist students and that they need not be thanked for doing what is expected of them. But it is courteous to acknowledge someone not connected with the academic community who assisted in locating sources or lent special materials.

Here is an example of a preface (to a paper on "Outsiders' Impressions of Mexican Border Towns: Right or Wrong?") that includes all of the parts:

Knowing full well that admitting to a fondness for Mexican border towns may class me as a boor, a degenerate, or a vice figure, I still like them. What really made me want to write this paper, though, was reading Ovid Demaris' Poso del Mundo (New York: Pocket Books, 1971), described on the cover as "a shocking exposé of the sin cities along the Mexican-American border." The book didn't tell exactly how long the writer stayed in the "sin cities," to whom he talked, or how he gathered his information; but his impressions, I fear, are the usual ones that outsiders carry away and perpetuate.

I do not feel like an outsider because I have lived along the border in various places for several years and have visited the towns extensively—from Matamoros to Tijuana, even the little ones like Nuevo Progresso and Ojinaga. Through the years and from many experiences, I have seen another side to these towns.

The available sources on this subject are many, including newspaper and magazine articles, tourist guides, and exposé books (other than the one by Demaris). One of the most interesting discoveries was a series of articles in the Los Angeles Examiner (April 1926) on Mexicali and Tijuana and

their effects on the neighboring California areas; these articles tended to show that the American citizens' attitude toward the border cities is historically ingrained. In addition, I carried out some interviewing and included the results
in the text.

    For their assistance, I would like to acknowledge the
many people I interviewed, even though their names are too
numerous to mention; Sr. Juan Trujillo of the Mexican Tourist Bureau, and several helpful librarians.

This preface hints at the approach to the subject, but it does not tell exactly how the paper will handle the subject; that is the job of the introduction and thesis statement. Thus, when you are writing a preface, be careful not to infringe on the territory of the introduction and thesis statement.

Table of Contents

When the text is divided into parts, a table of contents is necessary in order to provide an overview of the material and to give the page numbers of the various divisions. A table of contents is never needed in a short manuscript, but some instructors do require the inclusion of an outline, which serves as an overview but does not have page numbers.

Here is an example of a table of contents for a long paper on "Problems in Administering Urban Renewal Projects":

TABLE OF CONTENTS

	Page
PREFACE	ii
INTRODUCTION	1
CHAPTER	

Sometimes the introduction is considered as the first chapter and the conclusion as the final chapter.

List of Illustrations

Illustrations may be placed within the text or immediately following it. In either case, a list of illustrations, giving each illustration's title and/or number and the number of the page on which it will be found, follows the table of contents. Here is an example of a list of illustrations for the paper on "Problems in Administering Urban Renewal Projects."

This simplified list would be satisfactory in most cases. However, matters concerning the placement, numbering, and listing of illustrations vary according to subject area, kind of illustration, and the amount of illustrative matter. Thus, if you are making use of a number of illustrations, you should consult a textbook in your field as a sample or follow departmental regulations.

Appendix

Materials such as related bibliographies, documents, and specimen articles are often placed in an appendix, or appendixes if there are several different kinds of inclusions.

Although this material is related directly to the text, its incorporation would interrupt the flow of the text. In a sense, the reader is given a choice: He may or may not consider the appendixes, depending on his interest or particular needs.

Never use an appendix as a depository for leftover evidence that you could not use in the paper but thought was interesting anyway. An appendix should contain only material that amplifies and expands the text.

In case of several appendixes, designate each one, that is, appendix A, appendix B, and so on.

A short paper usually does not contain appendixes, but they are often included in a long paper, thesis, or dissertation.

Glossary

A glossary contains a listing of terms in a particular field or area and their definitions. Although it is not necessary for most papers, some research works (such as studies of specialized scientific subjects or foreign literature) do benefit from a glossary.

For the most part, it is preferable to define unfamiliar terms within the text of the paper.

Index

An index is an alphabetical listing of places, names, and topics and the page numbers on which they are discussed or mentioned. The three categories are listed either in a single index or in separate ones.

Subject-Matter Footnote

The subject-matter footnote, which gives additional information on specific matters mentioned within the text, is disappearing from modern research work because it tends to interrupt the flow of the text. If you are tempted to use a subject-matter footnote, ask yourself this question: If it is important enough to mention, then why not include it within the text?

Vita

Usually required for writers of theses and dissertations, the *vita* is a short autobiography (500 or fewer words), written in the third person. It includes the following information:

1. Basic biographical data: birthplace, birth date
2. Educational background: grammar and high school, college or university, degrees earned, honors received
3. Related experience: significant jobs or travel, publications
4. Future plans: educational, professional

Order of the Parts and Pagination

The order of the parts and the pagination (numbering of pages) are as follows.

SHORT PAPER OR REPORT

Title page	This is page i, small roman numeral; but the number does not appear.
Preface (optional)	Number the preface with small roman numerals: ii, iii, and so on.
Outline (optional)	Number the outline with small roman numerals, following the preface if there is one; following the title page if there is no preface.
Text Documentary note page (optional) Bibliography	Number these three parts consecutively with arabic numerals: 1, 2, 3, and so on.

LONG PAPER OR REPORT, THESIS, DISSERTATION

Title page	Do not number the title page.
Preface	Number with small roman numerals, beginning with "ii."
Table of Contents	Number with a small roman numeral or numerals, following the preface.
List of illustrations (if there is one)	Number with a small roman numeral or numerals, following the table of contents.

Introduction

Chapters

Conclusion

Note pages (if any)

Illustrations (if placed at end)

Glossary (if there is one)

Bibliography

Index (if there is one) or separate indexes (if any)

Number these parts consecutively with arabic numerals, beginning with 1.

MOVING TOWARD EXACTNESS

Research writing is a demanding task, but it can also be a rewarding one. Each time you carry out the research process—hypothesizing, investigating, analyzing, and synthesizing—you have added to your intellectual growth. And you have come nearer to being the "exact man" of whom Francis Bacon speaks.

Appendixes

Appendix A

Selected Bibliography of Basic Reference Works

1. Books about Books (Bibliographies)

1.1 Guides to Bibliographies

Bibliographic Index: A Cumulative Bibliography of Bibliographies. New York: Wilson, 1937—.

Courtney, Winifred, ed. *The Reader's Adviser: A Guide to the Best in Print.* 11th ed. New York: Bowker, 1969.

Winchell, Constance M. *Guide to Reference Books,* 8th ed. Chicago: American Library Association, 1967.

1.2 Guides to Books in Print

Books in Print: An Author-Title-Series Index to Publishers' Trade List Annual. New York: Bowker, annual.

British Books in Print. London: Whitaker, annual.

Cumulative Book Index: A World List of Books in the English Language. New York: Wilson, 1928—.

Paperbound Books in Print. New York: Bowker, monthly.

Vertical File Index: Subject and Title Index to Selected Pamphlet Material. New York: Wilson, monthly.

1.3 Guides to Books Being Published

American Book Publishing Record. New York: Bowker, monthly. (A list of titles published during previous month)

Forthcoming Books. New York: Bowker, quarterly. (A forecast of books to come with a cumulating author-title list of books published and postponed titles)

Monthly Catalog of U.S. Government Publications. Washington, D.C.: Government Printing Office, monthly and annually.

Publishers' Trade List Annual. New York: Bowker, annual. (A collection of catalogs of major publishers)

1.4 Guides to Books in Specific Libraries

National Union Catalog. Back issues republished by Ann Arbor, Mich.: Edwards, 1942—. Current issues from Washington, D.C.: Library of Congress, Card Division.

Book catalogs of specific libraries in the United States, Canada, and England

1.5 Guides to Book Reviews

Book Review Digest. New York: Wilson, 1905—. (A collection of excerpts from reviews appearing in magazines)

Book Review Index. Detroit: Gale Research, 1965—.

Choice: Books for College Libraries. Chicago: American Library Association, 1964—, monthly.

Library Journal. New York: Bowker, monthly.

Subscription Books Bulletin Reviews. Chicago: American Library Association, 1961—. (Reviews of reference books)

Wilson Library Bulletin. New York: Wilson, monthly.

Current periodicals and journals.

Newspapers, especially Sunday supplements such as *New York Times Book Review.*

2. Books about Periodicals, Documents, and Parts of Books

2.1 Directories to Periodicals

Ayer & Son's Directory of Newspapers and Periodicals. Philadelphia: Ayer, 1880—, annual.

Standard Periodical Directory. New York: Oxbridge, 1964—, annual.

Ulrich's Periodical Directory: A Classified Guide to a Selected List of Current Periodicals, Foreign and Domestic. 14th ed., 1970. New York: Bowker, triennially.

Union List of Serials in Libraries of the U.S. and Canada. 3d ed. 5 vols. New York: Wilson, 1965.

2.2 Directories to Government Documents

Androit, John L. *Guide to U.S. Government Serials and Periodicals.* 3 vols. McLean, Va.: Document Index, 1962—.

Brimmer, Brenda. *A Guide to the Use of United Nations Documents.* Dobbs Ferry, N.Y.: Oceana Publications, 1962.

Jackson, Ellen. *Subject Guide to Major U.S. Government Publications.* Chicago: American Library Association, 1968.

2.3 Indexes to the Contents of Magazines

Biography Index: A Cumulative Index to Biographical Material in Books and Magazines. New York: Wilson, 1946—, cumulative.

Library Literature Index. New York: Wilson, 1921—, cumulative.

Nineteenth Century Reader's Guide to Periodical Literature. 2 vols. New York: Wilson, 1944.

Poole's Index to Periodical Literature. 7 vols. New York: Peter Smith, 1938.

Public Affairs Information Service Bulletin. New York: PAIS, Inc., weekly and cumulated anually.

Reader's Guide to Periodical Literature. New York: Wilson, 1900—.

2.4 Indexes to the Contents of Newspapers

Facts on File. New York: Facts on File, 1940—, weekly, with annual bound volumes.

New York Times Index. New York: Times, 1913—, biweekly and annual.

2.5 Indexes to Composite Books

Essay and General Literature Index. New York: Wilson, 1900—, cumulative.

Granger's Index to Poetry. 5th ed. and supplement. New York: Columbia Univ. Press, 1962–1967.

Magill, Frank N. *Magill's Quotations in Context.* 2d series. New York: Salem Press, 1965–1969.

Monro, Isabel. *Index to Reproductions of American Paintings.* New York: Wilson, 1948–1964.

Ottemiller, John H. *Index to Plays in Collections.* New York: Scarecrow Press, 1964. (An author and title index to plays appearing in collections published between 1900 and 1962)

Play Index. New York: Wilson, 1949–1968. (Index to 2,616 plays in 1,138 volumes)

Short Story Index: An Index to 60,000 Stories in 4,320 Collections. (5 vols. New York: Wilson, 1953–1969.)

Sutton, Roberta Briggs. *Speech Index: An Index to 64 Collections of World Famous Orations and Speeches for Various Occasions.* New York: Wilson and Scarecrow, 1935–1961.

Wasserman, Paul, et al. *Statistics Sources: A Subject Guide to Data on Industrial, Business, Social, Educational, Financial, and Other Topics for the U.S. and Selected Foreign Countries.* 2d ed. Detroit: Gale Research, 1966.

3. Books about Audiovisual Materials

3.1 Guides to Films and Filmstrips

American Film Catalog. New York: Bowker, forthcoming.

Educators Guide to Free Films. Randolph, Wisc.: Educators Progress Service, Inc. (National Information Center for Educational Media), annual.

Index to 16mm Educational Films. New York: McGraw-Hill, 1967.

Catalogs from audiovisual centers of states, school districts, colleges, etc.

3.2 Guides to Microfilm and Microfiche

Bell & Howell Catalog. Cleveland, Ohio: Bell & Howell, current.

Prentice-Hall Editorial Staff, comp. *Educator's Complete ERIC (Educational Research Information Center) Handbook.* Phase One. Englewood Cliffs, N.J.: Prentice-Hall, 1967. (Microfiche and hard-copy pamphlets available through ERIC Document Reproduction Service, The National Cash Register Co., Box 2206, Rockville, Md. 20852.)

Xerox Catalog. Ann Arbor, Michigan: University Microfilms, current.

Catalogs of library holdings.

3.3 Guides to Records and Tapes
    Griffiths, Joan. *Records in Review*. Great Barrington, Mass:
        Wyeth Press, 1957—, annual.
    Schwann Record and Tape Guide. Boston: W. Schwann Inc.,
        monthly.
3.4 Guides to Reproductions of Paintings
    Bartran, Margaret. *A Guide to Color Reproductions*. New York:
        Scarecrow Press, 1966.
    Fine Art Reproductions of Old and Modern Masters. Greenwich,
        Conn.: New York Graphic Society, Ltd., 1968.
    Catalogs from specific art museums. (For addresses see *American
        Art Directory*, New York: Bowker, 1970.)

4. Books of Collected Information

4.1 General Encyclopedias
    Chambers's Encyclopaedia. New rev. ed. 15 vols. London: Inter-
        national Learning Systems Corp., Ltd., 1968.
    Collier's Encyclopedia. 24 vols. New York: Collier, 1971.
    Encyclopaedia Britannica. 24 vols. Chicago: Encyclopaedia Britan-
        nica, Inc., 1971.
    Encyclopedia Americana. 30 vols. New York: Encyclopedia Amer-
        icana, annual.
4.2 Desk Encyclopedias
    The Columbia Encyclopedia. 3d ed. New York: Columbia Univ.,
        1963.
    The Lincoln Library of Essential Information. Buffalo: Frontier
        Press Co., revised with each new printing.
4.3 Handbooks and Yearbooks
    Benét, William Rose. *The Reader's Encyclopedia*. 2d ed., New
        York: Crowell, 1965.
    The Book of the States. Chicago: Council of State Government,
        annual.
    Buras, Oscar Krisen. *Mental Measurements Yearbook*. Latest ed.
        1938–1959. Highland Park, N.J.: Gryphon.
    Douglas, George William. *The American Book of Days*. New
        York: Wilson, 1948.
    Information Please Almanac, Atlas, and Yearbook. New York:
        Simon & Schuster, annual.
    Publisher's World. New York: Bowker, annual.
    The World Almanac & Book of Facts. New York: New York
        World-Telegram, annual.
    Writer's Market. Cincinnati, Ohio: Writer's Digest, annual.
4.4 Books on Trends:
    The Europa Yearbook. London: Europa Publications, annual.
    The Statesman's Yearbook. New York: Macmillan, annual.
    U.S. Bureau of the Census. *Statistical Abstracts of the United
        States*. Washington, D.C.: Government Printing Office, annual.
    The World of Learning. London: Allen & Unwin, annual.

5. Books about Words

5.1 English-Language Dictionaries

The American Heritage Dictionary of the English Language. New York: American Heritage Publishing Co., 1969.

Craigie, William Alexander. *A Dictionary of American English on Historical Principles.* 4 vols. Chicago: University of Chicago Press, 1938–1944.

Funk & Wagnalls New Standard Dictionary of the English Language. New York: Funk & Wagnalls Co., 1961.

Murray, James Augustus Henry. *A New English Dictionary on Historical Principles* (also known as *Oxford English Dictionary*). 10 vols. Oxford: Clarendon Press, 1888–1928.

The Random House Dictionary of the English Language. New York: Random House, 1966.

Webster's Third International Dictionary of the English Language: Unabridged. Springfield, Mass.: Merriam, 1961.

5.2 Supplementary English-Language Dictionaries

ABBREVIATIONS: DeSola, Ralph. *Abbreviations Dictionary.* Rev. ed. New York: Hawthorne, 1967.

ETYMOLOGY: Partridge, Eric. *Origins* (A short etymological dictionary of modern English). 2d ed. London: Routledge & Paul, 1959.

FOREIGN TERMS: Guinagh, Kevin. *Dictionary of Foreign Phrases and Abbreviations.* New York: Wilson, 1965.

HANDBOOK: Wilson, Kenneth George. *Harbrace Guide to Dictionaries.* New York: Harcourt, Brace & World, 1963.

HISTORIES

Mencken, H. L. *The American Language.* New York: Knopf, 1936.

Pei, Mario. *The Story of Language.* New York: New American Library, 1960.

PHRASES: Funk, Charles E. *A Hog on Ice.* New York: Harper, 1948.

PRONUNCIATION: Bender, James Frederick. *NBC Handbook of Pronunciation.* 3d ed. rev. New York: Crowell, 1964.

RHYMING: Wood, Clement. *The Complete Rhyming Dictionary.* New York: Halcyon House, 1936.

SEMANTICS: Hayakawa, S. I. *Language in Thought and Action.* New York: Harcourt, Brace, 1949.

SLANG: Partridge, Eric. *A Dictionary of Slang and Unconventional English.* New York: Macmillan, 1961.

SYNONYMS: *Webster's Dictionary of Synonyms.* Springfield, Mass.: Merriam, 1951.

USAGE: Evans, Bergen. *A Dictionary of Contemporary American Usage.* New York: Random House, 1957.

5.3 Foreign-Language Dictionaries

Cassell & Heath publishes series in many languages in the following types:

1. Standard dictionary of foreign language
2. Bilingual dictionary (the foreign language with the English equivalent)
3. Polylingual dictionary (equivalents of several languages)

GUIDE TO FOREIGN-LANGUAGE DICTIONARIES: Collison, Robert L. *Dictionaries of Foreign Languages*. New York: Hafner, 1955.

6. Books about People

6.1 General Books

Dictionary of American Biography. 11 vols. New York: Scribner's, 1957.

Dictionary of National Biography. 27 vols. London: Oxford Univ. Press, 1959.

The National Cyclopedia of American Biography. New York: T. White & Co., 1891.

The New Century Cyclopedia of Names. 3 vols. New York: Appleton-Century-Crofts, 1954.

Webster's Biographical Dictionary. Rev. ed. Springfield, Mass.: Merriam, 1970.

Who Was Who (English). London: Black, 1897—.

Who Was Who in America. Chicago: Marquis Co., 1942—.

6.2 Current Books

Current Biography Yearbook. New York: Wilson, 1940—.

Who's Who (English). London: A. & C. Black, annual.

Who's Who in America. Chicago: A. N. Marquis Co., annual.

6.3 Directories

City directories.

Telephone directories.

Specialized directories of people in various professions and fields.

6.4 Directory of Biographical Material

Biography Index. New York: Wilson, 1946—.

7. Books about Places

7.1 Atlases

Bartholomew, John George. *Physical World Atlas*. 5th ed. New York: American Map Co., 1966.

Goode, John Paul. *Goode's World Atlas*. 15th ed. Chicago: Rand McNally, 1964.

National Geographic Atlas of the World. 3d ed. Washington, D.C.: National Geographic Society, 1970.

Pergamon World Atlas. Oxford: Pergamon Press, 1968.

Road Atlas of the U.S., Canada and Mexico. Chicago: Rand McNally, annual.

Bartholomew, John. *The Times Atlas of the World*. Midcentury ed. 5 vols. London: *Times* Publishing Co., 1955–1959.

7.2 Gazetteers

The *Columbia-Lippincott Gazetteer of the World*. New York: Columbia Univ. Press, 1962.

Larousse Encyclopedia of World Geography. New York: Odyssey Press, 1965.

Monkhouse, Francis John. *A Dictionary of Geography*. 2d ed. Chicago: Aldine Publishing Co., 1970.

Stewart, George Rippey. *American Place-Names*. New York: Oxford Univ. Press, 1970.

7.3 Special Atlases

Atlas of the Universe. Chicago: Rand McNally, 1961.

Atlas of Southeast Asia. London: Macmillan, 1964.

Fox, Edward Whiting. *Atlas of American History*. New York: Oxford Univ. Press, 1964.

Gilbert, Martin. *Recent History Atlas, 1870 to the Present Day*. New York: Macmillan, 1969.

North American Aviation, Inc. *Lunar Atlas*. New York: Dover, 1968.

Oxford Regional Economic Atlas: United States and Canada. Oxford: Clarendon, 1967.

Vilnay, Zee. *The New Israel Atlas, Bible to Present Day*. New York: McGraw-Hill, 1969.

7.4 Guidebooks and Travelers' Manuals

Baedeker, Karl. *Auto Guide to* [*various countries*]. New York: Macmillan, annual.

Fodor, Eugene. *Fodor's Guide to* [*various countries.*] New York: McKay, 1953—, annual.

Gresswell, R. Kay, and Huxley, Anthony. *Standard Encyclopedia of the World's Rivers and Lakes*. New York: Putnam, 1966.

Matthews, William H. *A Guide to the National Parks*. Garden City, N.Y.: Natural History Press, 1968.

Appendix B

Selected Bibliography of Specific Reference Works

Reference works, including bibliographies, for the major academic disciplines are listed here. The general Dewey decimal and Library of Congress designations appear after each heading. This bibliography is representative of the numerous reference works in the various areas.

1. Anthropology (570–573; G)

Frazer, J. G. *The Golden Bough.* 12 vols. London: Macmillan, 1911–1915.

International Bibliography of Social and Cultural Anthropology. Paris: UNESCO, 1955–1959, annual. Chicago: Aldine, 1960—.

Kroeber, A. L., ed. *Anthropology Today: An Encyclopedic Inventory.* Chicago: Univ. of Chicago Press, 1953.

2. Arts

2.1 General Works

Art Index: a cumulative author & subj. index to a selected list of f.a. periodicals. New York: Wilson, 1929—.

Larousse Encyclopedias
Prehistoric and Ancient Art (1962)
Byzantine and Medieval Art (1963)
Modern Art (1965)
(New York: Prometheus Press.)

Myers, Bernard S. *McGraw-Hill Dictionary of Art.* 5 vols. New York: McGraw-Hill, 1969.

Osborne, Harold. *The Oxford Companion to Art.* Oxford: Clarendon Press, 1970.

Read, Herbert, ed. *Encyclopaedia of the Arts.* New York: Meredith Press, 1966.

Runes, Dagobert D., and Schrickel, Harry G. *Encyclopedia of the Arts.* New York: Philosophical Library, 1946.

2.2 Architecture (720–729; NA NK)

Briggs, Martin. *Everyman's Concise Encyclopaedia of Architecture.* New York: Dutton, 1959.

Columbia University. *Avery Index to Architectural Periodicals.* 12 vols. Boston: G. K. Hall, 1963. Supplements: 1st, 1965; 2d, 1966; 3d, 1967; 4th, 1968.

Hatje, Gerd, ed. *Encyclopaedia of Modern Architecture.* London: Thames and Hudson, 1963.

2.3 Graphic Arts (740–749, 760–769; NC)

Who's Who in Graphic Art. Zurich, Switzerland: Amstutz and Herdeg Graphic Press, 1962.

2.4 Music (780–789; M)

Apel, Willi. *Harvard Dictionary of Music.* 2d ed. Cambridge, Mass.: Harvard Univ. Press, 1969.

Blom, Eric, ed. *Grove's Dictionary of Music and Musicians.* 9 vols. and supplement. New York: St. Martin's Press, 1970.

Cross, Milton, and Ewen, David. *The Milton Cross New Encyclopedia of the Great Composers and Their Music.* 2 vols. Garden City: Doubleday, 1969.

Lloyd, Norman. *The Golden Encyclopedia of Music.* New York: Golden Press, 1968.

Roxon, Lillian. *Rock Encyclopedia.* New York: Grosset & Dunlap, 1969.

Scholes, Percy A. *The Oxford Companion to Music.* London: Oxford Univ. Press, 1970.

Westrup, Jack. *Everyman's Dictionary of Music.* New York: Dutton, 1971.

2.5 Painting (750–759; ND)

Champlin, John Denison. *Cyclopedia of Painters and Paintings.* 4 vols. New York: Scribner's, 1913.

Lake, Carlton, and Maillard, Robert. *Dictionary of Modern Painting.* New York: Tudor Publishing Co., 1965.

Myers, Bernard S., ed. *Encyclopedia of Painting.* 3d ed. New York: Crown, 1970.

2.6 Performing Arts (Theater: 791–792, G; Ballet and Opera: 780–789, M)

Balanchine, George. *Balanchine's New Complete Stories of the Great Ballets.* Garden City: Doubleday, 1968.

Freedley, George, and Reeves, John A. *A History of the Theatre.* New York: Crown, 1955.

Green, Stanley. *The World of Musical Comedy.* Rev. ed. New York: A. S. Barnes & Co., 1968.

Hartnoll, Phyllis. *The Oxford Companion to the Theatre.* London: Oxford Univ. Press, 1951.

Loewenberg, Alfred. *Annals of Opera, 1597–1940.* Geneva: Societas Bibliographica, 1955. Vol. 1, text; Vol. 2, indexes.

Moore, Frank L. *Handbook of World Opera.* London: Arthur Barker, 1961.

Parker, John, ed. *Who's Who in the Theatre* (American Stage). New York: Pitman, 1967.

2.7 Photography (770–779; TR)

The Encyclopedia of Photography. 20 vols. New York: Greystone Press, 1963.

The Focal Encyclopedia of Photography. 2 vols. New York: McGraw-Hill, 1969.

Spottiswoode, Raymond. *The Focal Encyclopedia of Film and Television.* New York: Hastings House, 1969.

2.8 Sculpture and Related Arts (730–739; NB)

Koepf, Hans. *Masterpieces of Sculpture from the Greeks to Modern Times.* New York: Putnam's, 1966.

Selz, Jean. *Modern Sculpture: Origins and Evolution.* New York: Braziller, 1963.

3. Economics (330–339; H)

Bach, G. L. *Economics: An Introduction to Analysis and Policy.* 7th ed. Englewood Cliffs, N.J.: Prentice-Hall, 1971.

Bogue, Donald J., and Beale, Calvin L. *Economic Areas of the United States.* New York: Free Press, 1961.

Business Periodical Index. New York: Wilson, 1958––, monthly.

Chalmers, J. A., and Leonard, F. H. *Economic Principles: Macroeconomic Theory and Policy.* New York: Macmillan, 1971.

Economic Abstracts. The Hague: Martinus Nijhoff, 1953––, semimonthly.

Garcia, F. L. *Encyclopaedia of Banking and Finance.* 6th ed. Boston: Bankers Publishing Co., 1962.

Lipsey, Richard G., and Steiner, Peter O. *Economics.* 4th ed.   New York: Harper & Row, 1975.

4. Education (370–379; L)

Atkinson, Carroll, and Maleska, Eugene T. *The Story of Education.* New York: Chilton Co., 1962.

Ebel, Robert L. *Encyclopedia of Educational Research.* 4th ed. New York: Macmillan, 1969.

Education Index. New York: Wilson, 1929––, monthly.

Good, Carter V. *Dictionary of Education.* 3d ed. New York: McGraw-Hill, 1973.

Good, H. G., and Teller, James D. *A History of Western Education.* 3d ed. New York: Macmillan, 1969.

Harris, Chester, ed. *Encyclopedia of Educational Research.* 3d ed. New York: Macmillan, 1960.

5. Geography (900–919; G)

See "Books about Places," appendix A, p. 258.

6. History (920–999; D, E, F)

Adams, James Truslow, ed. *Dictionary of American History.* 4 vols., index. New York: Scribner's, 1940.

America: History and Life (A guide to periodical literature). Santa Barbara: American Bibliographical Center, 1964—.

Beard, Charles, and Beard, Mary. *The Rise of American Civilization.* 2 vols. New York: Macmillan, 1927.

Bury, John B., et al., eds. *Cambridge Ancient History.* 12 vols., text; 5 vols., plates. Cambridge: Cambridge Univ. Press, 1923–1939.

Carman, Harry J., et al., eds. *A History of the American People.* 2 vols. New York: Knopf, 1960.

Carruth, Gorton, ed. *Encyclopedia of American Facts and Dates.* 5th ed. New York: Thomas Y. Crowell, 1970.

Clark, George, et al., eds. *New Cambridge Modern History.* 14 vols., atlas. Cambridge: Cambridge Univ. Press, 1957—.

Encyclopedia Canadiana. 10 vols. Toronto: Grolier of Canada, 1966.

Fox, D. R., and Schlesinger, A. M., eds. *A History of American Life.* 12 vols. New York: Macmillan, 1950.

Gwatkin, Henry M., et al., eds. *Cambridge Medieval History.* 8 vols. Cambridge: Cambridge Univ. Press, 1911–1936.

History of Mankind. 6 vols. New York: Harper & Row, 1963–1966.

Langer, William L., ed. *An Encyclopedia of World History.* Boston: Houghton Mifflin, 1952.

Morris, Richard B., ed. *Encyclopedia of American History.* Rev. ed. New York: Harper & Row, 1976.

National Historical Publications Commission. *Writings on American History.* Washington, D.C.: Government Printing Office, 1908—, annual.

Ostrander, Gilman M. *A Profile History of the United States.* 2d ed. New York: McGraw-Hill, 1972.

Ridpath, John Clark. *History of the World.* 4 vols. New York: Merrill & Baker, 1897.

Story, Norah. *The Oxford Companion to Canadian History and Literature.* New York: Oxford Univ. Press, 1967.

Williams, Henry Smith. *The Historians' History of the World.* 25 vols. New York: Outlook Co., 1904.

Zabre, Alfonso Teja. *Guide to the History of Mexico: A Modern Interpretation.* New York: Pemberton Press, 1969.

7. Language (400–499; P)

See "Books about Words," appendix A, p. 257.

8. Law (340–349; K)

Black, Henry Campbell. *Black's Law Dictionary,* 4th ed. St. Paul, Minn.: West Publishing Co., 1951.

Gerhart, Eugene C., ed. *Quote It! Memorable Legal Quotations*. New York: Clark Boardman Co., 1969.

Index to Legal Periodicals. New York: Wilson, 1908—.

Jackson, Percival E. *Dissent in the Supreme Court*. Norman: Univ. of Oklahoma Press, 1969.

9. Literature

9.1 General Works (800–809; P)

Kunitz, Stanley. *Twentieth-Century Authors* (with supplement). New York: Wilson, 1942–1955.

Myers, Robin, ed. *A Dictionary of Literature in the English Language from Chaucer to 1940*. New York: Pergamon Press, 1970.

Shipley, Joseph T. *Dictionary of World Literature*. New York: Philosophical Library, 1943.

Smith, Horatio, ed. *Columbia Dictionary of Modern European Literature*. New York: Columbia Univ. Press, 1947.

Steinberg, S. H., ed. *Cassell's Encyclopaedia of World Literature*. 2 vols. New York: Funk & Wagnalls, 1954.

Thrall, William Flint, and Hibbard, Addison. *A Handbook to Literature*. Rev. and enl. C. Hugh Holman. New York: Odyssey Press, 1960.

9.2 American Literature (810–819; PS)

Hart, James D. *The Oxford Companion to American Literature*. 4th ed. New York: Oxford Univ. Press, 1961.

Herzberg, Max J. *The Reader's Encyclopedia of American Literature*. New York: Thomas Y. Crowell, 1962.

Hubbell, Jay B. *The South in American Literature, 1607–1900*. Durham, N.C.: Duke Univ. Press, 1954.

Leary, Lewis. *Articles on American Literature Appearing in Current Periodicals, 1900–1950*. Durham, N.C.; Duke Univ. Press, 1954.

Richards, Robert Fulton, ed. *Concise Dictionary of American Literature*. New York: Philosophical Library, 1955.

Spiller, Robert E., et al., eds. *Literary History of the United States*. 3d ed. New York: Macmillan, 1963.

9.3 English Literature (820–829; PR)

Bateson, F. W., ed. *Cambridge Bibliography of English Literature*. 4 vols. New York: Macmillan, 1941. Supplement, 1957.

Baugh, Albert C. *A Literary History of England*. New York: Appleton-Century-Crofts, 1948.

English Association. *The Year's Work in English Studies*. Oxford: University Press, 1921—, annual. (Recent editions include a section on American literature.)

Harvey, Paul, ed. *The Oxford Companion to English Literature*. Oxford: Clarendon Press, 1953.

Ward, A. W., and Waller, A. R. *The Cambridge History of English Literature.* 14 vols.; index. Cambridge: Cambridge Univ. Press, 1963.

9.4 Foreign Literature (830–899; P)

CHINESE: Giles, Herbert A. *A History of Chinese Literature.* With a supplement on the Modern Period by Liu Wu-Chi. New York: Frederick Ungar, 1967.

CLASSICAL

Duff, J. Wight. *A Literary History of Rome.* 3d ed. Ed. A. M. Duff. New York: Barnes & Noble, 1960.

Harvey, Paul, ed. *The Oxford Companion to Classical Literature.* Oxford: Clarendon Press, 1966.

FRENCH: Harvey, Paul, and Heseltine, J. E. *The Oxford Companion to French Literature.* Oxford: Clarendon Press, 1959.

GERMAN: Robertson, J. G. *A History of German Literature.* Rev. Edna Purdie. New York: British Book Centre, 1962.

ITALIAN: Wilkins, Ernest Hatch. *A History of Italian Literature.* Cambridge, Mass.: Harvard Univ. Press, 1962.

JEWISH: Waxman, Meyer. *A History of Jewish Literature.* 5 vols. New York: Thomas, Yoseloff, 1960.

MEXICAN: Peña, Carlos Gonzales. *History of Mexican Literature.* Dallas, Tex.: Southern Methodist Univ. Press, 1968.

POLISH: Milosz, Czeslaw. *The History of Polish Literature.* New York: Macmillan, 1969.

RUSSIAN

Waliszewski, K. *A History of Russian Literature.* New York: Appleton, 1927.

Mirsky, D. S. *A History of Russian Literature.* New York: Vintage-Knopf, 1960.

SCANDINAVIAN: Bach, Giovanni, et al. *The History of the Scandinavian Literatures.* New York: Dial Press, 1938.

SPANISH-AMERICAN: Anderson-Imbert, Enrique. *A History of Spanish-American Literature.* 2 vols. Detroit: Wayne State Univ. Press, 1969.

SPANISH: Ticknor, George. *History of Spanish Literature.* 6th ed. New York: Gordian Press, 1965.

10. Mathematics (510–519; QA)

Grazda, Edward E. *Handbook of Applied Mathematics.* Princeton, N.J.: Van Nostrand, 1966.

Hogben, Lancelot. *Mathematics for the Millions.* Rev. ed. New York: W. W. Norton, 1968.

Mathematical Reviews. Lancaster, Pa.: American Mathematical Society, 1940—, monthly, with annual cumulations.

Newman, James R., ed. *The World of Mathematics.* 4 vols. New York: Simon & Schuster, 1956.

11. Medicine (610–619; R)

Current Medical Information and Terminology. 4th ed. Chicago: American Medical Association, 1971.

Family Health Encyclopedia (An International Reference in the Health Sciences). 2 vols. Philadelphia: J. B. Lippincott, 1971.

Fishbein, Morris, ed. *New Illustrated Medical and Health Encyclopedia*. 8 vols. New York: H. S. Stuttman, 1971.

Gomez, Joan. *A Dictionary of Symptoms*. New York: Stein & Day, 1968.

Rothenberg, Robert E. *The New American Medical Dictionary and Health Manual*. New York: World, 1971.

Schmidt, J. E. *Medical Discoveries: Who and When*. Springfield, Ill.: Charles C. Thomas, 1959.

Thomson, William A., ed. *Black's Medical Dictionary*. 31st ed. New York: Barnes & Noble, 1976.

12. Military History and Science (355–359; U, V)

Albion, Robert G. *Introduction to Military History*. New York: AMS Press, 1971.

Dupuy, Ernest R., and Dupuy, Trevor N. *Encyclopedia of Military History*. Rev. ed. New York: Harper & Row, 1976.

Fuller, J. F. C. *Military History of the Western World*. 3 vols. New York: Funk & Wagnalls, 1954–1956.

Miller, W. R. *Bibliography of Books on War, Pacifism, Nonviolence and Related Studies*. Nyack, N.Y.: Fellowship of Reconciliation, 1960.

Naroll, Raoul, and Bullough, Vern L. *Military Deterence in History: A Statistical Survey*. Albany, N.Y.: State Univ. of New York Press, 1971.

Portway, Donald. *Military Science Today*. 3d ed. New York: Oxford Univ. Press, 1957.

Preston, Richard, and Wise, Sidney. *Men in Arms: A History of Warfare and Its Interrelationships with Western Society*. Rev. ed. New York: Praeger Publishers, 1970.

13. Philosophy, Psychology, and Related Disciplines (100–199; B)

Baldwin, James Mark, ed. *Dictionary of Philosophy and Psychology*. 3 vols. New York: Macmillan, 1911.

Brussel, James A. *The Layman's Guide to Psychiatry*. 2d ed. New York: Barnes & Noble, 1967.

Deutsch, Albert, ed. *The Encyclopedia of Mental Health*. 6 vols. New York: Franklin Watts, 1963.

Edwards, Paul. *The Encyclopedia of Philosophy*. 8 vols. New York: Macmillan, 1967.

Eidelberg, Ludwig, ed. *Encyclopedia of Psychoanalysis*. New York: Free Press, 1968.

Groth, Alexander J. *Major Ideologies: An Interpretative Survey of Democracy, Socialism and Nationalism*. New York: Wiley Interscience, 1972.

Psychological Abstracts. Lancaster, Pa.: American Psychological Association, 1927—, monthly, with annual cumulations.

Psychological Index. 42 vols. Princeton, N.J.: Psychological Review Co., 1894–1935. (Publication ceased in 1935.)

Redlich, Fredrick C. *The Theory and Practice of Psychiatry*. New York: Basic Books, 1966.

Snadowsky, Alvin M. *Social Psychology Research: Laboratory-Field Relationships*. New York: Free Press, 1972.

Urmson, J. O., ed. *The Concise Encyclopedia of Western Philosophy and Philosophers*. New York: Hawthorn Books, 1960.

14. Political Science (320–329; J)

Dunner, Joseph. *Dictionary of Political Science*. New York: Philosophical Library, 1964.

Emerson, Thomas I., and Haber, David. *Political and Civil Rights in the United States* (A Collection of Legal and Related Materials). 2 vols. Buffalo, N.Y.: Dennis & Co., 1958.

Harmon, Robert B. *Political Science: A Bibliographical Guide to the Literature*. New York: Scarecrow Press, 1965. Supplement, 1965.

International Bibliography of Political Science. Paris: UNESCO, 1953 —, annual.

McLaughlin, Andrew C., and Hart, Albert Bushnell. *Cyclopedia of American Government*. 3 vols. New York: Appleton, 1914.

Sperber, Hans, and Trittschuh, Travis. *American Political Terms*. Detroit: Wayne State Univ. Press, 1962.

15. Religion (200–299; B)

Ackroyd, P. R., and Evans, C. F. *The Cambridge History of the Bible*. 3 vols. Cambridge: Cambridge Univ. Press, 1970.

Brandon, S. G. F. *A Dictionary of Comparative Religion*. New York: Scribner's, 1970.

Bulfinch, Thomas. *Bulfinch's Mythology*. New York: Thomas Y. Crowell, 1913.

Catholic Periodical Index. New York: Catholic Library Association, 1939—, quarterly, with biennial cumulations.

Cross, F. L., ed. *The Oxford Dictionary of the Christian Church*. New York: Oxford Univ. Press, 1957.

Fox, William Sherwood. *The Mythology of All Races*. 13 vols. New York: Cooper Square Publishers, 1964.

Ellison, John W., comp. *Nelson's Complete Concordance of the Revised Standard Version Bible*. New York: Thomas Nelson and Sons, 1957.

The Interpreter's Bible. 12 vols. New York: Abingdon-Cokesbury Press, 1951–1957.

M'Clintock, John, and Strong, James. *Cyclopaedia of Biblical, Theological, and Ecclesiastical Literature.* 10 vols. New York: Arno Press, 1969.

Mead, Frank S. *Handbook of Denominations in the United States.* 4th ed. New York: Abingdon-Cokesbury, 1965.

Wace, Henry, and Piercy, William C. *A Dictionary of Christian Biography and Literature.* Boston: Little, Brown, 1911.

Wedeck, H. E., and Baskin, Wade. *Dictionary of Pagan Religions.* New York: Philosophical Library, 1971.

16. Sociology (300–309; HM)

International Encyclopaedia of the Social Sciences. 17 vols. New York: Macmillan, 1968.

Faris, Robert, ed. *Handbook of Modern Sociology.* Chicago: Rand McNally, 1964.

Gould, Julius, and Kolb, William L. *A Dictionary of the Social Sciences.* New York: Free Press, 1964.

Horton, Paul B., and Hunt, Chester L. *Sociology.* 3d ed. New York: McGraw-Hill, 1972.

Lindzey, Gardner, and Aronson, Elliot, eds. *The Handbook of Social Psychology.* 5 vols. Menlo Park, Calif.: Addison-Wesley Publishing Co., 1968.

Parsons, Talcott, et al., eds. *Theories of Society.* 2 vols. New York: Free Press, 1961.

Ricci, David M. *Community Power and Democratic Theory.* New York: Random House, 1971.

Sociological Abstracts. New York: Sociological Abstracts, Inc., 1952––, published several times yearly.

Vallier, Ivan, ed. *Comparative Methods in Sociology.* Berkeley: Univ. of California Press, 1971.

17. Science (500–599; Q) and Technology (600–699; T)

Alford, M. H., and Alford, V. L. *Russian-English Scientific & Technical Dictionary.* New York: Pergamon, 1970.

American Men of Science. 11th ed. New York: Bowker, 1968.

Applied Science and Technology Index. New York: Wilson, 1958––, monthly, with quarterly and annual cumulations.

Basic Bibliography of Science and Technology. New York: McGraw-Hill, 1966.

Biological Abstracts. Philadelphia: Univ. of Pennsylvania Press, 1926––, semimonthly, with annual cumulations.

Biological and Agricultural Index. New York: Wilson, 1964––, monthly.

Collocott, T. C., ed. *Chambers Dictionary of Science and Technology.* New York: Harper & Row, 1972.

Chemical Abstracts. Easton, Pa.: American Chemical Society, 1907––, biweekly, with annual cumulations.

Condon, E. U., and Odishaw, H. *Handbook of Physics*. 2d ed. New York: McGraw-Hill, 1967.

Cook's and Diner's Dictionary. New York: Funk and Wagnall's, 1968.

Dictionary of Scientific Biography. New York: Scribner's, 1970.

Encyclopedia of Science and Technology. 15 vols. New York: McGraw-Hill, 1971.

Forbes, Reginald Dundendale. *Forestry Handbook*. New York: Ronald Press, 1955.

Gray, H. J., ed. *Dictionary of Physics*. London: Longmans, Green, 1958.

Gray, Peter, ed. *The Encyclopedia of the Biological Sciences*. New York: Reinhold, 1961.

Henderson, I. F., and Henderson, W. D. *A Dictionary of Biological Terms*. Princeton, N.J.: Van Nostrand, 1963. (8th ed. by J. H. Kenneth.)

Hughe, L. E., et al. *Dictionary of Electronics and Nucleonics*. New York: Barnes & Noble, 1970.

International Encyclopedia of Chemical Science. Princeton, N.J.: Van Nostrand, 1964.

Johnson, Irma. *Selected Books and Journals in Science and Engineering*. 2d ed. Boston: Massachusetts Institute of Technology, 1959.

Jones, Franklin D., and Schubert, Paul B. *Engineering Encyclopedia*. New York: Industrial Press, 1963.

de Kerchove, Rene. *International Maritime Dictionary*. 2d ed. Princeton, N.J.: Van Nostrand, 1961.

Manly, Harold P. *Drake's Radio and Television Electronic Dictionary*. New York: Drake Publishers, 1971.

Nuclear Science Abstracts. Washington, D.C.: Atomic Energy Commission, 1948—, semimonthly.

Neidhart, P., ed. *Television Engineering and Television Electronics Technical Dictionary*. New York: Pergamon, 1964.

Physics Abstracts. London: Institute of Electrical Engineers, 1898—, monthly.

Rose, Arthur, and Rose, Elizabeth. *Condensed Chemical Dictionary*. 7th ed. New York: Reinhold, 1966.

Van Nostrand's Scientific Encyclopedia. 4th ed. Princeton, N.J.: Van Nostrand, 1968.

Winburne, John N., ed. *A Dictionary of Agricultural and Allied Terminology*. East Lansing: Michigan State Univ. Press, 1962.

Yearbook of Science and Technology (Preview of 1971 and Review of 1970). New York: McGraw-Hill, 1971.

Appendix C

Bibliography of Selected Works on Research and Writing

1. Research

1.1 General Works

Downs, Robert. *How to do Library Research*. Urbana: Univ. of Illinois Press, 1966.

Hillway, Tyrus. *Introduction to Research*. 2d ed. Boston: Houghton Mifflin, 1964.

Morse, Grant W. *The Concise Guide to Library Research*. New York: Washington Square Press, 1966.

1.2 Arts

Duffied, Holley G. *Problems in the Criticism of the Arts*. Scranton, Pa.: Chandler, 1968.

Osborne, Harold. *Art of Appreciation*. New York: Oxford Univ. Press, 1970.

Rosenberg, J. *On Quality in Art: Criteria of Excellence, Past and Present*. Bollinger Series, Vol. 35. Princeton, N.J.: Princeton Univ. Press, 1967.

Stolnitz, Jerome. *Aesthetics and Philosophy of Art Criticism*. Boston: Houghton Mifflin, 1959.

Wingless Pegasus: A Handbook for Critics. Baltimore: Johns Hopkins, 1950.

1.3 Social Sciences (Education, Psychology, Sociology)

Beckman, Leonard, and Henchy, Thomas. *Beyond the Laboratory: Field Research in Social Psychology*. New York: McGraw-Hill, 1972.

Gephart, William J., and Ingle, Robert B., eds. *Educational Research: Selected Readings*. Columbus, Ohio: Charles E. Merrill, 1969.

Good, Carter V., and Scates, Douglas E. *Methods of Research: Educational, Psychological, Sociological*. New York: Appleton-Century-Crofts, 1954.

Junker, Buford H. *Field Work: An Introduction to the Social Sciences.* Chicago: Univ. of Chicago Press, 1960.

McInnis, Raymond G., and Scott, James W. *Social Science Research Handbook.* New York: Barnes & Noble, 1975.

Phillips, Bernard S. *Social Research: Strategy and Tactics.* New York: Macmillan, 1966.

1.4 History

Barzun, Jacques, and Graff, Henry F. *The Modern Researcher.* Rev. ed. New York: Harcourt, Brace, 1970.

Baum, Willa K. *Oral History for the Local Historical Society.* Stockton, Calif.: Conference of California Historical Societies, 1969.

Dixon, Elizabeth I., and Mink, James V. *Oral History at Arrowhead* (The Proceedings of the First National Colloquium on Oral History). Los Angeles: Oral History Association, 1967.

Guide to Computer-Assisted Historical Research. Austin: Univ. of Texas Press, 1969.

Hockett, Homer Carey. *The Critical Method in Historical Research and Writing.* New York: Macmillan, 1955.

Kent, Sherman. *Writing History.* 2d ed. Appleton-Century-Crofts, 1967.

Vansina, Jan. *Oral Tradition: A Study in Historical Methodology.* Tr. H. M. Wright. Chicago: Aldine, 1965.

Vines, Kenneth; Newman, Alan; and Patterson, John. *Research in American Politics.* New York: Holt, Rinehart & Winston, 1971.

Winkes, Robin W., ed. *Historian as Detective: Essays on Evidence.* New York: Harper & Row, 1970.

1.5 Literature

Drewry, John E. *Writing Book Reviews.* Boston: The Writer, 1966.

Guerin, Wilfred, et al. *A Handbook of Critical Approaches to Literature.* New York: Harper & Row, 1966.

Hyman, Stanley Edgar. *The Armed Vision: A Study in the Methods of Literary Criticism.* Rev. ed. New York: Vintage Books, 1955.

Sanders, Chauncey. *An Introduction to Research in English Literary History.* New York: Macmillan, 1952.

1.6 Science and Technology

Ehrlich, Eugene, and Murphy, Daniel. *The Art of Technical Writing.* New York: Thomas Y. Crowell, 1964.

Emberger, Meta Riley, and Hall, Marian Ross. *Scientific Writing.* New York: Harcourt, Brace, 1955.

Freedman, Paul. *The Principles of Scientific Research.* New York: Pergamon Press, 1960.

Jones, W. Paul. *Writing Scientific Papers and Reports.* 6th ed. Dubuque, Iowa: William C. Brown Co., 1971.

Janis, J. Harold. *The Business Research Paper*. New York: Hobbs, Dorman & Co., 1967.

Mills, Gordon H., and Walter, John A. *Technical Writing*. New York: Holt, Rinehart & Winston, 1962.

Wilson, E. Bright, Jr. *An Introduction to Scientific Research*. New York: McGraw-Hill, 1952.

2. Writing

Brooks, Cleanth, and Warren, Robert Penn. *Modern Rhetoric*. 2d ed. New York: Harcourt, Brace & World, 1958.

Cousins, Norman, ed. *Writing for Love or Money* (A collection of 35 essays first appearing in *Saturday Review*). New York: Longmans, Green, 1949.

Gunning, Robert. *The Technique of Clear Writing*. New York: McGraw-Hill, 1968.

McCrimmon, James M. *Writing with a Purpose*. 5th ed. Boston: Houghton Mifflin, 1974.

Strunk, William. *The Elements of Style*. With revisions, an introduction and a new chapter on writing by E. B. White. New York: Macmillan, 1972.

Vrooman, Alan H. *Good Writing: An Informal Manual of Style*. New York: Atheneum, 1967.

Zinsser, William. *On Writing Well*. New York: Harper & Row, 1976.

3. Preparation of Visual Materials

Arkin, Herbert, and Colton, Raymond R. *Graphs: How to Make and Use Them*. New York: Harper and Brothers, 1940.

Brown, Lloyd A. *Map Making: The Art that Became a Science*. Boston: Little, Brown, 1960.

Gill, Bob, and Lewis, John. *Illustration: Aspects and Directions*. New York: Reinhold, 1964.

Papp, Charles E. *Scientific Illustration*. Dubuque, Iowa: William C. Brown Publishers, 1968.

Pitz, Henry C. *The Practice of Illustration*. New York: Watson-Guptill Publications, 1947.

Rogers, Anna C. *Graphic Charts Handbook*. Washington, D.C.: Public Affairs Press, 1961.

Schmid, Calvin F. *Handbook of Graphic Presentation*. New York: Ronald Press, 1954.

Spear, Mary Eleanor. *Practical Charting Techniques*. New York: McGraw-Hill, 1969.

Zaidenberg, Arthur. *Illustrating and Cartooning*. Garden City, N.Y.: Doubleday, 1959.

Zweifel, Frances. *A Handbook of Biological Illustration*. Chicago: Univ. of Chicago Press, 1961.

Appendix D

Forms for Documentary Notes

This guide gives the forms for documenting the major kinds of source materials. However, it is likely that you will occasionally encounter problems in documentation that are not covered in the following pages. Through applying the basic principles of documentation, along with a little common sense, you will be able to meet most problems.

Keep in mind that the documentary note (citation) provides information on the following four aspects in this order:

1. Authorship (if known)
2. Title of work
3. Publication information
4. Place in the work from which the information was taken

For further discussion and information on documentation, see the following sections in this book:

1. Purposes and procedures, chapter 6. p. 128.
2. Footnotes and note pages, chapter 9, p. 241.
3. Abbreviations, appendix F, p. 295.

In case of problems in a specific field, you should consult a standard work in that field to use as a model or a specialized handbook on research. Also, many departments publish style books that give instructions on documentary forms peculiar to specific areas of research.

Finally, remember that the form is only a means to an end. The real reason for documentation is to give proper credit for the sources you have used in your written work.

Key to Documentary Forms

This key first lists the basic sources: first citations and subsequent and continuing citations. It then gives an alphabetical listing of other sources. Each source is numbered to direct you to the specific section that treats the source in detail.

Forms for Basic Sources: First Citations
    1. Books with one author
    2. Signed periodical articles
    3. Unsigned periodical articles
Forms for Basic Sources: Subsequent and Continuing Citations
    4. Books with one author
    5. Signed and unsigned periodical articles
    6. Example of a series of citations
Forms for Other Sources: First, Subsequent, and Continuing Citations
    7. Abridged works (see 12.2)
    8. Afterwords (see 18)
    9. Anthologies and collections
  10. Bible
  11. Collaborations
  12. Edited, abridged, translated, and supplemented works
  13. Editions and series
  14. Encyclopedias
  15. Foreign language sources
  16. Government documents (see 23.2)
  17. Graphic materials
  18. Introductory material and afterwords
  19. Legal and legislative sources
  20. Literary sources
  21. Newspapers and newsmagazines
  22. Oral sources
  23. Pamphlets and government documents
  24. Reference works
  25. Reviews
  26. Secondary quotations
  27. Series (see 13)
  28. Special authorship
  29. Supplemented works (see 12.4)
  30. Translated works (see 12.3)
  31. Two or more authors
  32. Unpublished works
  33. Volumes

Forms for Basic Sources: First Citations

1. BOOKS WITH ONE AUTHOR

[1] Robert B. Downs, *Books That Changed America* (New York, 1970), p. 107.

1.1 Specifics of form
Indent the first line five spaces from the left-hand margin.
Place the number of the note slightly above the rest of the line.
List the author's name in natural order.
Underline the title to denote italics.
Enclose the city and year of publication within parentheses.
Separate the parts of the note with commas.
Place a period at the end of the note.

2. SIGNED PERIODICAL ARTICLES
   [2] Omar Williams, "A Canadian Experience," *Essence* (August 1971), 59.

2.1 Specifics of Form
Indent, number the note, and list the author's name just as you do with books.
Enclose the title of the article within quotation marks. Underline the name of the periodical to denote italics.
The volume and issue numbers may be omitted when the date of publication is given.
Omit "p." or "pp." before the page number or numbers in the first citation.

3. UNSIGNED PERIODICAL ARTICLES
   [3] "Comstock Country," *The American West* (September 1970), 34.

3.1 Specifics of form
The form is exactly the same as that for a signed article except that the title comes first.

Forms for Basic Sources: Subsequent and Continuing Citations

4. BOOKS WITH ONE AUTHOR

4.1 When citing a work immediately after a first citation note, if the page number is the same, use this form:
   [4] Downs.

4.2 When citing a work immediately after a first citation note, if the page number is different, use this form:
   [5] Downs, p. 93.

4.3 When citing a work after an intervening citation or citations, use this form:
   [6] Downs, *Books*, p. 91.

4.4 You may abbreviate the title whenever possible as long as it is clear.

4.5 You may use "ibid." instead of the author's name in the notes in 4.1 and 4.2. However, the author's name is just as easy to write, and it is clearer to the average reader.

4.6 When there have been intervening citations, it is preferable to repeat the page number, even if it is the same page number that appeared in the earlier citation.

5. SIGNED AND UNSIGNED PERIODICAL ARTICLES

5.1 When citing an article immediately after a first citation note, if the page number is the same, use the appropriate form:
Signed article
   ⁷ Williams.
Unsigned article
   ⁸ "Comstock Country."

5.2 When citing an article immediately after a first citation note, if the page number is different, use this form:
Signed article
   ⁹ Williams, p. 60.
Unsigned article
   ¹⁰ "Comstock Country," p. 36.

5.3 When citing an article after an intervening citation or citations, use this form:
Signed article
   ¹¹ Williams, "Experience," p. 60.
Unsigned article
   ¹² "Comstock Country," p. 36.

5.4 You may abbreviate the title of the article whenever possible. However, it would not be wise to abbreviate a title such as "Comstock Country" in 5.3, because it is essentially a single term.

6. EXAMPLE OF A SERIES OF CITATIONS

For continuing citations, follow the same principles that apply to first and subsequent citations, as illustrated in this example of a series of citations:

First citation

   ¹ Robert B. Downs, *Books That Changed America* (New York, 1970), p. 107.

Subsequent citation; different page number

   ² Downs, p. 120.

Continuing citation; same page number as note 2

   ³ Downs.

First citation

   ⁴ Omar Williams, "A Canadian Experience," *Essence*, (August 1971), 59.

Continuing citation; different page number	[5] Downs, p. 123.
Subsequent citation; same page number as note 4	[6] Williams, "Experience," p. 59.
First citation	[7] "Comstock Country," *The American West*, (September 1970), 34.
Continuing citation; different page number	[8] Williams, "Experience," p. 60.
Continuing citation; same page number as note 5	[9] Downs, *Books*, p. 123.
Subsequent citation; different page number	[10] "Comstock Country," p. 36.

Forms for Other Sources: First, Subsequent, and Continuing Citations

Only the first citation form is given for the numerous other sources unless special directions are necessary. Otherwise, apply the same principles that directed the subsequent and continuing citations for basic sources.

7. ABRIDGED WORKS (SEE 12.2)

8. AFTERWORDS (SEE 18)

9. ANTHOLOGIES (ALSO CALLED COLLECTIONS)

9.1 Titled introductory material from an anthology

[1] Dorothy Van Ghent and Joseph S. Brown, eds., "The Ancient World," *Continental Literature* (Philadelphia, 1968), p. 5.

9.2 Untitled introductory material from an anthology
The introductory material is not always titled, or it may simply be called "Preface" or "Introduction." When citing untitled material, use either the single word ("Introduction" or "Preface") or enlarge on the title by adding descriptive words and placing them in brackets, as in this example:

[2] Irving Howe, ed., "Introduction [to *The Pupil*]," *Classics of Modern Fiction* (New York, 1968), p. 219.

9.3 Specific work from an anthology

⁴ Leonard J. Duhl, "Environmental Health: Politics, Planning, and Money," *The Vanishing Landscape,* ed. Donald G. Douglas and John R. Stewart (Skokie, Ill., 1970), p. 125.

10. BIBLE

10.1 First citation note
 ⁵ Jeremiah 5:14–17, The New English Bible.
 ⁶ Matthew 26:1, Revised Standard Version.

10.2 Parenthetical notes
After the version has been established in the first citation note, the following citations may be noted parenthetically, that is, enclosed in parentheses in the text. (See p. 133 for further discussion of parenthetical notes.) The names of the books of the Bible may also be abbreviated in the first citation note and in the parenthetical notes, as in these examples:
     (Jer. 5:14–17)
     (Matt. 26:1)

11. COLLABORATIONS

11.1 First citation note
Some books are "told to" another person or are written with the assistance of another person. For these works, the writer named first is the actual authority and receives the major credit. When citing a collaboration, use this form:
 ⁶ Malcolm X, with the assistance of Alex Haley, *The Autobiography of Malcolm X* (New York, 1965), p. 23.

11.2 Subsequent notes
The work would be identified by the first author in subsequent citations, as in these examples:
 ⁷ Malcolm X, p. 25.
 ⁸ Malcolm X, *Autobiography,* p. 217.

12. EDITED, ABRIDGED, TRANSLATED, AND SUPPLEMENTED WORKS

12.1 Major figure's work that has been edited
 ¹ Alexander Pope, *The Best of Pope,* ed. George Sherburne (New York, 1929), p. 78.

12.2 Major figure's work that has been abridged
 ² James Boswell, *Life of Johnson,* abridged by Charles G. Osgood (New York, 1945), p. 155.

12.3 Translated work
 ³ Jan Vansina, *Oral Tradition: A Study in Historical Methodology,* trans. from French by H. M. Wright (Chicago, 1965), p. 31.

12.4 Combinations
A single work may have been edited, abridged, translated, and

supplemented, or any combination of these. Here are examples showing how you would handle such works:

[11] Dietrich Bonhoeffer, *No Rusty Swords*, ed. and introd. by Edwin H. Robertson, trans. by Edwin H. Robertson and John Bowden (New York, 1965), p. 21.

[12] William Strunk, *The Elements of Style*, with revisions, an introduction, and a chapter on writing by E. B. White (New York, 1972), p. 20.

12.5 Variations in form
> The word "by" may be omitted in these notes, as in 12.1; however, its inclusion adds clarity to the citations.
> In some instances, you may omit the information regarding editing and the like if it does not seem important to the documentary note. However, the information should appear in the bibliographical entry.

13. EDITIONS AND SERIES

Books that stay in print over a number of years are often revised so that they will remain current. Give the edition or series number in the documentary note.

[2] W. Paul Jones, *Writing Scientific Papers*, 6th ed. (Dubuque, Iowa, 1971), p. 253.

[3] Frank N. Magill, ed., *Magill's Quotations in Context*, 2d series (New York, 1969), p. 211.

14. ENCYCLOPEDIAS

14.1 Signed articles
[1] John Bell Condliffe, "Free Trade," *Encyclopaedia Britannica* (1968), 853.

14.2 Unsigned articles
[2] "Gerard Ter Borch," *Encyclopedia Americana* (1965), 440.

14.3 Information on authors
> Most encyclopedia articles are signed, but some short ones are not. In some works, as in the *Britannica*, only initials appear at the end of each article. Full names are given elsewhere, for example, in the *Britannica* index volume.

15. FOREIGN-LANGUAGE SOURCES

15.1 Basic forms
> Follow the same forms as you would for English works. Write in accent marks, umlauts, and tildes as necessary. See the discussion of capitalization of titles in 15.2.

[1] "Biologia," *Monitor, enciclopedia salvat para todos* (1966), I, 315.

[2] A. Albert-Petit, *Histoire de Normandie* (Paris, 1911), p. 81.

[3] Erich Maria Remarque, *Der Himmel kennt keine Günstlinge* (Berlin, 1961), p. 207.

[4] Marcelino Menendez y Pelayo, *Historia de las ideas estéticas en españa* (Madrid, 1961), p. 161.

15.2 Capitalization of titles
      15.2.1 French and Italian
          Capitalize the initial article, the following noun, and an adjective that may come between the article and the noun. If a title begins with a word other than an article or an adjective, the following words, with the exception of proper nouns, are not capitalized.
      15.2.2 German
          Capitalize all nouns. Capitalize other words only when they are initial words.
      15.2.3 Greek and Latin
          Capitalize the first word only
      15.2.4 Spanish
          Capitalize the first word only.

16. GOVERNMENT DOCUMENTS (SEE 23.2)

17. GRAPHIC MATERIALS

When using reproductions of graphic materials, give credit to the source immediately after the caption. (See chapter 8, p. 183, for examples.) Give full bibliographical information in the bibliography.

18. INTRODUCTORY MATERIAL AND AFTERWORDS

18.1 Basic form
    When you are citing material in a work written by someone other than the author, follow this form:

[5] M. S. Handler, Introduction to *The Autobiography of Malcolm X* (New York, 1965), p. xiii.

[6] John Reilly, Afterword to *Native Son* by Richard Wright (New York, 1966), p. 397.

18.2 Variations
    When it is obvious who wrote the work, you do not need to include the major author's name, as in note 5 in 18.1; but when the title does not reveal the major author, you should include his name, as in note 6 in 18.1.
    18.2.1 Major author revealed in title

[7] F. N. Robinson, Introduction to *The Poetical Works of Chaucer* (Boston, 1933), p. xxi.

18.2.2 Major author not revealed in title

[8] Robert Brustein, Introduction to *The Old Glory* by Robert Lowell (New York, 1965), p. xii.

18.3 When you are citing introductory material or afterwords written by the author of the work, use this form:

[9] T. Harry Williams, Preface, *Huey Long* (New York: Knopf, 1970), p. ix.

19. LEGAL AND LEGISLATIVE SOURCES

19.1 Congressional bills
H. R. stands for "House and Senate Bill," 70 for the number of the bill.
19.1.1 First citation

[1] H. R. 70, 81st Cong., 1st Sess. (1949), p. 3.

19.1.2 Subsequent citations

[2] H. R. 70, p. 4.

19.2 *Congressional Record*
The page numbers in the bound volumes and the daily editions are not the same; thus, when citing from the daily edition, it is necessary to give the full date. The numbers immediately after *Cong. Rec.* denote the page number.
19.2.1 Bound volumes

[3] 94 *Cong. Rec.* 9761 (1948).

19.2.2 Daily editions

[4] 94 *Cong. Rec.* 9917 (Aug. 4, 1948).

19.3 Supreme Court cases
The numbers preceding "U.S." stand for the volume number; those after "U.S." stand for the page number.

[6] Jones v. Jones, 362 U.S. 258 (1960).

19.4 The same forms would apply to state and local legal documents. For a complete guide to documenting legal and legislative sources, see Miles O. Price and Harry Bitner, *Effective Legal Research,* 3d ed. (Boston: Little, Brown, 1969).

20. LITERARY SOURCES

20.1 Well-known literary works
When citing from a well-known literary work, you may omit publication details and the writer's first name. Even the writer's last name may be omitted from the note if his name is mentioned in the text. Of course, you will have to exercise your own judgment on how well known the work is. Another factor to consider is the audience for which you are writing. When the information regarding publication and author seems important,

then you should include it. Keep in mind, however, that these facts will always appear in the bibliography.

20.2 Essays

Enclose the title of the essay in quotation marks. The name of the work from which it is taken is not important in the documentary note.

[10] Bacon, "Of Cunning," p. 37.

[11] James, "The Art of Fiction," p. 12.

20.3 Novels

The chapter number will be helpful to the reader who does not have the edition from which you are quoting. However, it is not absolutely necessary to include it.

[12] Hawthorne, *The Scarlet Letter*, ch. 4, p. 65.

20.4 Prose works divided into titled parts

If it is clear in the text exactly what the name of the whole work is, you do not need to include that title in the citation; you may use only the title of the part.

[13] Swift, "A Voyage to Lilliput," p. 61.

[14] Swift, "A Voyage to Lilliput," *Gulliver's Travels*, p. 61.

20.5 Plays

Capital roman numerals denote the act; small roman numerals, the scene; and arabic numerals, the lines. Usually the denotations, "Act," "sc." for scene, and "l." or "ll." for line or lines, are omitted. It would not be incorrect, however, to include them for the sake of clarity in some instances.

[5] Shakespeare, *King Lear*, IV. ii. 11–13.

20.6 Short poems not divided into books or parts

The names of the poems (enclosed within quotation marks), not the anthologies or works from which they were taken, are the important matters in the citations.

[6] Arnold, "Dover Beach," l. 20.

[7] Whitman, "When I Heard the Learn'd Astronomer," ll. 4–6.

20.7 Long poems divided into books or parts

[8] Dante, *Purgatorio*, Canto II, ll. 95–96.

[9] Whitman, *Song of Myself*, Sec. 10, ll. 175–179.

[10] Browning, *The Ring and the Book*, Book V, l. 20.

20.8 Classical references

When citing from a classic Greek or Roman work, omit all commas and separate the elements of the actual reference by periods. The roman numeral denotes the book; the arabic numerals, the lines; as applicable, the small roman numeral denotes the chapter.

[1] Homer *Iliad* XXII. 24–25.

[2] Sophocles *Antigone* 880.

[3] Lucretius *On the Nature of the Universe* II. 806–810.

[4] Aristotle *The Nicomachean Ethics* II. i. 4–6.

21. NEWSPAPERS AND NEWSMAGAZINES

21.1 Basic forms for newspaper articles
21.1.1 With sections

[5] "Saigon under Guard on Eve of Elections," St. Louis *Post-Dispatch*, 28 Aug. 1971, sec. A, p. 1.

21.1.2 Without sections

[6] "The Summer of 1931," *Journal of Commerce*, 26 Aug. 1971, p. 4.

21.2 Name of edition
Some newspapers have several editions, and the particular edition from which you are quoting might be of interest to the reader.

[3] Florence Mouckley, "On Working Vacations," *Christian Science Monitor*, Western Edition, 28 Aug. 1971, sec. 1, p. 1.

21.3 Place of publication
The place of publication is often included in the name of the newspaper; but if it is not and the fact is important, then you should add the city (and possibly state) of publication.

[4] Don McLeod, "Citizen Lobby Power Grows," *Times-Picayune* (New Orleans), 30 Aug. 1971, sec. 4, p. 15.

[5] "World Language Students Complete Three Intense American Weeks," *World Tribune* (Santa Monica, Calif.), 1 Sept. 1971, p. 5.

21.4 Underlining the name of the newspaper
When the name of the city is a part of the newspaper's name, it should not be underlined in the note; also, you may drop "The" from the name. In the bibliographical entry, though, include "The" and underline it, as well as the name of the city.

[6] "Saigon under Guard on Eve of Elections," St. Louis *Post-Dispatch*, 28 Aug. 1971, sec. A, p. 1.

21.5 Newsmagazines
When citing a widely known weekly newsmagazine (such as *Time, U.S. News & World Report*, or *Newsweek*), you may treat it in the same manner as a newspaper.

[7] "A Search for Peace and Understanding," *U.S. News and World Report*, 14 June 1971, p. 19.

22. ORAL SOURCES

22.1 Interviews
22.1.1 Personal interviews

[1] John D. Jones, Superintendent of School District 19, Personal Interview on School Financing, Middletown, Iowa, 15 June 1970.

22.1.2 Taped interviews

[2] John D. Jones, Superintendent of School District 19, Taped Interview on School Financing, Middletown, Iowa, 15 June 1970.

22.2 Lectures

[3] Marilyn Schmidt, Director of City Museums, "Saving Our Art Treasures," Lecture, Conway Museum, Middletown, Iowa, 15 Apr. 1971.

22.3 Radio and television broadcasts
      22.3.1 Individual talks

[4] Miram Holmes, free-lance writer, "The Change in Popular Magazines," Radio Talk, KLIK, Middletown, Iowa, 28 Feb. 1970.

22.3.2 Programs

[5] "The Ocean's Resources," Special Program, NBS, 15 May 1969.

23. PAMPHLETS AND GOVERNMENT DOCUMENTS

Pamphlets, which comprise many and varied publications, and government documents usually contain the same information on publication as books do. However, some pamphlets omit certain facts regarding publication; when citing such a pamphlet, record as much information as is available.

23.1 Pamphlets

[1] *Legacy for All, A Record of Achievements by Black American Scientists* (1971), p. 3.

[2] Willa K. Baum, *Oral History for the Local Historical Society* (Stockton, Calif., 1969), p. 15.

23.2 Government documents

[1] J. R. Parker and R. V. Connin, *Grasshoppers, Their Habits and Damage,* Agricultural Information Bulletin No. 287 (Washington, D.C., 1964), p. 15.

23.3 Programs

Many special programs contain helpful information. When citing such programs, treat them as pamphlets, giving as much information as is available.

[2] *Souvenir Program, Oregon Shakespearean Festival* (Ashland, 1968), p. 21.

24. REFERENCE WORKS

24.1 Works with one or two authors, editors, or compilers

[3] Donald Portway, *Military Science Today,* 3d ed. (New York, 1957), p. 31.

[4] James A. Brussel and George L. Cantzlaar, *The Layman's Dictionary of Psychiatry* (New York, 1967), p. 50.

[5] Gardner Lindzey and Elliot Aronson, eds., *The Handbook of Social Psychology* (Menlo Park, Calif., 1968), V, 43.

24.2 Works with three or more authors, editors, or compilers

It is not necessary to list several names for works with multiple authors and the like. Use the first name given and thereafter "et al.," meaning "and others."

[4] Talcott Parsons, et al., eds., *Theories of Society* (New York, 1961), I, p. 75.

24.3 General dictionaries

It is not necessary to give the names of editors or publishers for general dictionaries.

[6] *Webster's Third International Dictionary of the English Language: Unabridged* (1961), p. 171.

It would be permissible to shorten the title.

[7] *Webster's Third International* (1961), p. 171.

24.4 Specific dictionaries

[8] Ralph Desola, ed., *Abbreviations Dictionary*, rev. ed. (New York, 1967), p. 51.

24.5 Other works without special authorship

[9] *The Statesman's Yearbook* (New York, 1970), p. 51.

25. REVIEWS

[1] Dan Walker, rev. of *Boss: Richard J. Daley of Chicago* by Mike Royko, *Saturday Review*, 24 Apr. 1971, 28.

[2] Louise Sweeney, rev. of *A Gunfight, Christian Science Monitor*, Western Edition, 28 Aug. 1971, sec. 2, p. 8.

[3] Henry Hewes, rev. of *Home* by David Storey, *Saturday Review*, 12 Dec. 1970, 16.

26. SECONDARY QUOTATIONS

It is always preferable to quote from the original source, but when that is not possible, use these forms.

[4] George A. Ellis, *A Half-Century of the Unitarian Controversy*, as quoted in R. W. B. Lewis, *The American Adam* (Chicago, 1965), pp. 30–31.

[5] Judy Clavir and John Spitzer, eds., *The Conspiracy Trial*, as quoted in Henry S. Resnik "The Shadows Cast by Chicago," *Saturday Review*, 12 Dec. 1970, 29.

27. SERIES (SEE 13)

28. SPECIAL AUTHORSHIP

When a work has an unusual or significant authorship, usually by an important organization, note this fact.

[6] UNESCO, *World Survey of Education II, Primary Education* (London, 1958), p. 253.

29. Supplemented Works (See 12.4)

30. Translated Works (See 12.3)

31. Two or More Authors

31.1 Two authors

[7] Jacques Barzun and Henry F. Graff, *The Modern Researcher* (New York, 1962), p. 90.

31.2 Three or more authors

Generally, when a work has three or more authors, name the first author only and use "et al." ("and others") to note additional writers. However, if it is important that all the writers be named, you should do so.

[8] Wilfred Guerin, et al., *A Handbook of Critical Approaches to Literature* (New York, 1966), p. 200.

32. Unpublished Works

32.1 Diaries and personal histories

[9] Margaret Mattson, Diary, June 1920–Sept. 1931, p. 10.

[10] Samuel Bridges, Personal History, Sept. 1941, p. 15.

32.2 Letters

[1] Matthew Brownlee, Personal Letter, 20 June 1970, p. 2.

In some cases, you may want to identify the writer and specify the subject of the letter.

[2] Matthew Brownlee, President of National City Bank, Personal Letter on Experiences in Banking, Middletown, Iowa, 20 June 1970, p. 4.

32.3 Theses, dissertations, and other unpublished works

If the school at which the thesis or dissertation was written is not well known, include the name of the city and state, unless the latter is obvious.

[3] Ronald Swift, "Economic Problems in Quintana Roo," MA Thesis Everystate University 1970, p. 21.

[4] Charles Mack, "Artistic Problems in Sculptural Reproductions," PhD Diss. Anystate College Middletown, Iowa, 1960, p. 45.

[5] Millier Flanders, The History of the Flanders Family (Typed Paper in Public Library, Middletown, Iowa, 1955), p. 15.

32.4 Approximate or unknown dates

The dates of unpublished material are not always certain or known. If you can determine the approximate date from in-

ternal evidence, place "ca." ("about" or "approximately") before the date. If the date is unknown, state this fact, using
"n.d." for "no date."

[1] Margaret Mattson, Diary, ca. 1920–1930, p. 5.

[2] Samuel Bridges, Personal History, n.d., p. 3.

33. Volumes

When citing from a work that covers two or more volumes, give
the volume number just before the page number. Omit the abbreviation "p." or "pp." when the page number follows a volume number.

[11] Eric Blom, ed., *Grove's Dictionary of Music and Musicians*
(New York, 1961), VIII, 103.

Appendix E

Forms for Bibliographical Entries

Bibliographical forms for the major kinds of sources are illustrated in this guide. For directions concerning the formation of the total bibliography, see chapter 9, p. 241. Abbreviations commonly used in bibliographies are given in appendix F, p. 295.

The main parts (each separated by a period) of the bibliographical entry are as follows:

1. Authorship (if known)
2. Name of work
3. Publication information

In some instances, other facts are added, such as edition numbers, volume numbers, and series. Study the variant forms carefully.

For problems not covered in this guide, see standard works in your field.

Key to Bibliographical Forms

This key first lists the basic sources. It then gives an alphabetical listing of other sources. Each source is numbered to direct you to the specific section that treats the source in detail.

Forms for Basic Sources

1. Books
   1.1 With one author
   1.2 With two authors
   1.3 With three or more authors
   1.4 With no given authorship
   1.5 With special authorship
2. Periodical articles
   2.1 Signed periodical articles
   2.2 Unsigned periodical articles

Forms for Other Sources

3. Abridged works (see 8.2)
4. Afterwords (see 14)
5. Anthologies and collections
6. Bible
7. Collaborations
8. Edited, abridged, translated, and supplemented works
9. Editions and series
10. Encyclopedias
11. Foreign-language sources
12. Government documents
13. Graphic materials
14. Introductory material and afterwords
15. Literary sources
16. Newspapers and newsmagazines
17. Oral sources
18. Pamphlets and government documents
19. Privately printed works
20. Reference works
21. Reviews
22. Secondary quotations
23. Series (see 9.2 and 9.3)
24. Supplemented works (see 8.4)
25. Translated works (see 8.3)
26. Unpublished works
27. Volumes

Forms for Basic Sources

1. BOOKS

1.1 With one author
Downs, Robert B. *Books That Changed America.* New York: Macmillan, 1970.
1.2 With two authors
Barzun, Jacques, and Graff, Henry F. *The Modern Researcher.* New York: Harcourt, Brace, 1962.
1.3 With three or more authors
1.3.1 If it does not seem important to list all the authors, list the name given first, followed by "et al." ("and others").
Guerin, Wilfred, et al. *A Handbook of Critical Approaches to Literature.* New York: Harper & Row, 1966.
1.3.2 If it is necessary to list all the authors, follow this form.
Guerin, Wilfred; Labor, Earl G.; Morgan, Lee, and Willingham, John R. *A Handbook of Critical Approaches to Literature.* New York: Harper & Row, 1966.
1.4 With no given authorship
The Book of the States. Chicago: Council of State Government, 1970.

1.5 With special authorship
     North American Aviation, Inc. *Lunar Atlas.* New York: Dover, 1968.

2. PERIODICAL ARTICLES

2.1 Signed articles
     Letiche, J. M. "Soviet Views of Keynes." *The Journal of Economic Literature* (June 1971), 442–458.
2.2 Unsigned articles
     "Comstock Country." *The American West* (September 1970), 34–43.

Forms for Other Sources

3. ABRIDGED WORKS (SEE 8.2)
4. AFTERWORDS (SEE 14)
5. ANTHOLOGIES (ALSO CALLED COLLECTIONS)

5.1 Titled or untitled introductory material from an anthology
     Van Ghent, Dorothy, and Brown, Joseph S., eds. "The Ancient World." *Continental Literature.* Philadelphia: J. B. Lippincott, 1968.
     Howe, Irving, ed. "Introduction [to *The Pupil*]." *Classics of Modern Fiction.* New York: Harcourt, Brace, & World, 1968.
5.2 Specific work from an anthology
     Duhl, Leonard J. "Environmental Health: Politics, Planning, and Money." In *The Vanishing Landscape.* Eds. Donald G. Douglas and John R. Stewart. Skokie, Ill.: National Textbook, 1970.

6. BIBLE

6.1 Short entry
     Holy Bible, Revised Standard Version.
6.2 Complete entry
     You may want to use a complete form for new or special versions of the Bible.
     The New English Bible with the Apocrypha. Joint Committee on the New Translation of the Bible. Cambridge: Cambridge Univ. Press, 1970.

7. COLLABORATIONS

     Malcolm X, with the assistance of Alex Haley. *The Autobiography of Malcolm X.* New York: Grove Press, 1965.

8. EDITED, ABRIDGED, TRANSLATED, AND SUPPLEMENTED WORKS

8.1 Edited works
     Whitman, Walt. *Leaves of Grass.* Ed. by Harold W. Blodgett and Sculley Bradley. New York: W. W. Norton, 1965.
8.2 Abridged works

Boswell, James. *Life of Johnson.* Abr. by Charles G. Osgood. New York: Scribner's, 1945.

8.3 Translated works

Vansina, Jan. *Oral Tradition: A Study in Historical Methodology.* Trans. from French by H. M. Wright. Chicago: Aldine, 1965.

8.4 Supplemented works

Strunk, William. *The Elements of Style.* With revisions, an introduction, and a new chapter on writing by E. B. White. New York: Macmillan, 1972.

You could use several abbreviations in the above entry.

Strunk, William. *The Elements of Style.* With revs., an introd., and a new ch. on writing by E. B. White. New York: Macmillan, 1972.

9. EDITIONS AND SERIES

9.1 Editions

Jones, W. Paul. *Writing Scientific Papers.* 6th ed. Dubuque, Iowa: William C. Brown, 1971.

9.2 Series (new editions)

Magill, Frank N., ed. *Magill's Quotations in Context.* 2d series. New York: Salem Press, 1969.

9.3 Series (related works published separately)

It is not always necessary to state the name of the series of which a particular work is a part, but when this information should be included, use the following form:

Turner, Arlin. *Nathaniel Hawthorne.* American Authors and Critics Series, AC 2. New York: Barnes & Noble, 1961.

10. ENCYCLOPEDIAS

10.1 Short form

Use this form when the encyclopedia was used as a reference work but was not cited directly.

Chambers's Encyclopaedia. New rev. ed. 15 vols. 1968.

Encyclopaedia Britannica. 24 vols. 1971.

10.2 Complete form

Use this form when you have cited a specific article directly.

Condliffe, John Bell. "Free Trade." *Encyclopaedia Britannica* (1968), IX, 853–854.

"Gerard Ter Borch." *Encyclopedia Americana* (1965), XXVI, 440.

11. FOREIGN-LANGUAGE SOURCES

Give the information exactly as you would with English-language sources.

Remarque, Erich Maria. *Der Himmel kennt keine Günstlinge.* Berlin: Kiepenheuer and Witsch, 1961.

"Biologia." *Monitor, enciclopedia salvat para todos* (1966), I, 315.

12. Government Documents (See 18.2)

13. Graphic Materials

When you have used reproductions of graphic materials from specific sources, give full bibliographical information, including the name of the illustrator.

Papp, Charles S. *Scientific Illustration.* Illus. by the author. Dubuque, Iowa: William C. Brown, 1968.

14. Introductory Material and Afterwords

Give the name of the major author only when it is not clear in the title, as in the second entry.

Handler, M. S. Introduction to *The Autobiography of Malcolm X.* New York: Grove Press, 1965.

Reilly, John. Afterword to *Native Son* by Richard Wright. New York: Harper & Row, 1966.

15. Literary Sources

Although documentary notes may be abbreviated, it is a good idea to give complete information in the bibliography.

15.1 Works from anthologies

Hawthorne, Nathaniel. "My Kinsman, Major Molineux." *Masters of American Literature.* Ed. by Leon Edel et al. Boston: Houghton Mifflin, 1959.

15.2 Works from editions

Whitman, Walt. "As Toilsome I Wander'd Virginia's Woods." *Leaves of Grass.* Ed. by Harold W. Blodgett and Sculley Bradley. New York: W. W. Norton, 1965.

15.3 Single works with special information

Hesse, Herman. *Steppenwolf.* Trans. by Basil Creighton. Trans. updated by Joseph Mileck. New York: Bantam, 1969.

15.4 Classics

Homer. *The Odyssey.* New verse trans. by Albert Cook. New York: W. W. Norton, 1967.

16. Newspapers and Newsmagazines

16.1 Newspapers

Underline the name of the city and include and underline "The" when they are part of the newspaper's name. Give sections, editions, and cities as necessary. (See appendix D, sec. 21, for fuller discussion of newspapers.)

"Saigon under Guard on Eve of Elections." *St. Louis Post-Dispatch,* 28 Aug. 1971, sec. A, p. 1.

Mouckley, Florence. "On Working Vacations." *The Christian Science Monitor,* Western Edition, 28 Aug. 1971, sec. 1, p. 1.

"World Language Students Complete Three Intense American

Weeks." *World Tribune* (Santa Monica, Calif.), 1 Sept. 1971, p. 5.

16.2 Newsmagazines

Weekly newsmagazines may be treated as newspapers in the bibliography.

"A Search for Peace and Understanding." *U.S. News & World Report*, 14 June 1971, p. 19.

In some instances, however, you may want to follow the regular periodical form, as given in sec. 2.

17. ORAL SOURCES

17.1 Interviews

Jones, John D., Superintendent of School District 19. Personal Interview on School Financing. Middletown, Iowa, 15 June 1970.

17.2 Lectures

Schmidt, Marilyn, Director of City Museums. Lecture. "Saving Our Art Treasures." Conway Museum, Middletown, Iowa, 15 April 1971.

17.3 Radio and television broadcasts

Holmes, Miram, free-lance writer. Radio Talk. "The Change in Popular Magazines." KLIK, Middletown, Iowa, 28 Feb. 1970.

18. PAMPHLETS AND GOVERNMENT DOCUMENTS

18.1 Pamphlets

Give as much information as is available. The first example does not include city of publication, which was not listed on the pamphlet; this is noted by "n.p.," meaning "no place of publication given." The second entry is complete.

Legacy for All, A Record of Achievements by Black American Scientists. n.p.: Western Electric, 1971.

Baum, Willa K. *Oral History for the Local Historical Society.* Stockton, Calif.: Conference of California Historical Societies, 1969.

18.2 Government documents

Give the name and number of the bulletin. The second note covers a more specialized government publication.

Parker, J. R., and Connin, R. V. *Grasshoppers, Their Habits and Damage.* Agricultural Information Bulletin No. 287. Washington, D.C.: Government Printing Office, 1964.

Mitchell, Shizuko; Tanaka, Norimitsu, and Steiner, Loren F. *Methods of Mass Culturing Melon Flies and Oriental and Mediterranean Fruit Flies.* Bulletin 33–104. Beltsville, Md.: Department of Agriculture, Research Service, 1965.

18.3 Special programs

Souvenir Program. Ashland: Oregon Shakespearean Festival, 1968.

19. PRIVATELY PRINTED WORKS

When a work has been published by an individual or an organization, give the individual or organization as the publisher, even though a printing company may be listed on the title page.
Smith, Mary Jane. *The Complete Poems of Mary Jane Smith.* Denver: The Author, 1931.

20. REFERENCE WORKS

Brussel, James A., and Cantzlaar, George L. *The Layman's Dictionary of Psychiatry.* New York: Barnes & Noble, 1967.
Parsons, Talcott, et al., eds. *Theories of Society.* 2 vols. New York: Free Press, 1961.

21. REVIEWS

Walker, Dan. rev. of *Boss: Richard J. Daley of Chicago* by Mike Royko. *Saturday Review,* 24 Apr. 1971, 28.

22. SECONDARY QUOTATIONS

Ellis, George A. *A Half-Century of the Unitarian Controversy.* As quoted in R. W. B. Lewis, *The American Adam.* Chicago: Univ. of Chicago Press, 1965.

23. SERIES (SEE 9.2 AND 9.3)

24. SUPPLEMENTED WORKS (SEE 8.4)

25. TRANSLATED WORKS (SEE 8.3)

26. UNPUBLISHED WORKS

Mattson, Margaret. Diary. Boulder, Colorado, June 1920–Sept. 1931.
Brownlee, Matthew. Personal Letter. Middletown, Iowa, 20 June 1971.
Swift, Ronald. "Economic Problems in Quintana Roo." MA Thesis Anystate College Middletown, Iowa, 1960.

27. VOLUMES

Even if you cite only one volume of a multivolume work, give the number of volumes. Works of several volumes may be published over a period of years; note this fact, as in the first entry.
Gwatkin, Henry M., et al., eds. *Cambridge Medieval History.* 8 vols. Cambridge: Cambridge Univ. Press, 1911–1936.
Ridpath, John Clark. *History of the World.* 4 vols. New York: Merrill & Baker, 1897.
In some cases, it might be preferable to use this form:
Ridpath, John Clark. *History of the World.* Vol. 2 of 4 vols. New York: Merrill & Baker, 1897.

Appendix F

List of Standard Abbreviations

A.D., a.d.   (no space between) *anno Domini;* in the year of the Lord
anon.   anonymous
ante   before
b.   born
B.C., b.c.   (no space between) before Christ
bk., bks.   book, books
ca., c.   *circa;* about; used with approximate dates
cf.   *confer;* compare to another idea; does not mean "see"
ch., chs.   chapter, chapters
col., cols.   column, columns
d.   died
ed.   edited*
ed., eds., edn., edns.   edition, editions
ed., eds., edd. (pl.)   editor, editors
e.g.   (no space between) *exempli gràtia;* for example
enl.   enlarged*
et al.   *et alii;* and others
etc.   *et cetera;* and so forth. (Avoid using in text.)
fac., facsim.   facsimile
fig., figs.   figure, figures
ibid., ib.   *ibidem;* in the same place; refers to the note immediately
preceding. (Using the author's last name in place of ibid. simplifies
matters.)
i.e.   (no space between) *id est;* that is
illus.   illustrator, illustration, illustrations, illustrated*
introd.   introduction, introduced by*
l., ll.   line, lines
loc. cit.   *loco citato;* in the place cited; the passage referred to in a
note prior to the intervening citations. (The note would read [2] Jones,
loc. cit.; to simplify matters, abbreviate the title so that the note
reads [2] Jones, *History.*)
MS, MSS   manuscript, manuscripts. (Place a period after MS when
referring to a specific manuscript, as in Quimby MS., but do not
use a period otherwise.)

n., nn.   note, notes, either documentary or subject matter

n.d.   no date given

no., nos.   number, numbers

n.p.   no place of publication given

numb.   numbered

op. cit.   *opere citato;* in the work cited. (This abbreviation refers to a different page in a work recently cited, as in [3] Jones, op. cit., p. 50; to simplify matters, use an abbreviated title, as in [4] Jones, *History*, p. 50.)

periodicals   Names of periodicals, scholarly journals, and standard works may be abbreviated in documentary notes and bibliographical entries. See a work in your field for a list of accepted abbreviations.

p., pp.   page, pages; never capitalize. (Omit p. or pp. when volume precedes, as in 2, 311, not 2, p. 311.)

pl., pls.   plate, plates

pref.   preface

pseud.   pseudonym; a writer's pen name

pt., pts.   part, parts

pub., publ., pubs.   published, publication, publications

reg.   registered

rev.   revised,* revision

sc.   scene

sec., sect., secs.   section, sections

sic   thus; as it was in the original. (Avoid overusing this word.)

sig., sigs., sigg.   signature, signatures

scholarly journals and standard works   (See **"periodicals"**)

st.   stanza

St., SS.   saint, saints

Ste.   female saint

trans., tr.   translator, translation, translated*

v., vv., vs., vss.   verse, verses

viz.   (with or without period) *videlicet;* namely

vol., vols.   volume, volumes (Omit the abbreviation "vol." when the page number is also given, as in [6]*Encyclopedia Americana*, 4, 211.)

vs.   *versus;* against; appears as v. in legal references

---

* The word "by," as in "ed. by," "introd. by," "rev. by," "trans. by," and so forth, may be omitted; including it, however, sometimes adds clarity.

Index